CHRIST, FAITH AND HISTORY

CHRIST
FAITH AND HISTORY

CAMBRIDGE STUDIES IN
CHRISTOLOGY

EDITED BY

S. W. SYKES AND J. P. CLAYTON

CAMBRIDGE
AT THE UNIVERSITY PRESS

1972

Published by the Syndics of the Cambridge University Press
Bentley House, 200 Euston Road, London NW1 2DB
American Branch: 32 East 57th Street, New York, N.Y. 10022

Library of Congress Catalogue Card Number: 70-176257

ISBN: 0 521 08451 2

Printed in Great Britain by
Alden & Mowbray Ltd
at the Alden Press, Oxford

CONTENTS

PREFACE

In the Introduction to *Soundings*, whose tenth anniversary this is, Alec Vidler expressed the collective opinion of the contributors that 'there are very important questions which theologians are now being called upon to face, and which are not yet being faced with the necessary seriousness and determination' (p. xi). Whatever critics found to criticise in that volume, they could not fault it on the score of determination. Moreover, the publication of *Soundings* inaugurated a decade of theology in Cambridge which has been marked by an increasing resolution to accept its challenge to do some hard thinking about fundamental philosophical and historical problems which inhere in Christian theology.

One of the manifestations of this resolution has been the formation of a graduate christology seminar, inaugurated by Professor Wiles in 1965 when he was a lecturer in the Faculty of Divinity. Most of the essays in this volume have been heard at recent meetings of that seminar, and bear the marks of improvements suggested in discussion. But, although the seminar has met regularly over the last few years, we – like the editor of *Soundings* – are unable to report on anything resembling a common mind.

We present this volume of essays, therefore, as a series of investigations into aspects of christology, in the belief that the differences of approach which are bound to exist in any lively faculty of theology need to be opened for examination. From the beginning the editors neither expected nor desired the essays to reflect a single point of view, whether 'liberal', 'orthodox' or 'radical'. They only asked that the contributions be constructive as well as critical. We have thus tried not merely to raise questions, but to argue (sometimes against each other) for answers. From a variety of religious backgrounds, including that of Jewish faith, the contributors have taken up themes which they believe are being mishandled or overlooked in contemporary christological discussion. The result is a volume which reflects our current preoccupation with the relation between history and faith and which, while giving evidence (as we hope) of such 'necessary seriousness and determination' as befits those who are most

directly indebted to the work of the *Soundings* group, pays the
editor and contributors of *Soundings* the compliment of not
having tried to imitate them. For it was precisely imitative
theology which they were most determined to counter.

S.W.SYKES

Cambridge, 1972   J.P.CLAYTON

PART I

BEGINNING ALL OVER AGAIN?

I

DOES CHRISTOLOGY REST ON A MISTAKE?[1]

M. F. WILES

So presumptuous a title calls for some justification. Christology has never ceased to puzzle and to perplex the minds of Christians from earliest times. It would be outrageous to assert that because something in the realm of theology remains mysterious it must for that reason alone be being misunderstood. Nevertheless modern historical thought has posed the problem of the intelligibility of traditional christology in a particularly acute way and this fact places an obligation upon Christians to ask once again whether it is unmistakably clear that their christological beliefs do represent the faithful response to a mystery and are not the outcome of some mistake.

I do not intend in this paper to discuss directly the historical evidence about Jesus himself. In any full treatment of christology such a discussion would be essential and fundamental. I can only state here somewhat dogmatically that that evidence by itself appears to me to be ambiguous and inconclusive. The New Testament certainly includes evidence that has not unreasonably led the church to its affirmation of Christ's consubstantial divinity, but it also seems to me to include evidence that remains very puzzling on an orthodox christological interpretation. If that is a sound judgment, then the interpretative context and the basic assumptions in the light of which that evidence has been understood will be matters of vital significance. It is with these that I am particularly concerned.

Certainly neither the life of Christ nor belief in him as incarnate Son of God are things that can be considered as if they existed in a vacuum. The life of Jesus happened in a particular historical context and to speak of him as Christ is already to place him in a

[1] Reprinted with permission from *Religious Studies*, VI (1970), 69–76.

very specific context of historico-theological interpretation. Similarly belief in him as incarnate Son of God did not arise as an isolated phenomenon; it developed in relation to other specific theological beliefs. That pattern of beliefs could be spelt out in various ways; one obvious and basic way of spelling it out is to say that belief in the incarnation arose within the complex of beliefs—creation, fall, redemption. When Jesus was thought of as second Adam, this implied both that his work was a continuation and completion of the work of creation and that it was a reversal of the disaster of the fall. Irenaeus may stress one aspect, Augustine another; but in the full tradition both ideas are present. Moreover, this complex of beliefs is not merely a wider setting into which belief in the incarnation had at some later stage to be fitted. Rather it is the matrix within which the earliest examples of mature christological reflection took their origin. Evidence for that claim is provided not only by the presence of the second Adam idea (already referred to) in Romans and I Corinthians, but also by the Adam typology of Philippians ii, the image concept of Colossians and the notion of the Logos in the Johannine prologue. If then the doctrine of the incarnation has been from its earliest origins so closely interwoven with the doctrines of creation and of the fall, it seems sensible to reflect upon it in very close relationship with those two other doctrines.

When one considers the history of these two doctrines – the creation and the fall – a striking point of similarity between them emerges. In both cases it was for a very long time felt that a certain specific action in history was essential to the possibility of affirming the doctrine, essential to its survival as a meaningful theological doctrine at all. The actions involved were of a very different kind – one divine, one human – so that discussion of them needs to be developed separately; but the similarity remains nonetheless and is a fact of considerable significance.

With regard to the doctrine of creation, there is no need to do more than to recall in briefest outline the response aroused by the development of evolutionary theory 100 years ago. The difficulty felt was not simply that evolution contradicted the account of Genesis understood in a literal, fundamentalist sense. In a broader, more theological way it was felt by some to contradict the basic affirmation of God's creation of man in his own image. Many who accepted the general truth of evolutionary theory sought to maintain a place for the specific creative action of God in the gap between inorganic matter and life or in the gap between man as a rational being and irrational animals. A position of this general kind is still frequently affirmed in Roman Catholic teaching. Thus we can read for example in a recent dictionary of theology:

> We can say that from amoeba to physical man, as it were, the process of evolution was complete and continuous. God could have willed the process to stop there, but instead something new was created, something which was not part of the biological process occurred. Something was gratuitously *added* to the evolutionary process in that God created a human spiritual soul which had no biological connections with any organism previous to that which it now informed.[1]

But very many Christians today would regard this kind of an approach, which looks for some specific creative act of God within the evolutionary process even though not as part of it, as a mistaken one. Those of us who do so ought to recognise that we do so not because we have evidence that can show it to be false, but because it embodies a method of reasoning with which we do not and cannot identify ourselves. Moreover the grounds of this objection are religious as much as scientific. Already in the nineteenth century, Aubrey Moore could write: 'Apart from the scientific evidence in favour of evolution, *as a theory* it is infinitely more Christian than the theory of "special creation"... *A theory of occasional intervention implies as its correlative a theory of ordinary absence.*'[2] In other words, whereas to some the idea of a specific divine act of the creation of man – or at least man's soul – seemed essential to the doctrine of creation, to others it has come to seem not only unnecessary but even inimical.

Recent attitudes to the doctrine of the fall are, if anything, even more familiar. Denial of the historicity of the Adam story was seen by some as undermining an essential Christian doctrine. Here again this was not simply a matter of contradicting the

[1] P. G. Fothergill, 'Evolution', *A Catholic Dictionary of Theology* (1967), II, 259–60.
[2] Cited by A. R. Vidler, *The Church in an age of Revolution* (1961), p. 121.

Genesis story. The difficulty could also be felt in a more sophisticated way as for example in the defence of monogenism in *Humani Generis*, where it is affirmed that 'original sin is the result of a sin committed, in actual historical fact, by an individual man named Adam, and it is a quality native to all of us, only because it has been handed down by descent from him'. The reason given for this judgment is that no other view is compatible with the doctrine of original sin. But once again many Christians react very differently and are more likely to agree with J. S. Whale when he wrote: 'The Fall relates not to some datable aboriginal calamity in the historic past of humanity but to a dimension of human experience, which is always present – namely, that we who have been created for fellowship with God repudiate it continually; and that the whole of mankind does this along with us.'[1] Moreover so far from regarding such an interpretation as undermining the doctrine of the fall, they would be more likely to claim that it helps to rescue that doctrine from certain embarrassments (e.g. concerning the manner of the transmission of original sin) which belong to it in any form which stresses the historicity of Adam's primordial transgression.

In both these cases, then, we see a tendency to regard the doctrines concerned as logically tied to particular events. I believe that we now have grounds for claiming that the attitude was a mistaken one. This gives us no right to feel superior or scornful in relation to our predecessors on that score. Their attitude was not unreasonable. The doctrines do seem to lose something of their toughness, something of their cutting edge with the loosening of what was once thought to be a firm logical bond. Something of the direct divine element in the doctrine of creation does seem to go if we do not speak of any specific divine act within the process by which human existence was brought into being. Nevertheless I do think that the old view was mistaken; I do think that the untying of the old bond not only frees us from an embarrassment in relation to scientific thought but also enables us to affirm divine creation in a fuller and more transcendent sense

[1] *Christian Doctrine* (1941), p. 49: cited by F. W. Dillistone, 'The Fall: Christian Truth and Literary Symbol' in *Comparative Literature Studies*, II (1965), 359.

as religious thought itself requires. Thus older forms of the doctrine of creation and of the fall did rest on a mistake – albeit a very respectable and not easily detectable mistake.

Now I have already argued that the doctrine of the incarnation arose in the closest conjunction with these two doctrines, both of which had this kind of mistake built into them. It does not therefore seem unreasonable to ask whether it also, in its traditional form, grew up with the same kind of mistake built into it. When we compare the doctrines in this way, the parallels are, I think, striking.

The first disciples and countless Christians down the ages have been convinced that through Christ the redeeming grace of God was at work; it was at work in a way which they could not describe in lesser terms than the crowning of God's creative work and the reversal of the fall. But how could that be? Creation was in a special sense God's act; the redemption which was the climax and the crown of that creation must be God's work in every bit as full a way. The fall was a single act with universal consequences for ill; as its reversal, Christ's redeeming act must embody an equally universal transformation of the human situation for righteousness. Divine action of a quite special kind must be embodied in Christ's person and in his saving activity. Only so could the redeeming grace of Christian experience be adequately accounted for. But we have seen that in spite of what might reasonably be anticipated, the doctrine of creation does *not* require the postulation of any specific divine act within the process as a whole; indeed such an act would be an embarrassment to the expression of that doctrine in its full transcendent reality. Can we not say the same of the doctrine of redemption? It is perhaps possible that the truth of that doctrine would even stand out more clearly if it were not tied to one particular act or life differing in kind from the rest of the series of human acts and human lives? If the doctrine of the fall 'relates not to some datable aboriginal calamity in the historic past ...but to a dimension of human experience', may not the same both negatively and positively be said of the doctrine of redemption?

The heart of the suggestion, therefore, that I want to put forward in this paper is that traditional christology rests on a mistake in this sense. It arose because it was not unnaturally, yet nonetheless mistakenly, felt that the full divine character of redemption in Christ could only be maintained if the person and act of the redeemer were understood to be divine in a direct and special sense. In the parallel cases of creation and fall our forefathers had to learn – and it was a painful process – that what they thought was a logically necessary link between the theological assertion and particular occurrences in history was not as logically necessary as they thought it to be. Are we perhaps at the equivalent – and even more painful – moment of learning the same truth about the doctrine of redemption?

That is the heart of what I want to suggest. But it seems appropriate to go on and give some brief indication of what more positive lines of thought might take the place of a traditional christological approach, if it were to be concluded that that did indeed rest on a mistake. And here too there is help to be found in a consideration of the doctrine of creation. If we do not accept the idea of a special act of creation at some point within the evolutionary process, in what sort of way do we give fuller expression to the doctrine? What do we say about it beyond a bald affirmation of God's creatorhood? It seems to me that what we do is to tell two different kinds of story. On the one hand we tell the scientific story of evolution; it is the real world as it has really developed with which the doctrine of creation is concerned, not with some ideal world of the theological imagination. But in addition we tell a frankly mythological story about the spirit of God moving on the face of the chaotic waters, about God taking the dust of the earth, making man in his own image, and breathing upon him so that he becomes a living soul. If we know what we are doing we can weave the two stories together in poetically creative ways – as indeed the poet combines logically disparate images into new and illuminating wholes. But we don't try to bind the two stories together at some specific point, claiming divine action to be at work in a special sense in the emergence of a first man with a distinct spiritual soul. Nevertheless, although we would regard it as falling back into the old mistake to isolate such a moment as different in kind from other moments in the process, we would still regard that aspect of the evolutionary story – the emergence of the distinctively human – as a part of the whole story which has special significance for the doctrine of creation. We have to be concerned with the whole story; we do not see that moment within the story as related in a different way to the divine or mythological story, but we still regard it as a part of the story which sheds a particular light on the significance of the story as a whole.

Can we not speak in a similar way of incarnation and redemption? Here too, I suggest, we will need to tell two stories. In the first place a human story of the partial overcoming in human lives of that repudiation of the fellowship with God of which the doctrine of the fall speaks. And also a mythological story of God's total self-giving, God's compassionate acceptance of pain and evil whereby that overcoming is made possible and effective. We may interweave these two stories in various ways; in the gospels themselves they are already so interwoven and for religious purposes we need to have it so. But we do not need – indeed on this analysis we would be wrong – to tie the two stories together by claiming that at one particular point, namely the life, death and resurrection of Jesus of Nazareth, the two stories are literally united with one another. Nevertheless it could still be reasonable to give to the life of Jesus a special place as illuminating, as no other life, the significance of the whole story, as bringing home to us effectively the transcendent divine truth which the mythological story in its own way is designed to proclaim.

The inevitable – and quite proper – question is why *this* story? Why should the life of Jesus fulfil this role as no other life, if it is not united to the divine, mythological story in any distinctively different way? We are faced here once again with the apparent Achilles heel of all reductionist christologies. The traditional answers are familiar; we can speak of the perfect measure of his obedience to God, the creative character of his life as seen in the transformation of the disciples and the emergence of the church. But such answers, as we know, have always seemed to the majority of Christians to be inadequate, to leave unsaid the one thing needful. Is there any point then in trotting them out once again? Only this. It has been the burden of this paper to try to show how it might be that the church should have so persistently felt the need to say something more and yet have been mistaken in that persistent feeling. The theological conviction of the reality of divine redemption was felt to require the underpinning of a distinct divine presence in Jesus; but in the light of the comparison with other related doctrines it seems reasonable to suggest that that very natural feeling rests on a mistake. In that case the inadequacy of what I have called the reductionist accounts of the specialness of Jesus – though they certainly have their weaknesses and their problems – need not be as fundamental as has normally been assumed.

It would be premature to assess how such discussion of the specialness of Jesus might develop in detail if it were freed from the anxious concern to give an account of that something more which Christian consciousness has seemed to demand. The precise form of the answer to the question, 'Why *this* story?', would need to depend very largely on the context within which it was being raised. If it is raised in a specifically Christian context, where the alternative stories in mind as possible focal embodiments of the doctrine of redemption might be the stories of an Augustine or a Francis, it would be pertinent to point to the directness of the relation of Jesus to God in contrast to the mediatorial role of the person of Jesus himself in Augustine's and Francis' own understandings of their relationship with God. In other words the story of Jesus is not an arbitrarily chosen story; from a Christian standpoint, it is the story of that historical happening which did in fact create a new and effective realisation of divine redemption at work in the lives of men, and which has remained the inspirational centre of the community of faith to which we belong from that day until now. There are certainly grave problems concerned with how much we can know with confidence of that story in its original historic form and of how far we can enter into the very different thought-forms and assumptions of that earlier period. But I do not think that these difficulties need undermine the centrality of the story of Jesus for faith. The difficulties are just as real for an orthodox christology which takes seriously its affirmation of the humanity of Jesus.

If on the other hand the question is raised in an inter-religious context, as is bound increasingly to be the case, it raises further problems and will have to be approached in a very different way. In many discussions of basic issues there comes a point at which we reach a limit question, where we have to say 'I can give no further reasons for seeing the thing as I do; this is my vision; do you not feel drawn to share it too?' Two historians may agree on all critical questions in assessment of the available evidence on some issue, and yet tell the resultant historical story in very different terms. Two moralists may agree on the factual aspects of a particular situation and on the moral issues involved, and yet make divergent moral judgments on what ought to be done in the situation. Discussion of the facts of the case and of the relevant criteria are important and in many cases may lead one person or the other to revise his judgment; but there may come a point at which, having been through such a process, there are no more reasons to be given. Each can only commend his vision to the other. Something like this is true, I believe, with regard to the basic affirmation of theism. May it not be so with the Christian's understanding of the specialness of Christ? There are many things to be said which give grounds for seeing the life and death of Jesus as a part of the human story which is of unique significance in relation to seeing the human story as a whole as a true story of divine redemption at work. To ask for some further ontological justification of that vision would be to succumb to the category mistake of confusing the human historical story with the divine mythological story.

I began by acknowledging the presumptuous nature of the question embodied in the title of the paper; I must end by acknowledging the presumptuous nature of the answer embodied in the paper itself. That presumption may perhaps be mitigated somewhat by an insistence that the answer proposed is put forward tentatively as an intended stimulus to further discussion. But there is a kind of presumption of which it may be accused to which I would plead firmly not guilty. There are parallels between what I have been trying to say and what John Knox has written in his *Humanity and Divinity of Christ*. Dr Mascall has accused him in that book of 'dismissing...the whole of the classical Christology from Athanasius and Cyril...to Augustine and Aquinas and beyond' and of implying that 'the great thinkers of the Christian church' were 'incurably boneheaded'.[1] It is true that, if I am right, the whole of the classical christology would have to be dismissed as resting on a mistake – in the specific form in which it was undertaken though not in all the insights lying behind the attempt. But this, I would insist, does not imply in any way at all that those early thinkers were 'incurably bone-headed', any more than to deny the inerrancy of scripture involves passing an unfavourable judgment on the intelligence of those earlier generations who accepted it without question. What I have suggested may well be wrong; but I do not believe that it can rightly be dismissed on the basis of any claim that it would entail regarding all earlier christological discussion as a form of meaningless gibberish or all earlier faith in the divinity of Christ as regrettable superstition. No such entailment is involved.

[1] *Theology and the Future* (1968), pp. 105–6.

2

A DELIBERATE MISTAKE?

PETER R. BAELZ

In his contribution entitled 'Does christology rest on a mistake?'
Professor Wiles has suggested that traditional attempts to characterize the unity of God and man in the person of Jesus Christ are
the outcome of a logical mistake rather than the fruit of a faithful
response to a real mystery. The mistake arises, he alleges, from an
illegitimate mixture of two different languages. In speaking of
the significance of Jesus Christ for Christian faith we must indeed
use two languages, the one human and historical, the other divine
and mythological, each with its own distinctive function and
logic. It is, however, a mistake to think that we can combine these
two separate languages into a single, new and logically coherent
language, and any attempt to do so results not in an increase of
theological understanding but in a nonsensical hybrid which is
neither one thing nor another. He argues for this thesis on the
grounds that the doctrine of the incarnation is internally related
to the doctrines of the creation and of the fall, and that developments in our understanding of the latter doctrines demand a
related and similar development in our understanding of the
former. A logical mistake which has been discerned and
rectified in the one case needs to be discerned and rectified in the
other.

Let me confess straightaway that I find Wiles' suggestion
attractive. His arguments are forceful. He is surely correct when
he insists that the doctrines of creation, the fall and redemption are
parts of a single conceptual scheme and must on that account be
treated in relation to one another. Furthermore, his distinction
between two logically separate languages promises a gain in
clarity. Problems which have never ceased to worry traditional
theology are thereby dismissed as non-problems. A certain
economy of thought and utterance is thus achieved. Nevertheless,

clarity and economy are not the sole criteria of theological success. Adequacy must also be sought. Does the suggested scheme do justice to all that needs to be said? Has the notion of distinct logical languages, a notion which has been deployed with considerable success in various branches of linguistic and philosophical analysis, been applied by Wiles with equal success to the definition of the logical structure of Christian doctrine? When the implications of Wiles' suggestion have been worked out in detail, will they be seen to involve not simply a different way of understanding our talk about the Christian faith but rather a different talk and consequently a different faith? If the latter, two questions at once arise: first, whether the new faith is sufficiently close to the old to deserve still to be called a form of *Christian* faith, or whether it is so changed that we ought no longer to call it by the same name; and second, and more important, whether it is nearer the truth. What is the right way to go about answering the latter question is itself an exceedingly difficult question. If, however, we can somewhere detect a logical error, and agree that it is nothing but a logical error, we shall at least have made a little progress. Consequently it is primarily with logical considerations that I myself shall be concerned. In what follows I shall be using Wiles' paper as a starting-point, but I shall wander well beyond its confines, and I do not wish to attribute to him, directly or by implication, views which he may or may not himself espouse.

What I propose to consider in this paper is, first, the precise nature of the changes in the doctrines of creation and the fall which have won wide acceptance in recent times; second, the application of the notion of complementary languages to Christian doctrine in general; and finally, the underlying function of christology and the kinds of language which this appears to demand.

I

We begin with the doctrine of man's creation. The problem arises from the difference between the biblical account of God's creation of Adam and the evolutionary account of man's animal ancestry. They appear to contradict each other, and if that is the case they cannot both be true. Can they, however, be harmonized? And if so, how?

The first and obvious move is to distinguish between a theological and a scientific account of man's origins. The Genesis story is fundamentally theological, the evolutionary story is fundamentally scientific. The two stories treat of the same subject from different angles and in different categories. The one claims to be theologically true, the other scientifically true.

So far, so good. We have made a distinction, and eliminated a contradiction. Further reflection, however, suggests that this simple distinction is not sufficient to remove the contradiction. It appears again in another place. In so far as the two accounts purport to treat of the same subject, the origin of man, they must be compatible with each other. Granted that it is not the function of the theological account to answer scientific questions, nor the function of the scientific account to answer theological questions, nevertheless it is necessary to ask precisely how the two accounts are to be related to each other and to this extent, at least, to harmonize them. On the face of it the theological account will accept the scientific account *as far as it goes*, but will wish to say '*more*' than is said by that account. Although this 'more' will not be a scientific 'more', it must still leave logical room for the scientific account and be logically compatible with it.

Now Wiles observes that some theologians have attempted to achieve such a harmony by speaking of 'a specific creative action of God in the gap between inorganic matter and life or in the gap between man as a rational being and irrational animals', and, again, of 'some specific act of God within the evolutionary process even though not as part of it'. He rejects this attempt to harmonize the two accounts, not on the grounds that we possess sufficient evidence to demonstrate that it is false, but on the grounds that 'it embodies a method of reasoning with which we do not and cannot identify ourselves'. He adds the further comment that 'the grounds of this objection are religious as much as scientific', and quotes Aubrey Moore's words: 'Apart from the scientific evidence in favour of evolution, *as a theory* it is infinitely more Christian than the theory of "special creation"...A theory of occasional intervention implies as its correlative a theory of ordinary absence.'

At this point, if we are to be clear what is going on, certain comments must be made. It might be questioned, for example, whether we should speak of *scientific* objections to a *theory* of special creation unless that 'theory' itself claimed some sort of scientific status, that is, unless it were the kind of theory which might be the outcome of a properly scientific method. But are they competing theories, offering different explanations, but of the same logical kind? It would appear not. God-hypotheses do not belong to scientific language. They have no scientifically explanatory power. The doctrine of a special creation does not belong to the language of scientific theory. Its function, if it has a valid function, is to be sought elsewhere.

There might, however, be reason to speak of a 'scientific' objection to the doctrine of a special creation if the doctrine entailed the view that evolutionary theory was *scientifically* deficient. Talk about 'gaps' may suggest that this is what is in fact intended. Now there may or there may not be certain empirical facts which an evolutionary theory finds it difficult to cover. If there are, we may then speak of 'gaps' in the evolutionary process, meaning by that gaps in the evolutionary story which we wish to tell. But the development of evolutionary theory has consistently narrowed such gaps, and in so far as it can give an ordered, consistent and continuous account of the way in which things have come to be as they now are – and this will include an account of the developing conditions under which novel features have appeared in the process – there will be no gaps left. It will then be a mistake to speak of the gap between inorganic matter and life, or between the sub-human animals and man. Despite the fact that real novelty has indeed occurred there will be nothing left unexplained. The evolutionary story is a complete story.

But, it may be retorted, is not novelty itself a kind of gap? Because it is new, is it not unexplained? At this point we are moving from science to metaphysics. Can the appearance of what is new be accounted for in terms of what preceded it and, by definition, lacked the properties which newly appeared? Can the non-living account for the living, and the irrational for the rational? Considered empirically, the answer may be 'yes'. It has happened – and this is the way in which it has happened. Furthermore, in our laboratories we may be able to make it happen again. Considered metaphysically, however, the question may still be pressed. How is the newness of what is new to be explained? Has matter the 'power' to produce life, and has life the 'power' to produce spirit? *Ex nihilo nihil fit.* The spiritual cannot be explained in terms of the material, which is by definition non-spiritual. There remains a gap, and it is this 'gap' which the 'special' creative action of God is introduced in order to 'explain'.

The scientist may dismiss all such talk of 'power' and metaphysical explanation as nonsense. Or he may assert a counter-metaphysic, for example, some form of materialism. He may claim that the material world of physical objects is the only real world – not in the sense in which 'real' and 'unreal' are distinguished within scientific discourse, but in a deeper and more ultimate sense. Or, again, he may put forward the view that there is a mental pole as well as a material pole to all natural processes and that mind and matter are ultimate and universal categories. These claims, however, are metaphysical claims, and it is a logical mistake to think that they can be proved by a simple appeal to the success of scientific explanation. Similarly, it is a logical mistake if the theologian, for his part, thinks he can prove his case by an appeal to some alleged failure of scientific explanation. The success or failure of scientific explanation does not touch the metaphysical issues. A different kind of 'explanation' is being canvassed. There is nothing but confusion if the two are not distinguished. Thus extreme caution must be exercised in speaking of a scientific objection to the doctrine of a special creative act of God. Everything depends on the account that is given of such an act and the kinds of reasons which are adduced to support it.

When we turn to consider the *theological* objection to the doctrine of a special creative act of God we must once again exercise logical care. It is said that 'a theory of occasional intervention implies as its correlative a theory of ordinary absence'. Let us at once admit that a theory of ordinary absence sounds theologically intolerable. On religious grounds we refuse to allow the possibility that God is ever absent from his world. Were he so, there would cease to be a world. At least, that I take to be the implication of the doctrine that God is creator and sustainer. Furthermore, we may agree that the ordinary use of the word 'intervention' carries with it the implication of coming into a situation from which one was previously absent, of getting involved when one was previously not involved. Consequently the theological objection to special creation seems to be well founded.

On the other hand, we may question whether it is theologically necessary to characterize God's special activity as an 'intervention'. In the first place it may be said that such a term carries with it too many overtones of physical interposition, for example, of putting one's own body in between the bodies of two contestants. In this case the intervention is observable and consequently is open to empirical description. But God's activity is not observable. Even if we wish to speak of God as 'intervening' we must remember that we are not using the word in its literal sense. In the second place there may be good theological reasons for distinguishing between God's 'general' activity and his 'special' activity, and this distinction may not carry with it the unfortunate implication that we are comparing his special activity and his general inactivity. In ordinary language, it is true, we tend to contrast action and inaction. Either a person is doing something or he is not. We do indeed speak of a person's being more or less active, but such language seems to refer to the physical aspects of activity. It is not easy to see what a distinction between general and special activity could mean when applied to God. However, such a distinction is sometimes made, and good reasons can be offered for making it. This issue cannot be fully discussed here, but the following brief points may be relevant. Religiously we *do* sometimes speak of the absence of God. In fact contemporary theologians make much use of this notion. Would it be accepted as sufficient comment to say of Jesus' cry of dereliction on the cross that God only seemed to be absent? I do not think so. (Nor, however, do I think it would be true to say, *tout court*, that he was really absent!) Again, the concept of activity is closely tied to the concepts of responsibility, purpose, fulfilment and the like. Are we prepared to say that God is equally responsible for everything that happens in the world, that his purposes are everywhere equally fulfilled? Here again I suggest that our immediate answer would be 'no', and that even if further reflection introduced a more hesitant note, we should still wish to make certain distinctions which did justice to the facts which evoked our initial 'no', facts of which evil in all its manifold forms is the signal example. Lastly, if the concept of special activity raises problems, the concept of general activity raises problems too. Can we rescue it from disappearing into some impersonal concept like that of force? Are we prepared to think of God's activity as similiar to the constant pressure of a uniform force? Such forces take no note of the individual needs of individual persons, and persons are nothing if not individual. It is shortsighted to think that awkward problems arise only when we attempt to relate God's creative activity to this or that event in time: they are present in attempts to relate God's being and activity to the temporal process as a whole.

What is the import of our discussion so far? Perhaps not very much, except to show that it is not enough simply to distinguish between scientific and theological languages. The full nature of the distinction must be explored. Furthermore, if both languages are about one and the same world, what is said in the one cannot be irrelevant to what is said in the other. The connections must be displayed as well as the differences. To distinguish is not the same thing as to divorce.

II

We can for our own purposes deal with the doctrine of the fall more briefly. Here we are not concerned with the difficulties inherent in language about God. If God is anywhere absent, he is surely absent in the fall!

Obviously the Genesis account of the fall is not to be taken as it stands as straightforwardly historical. Talking serpents, to say the least, are figments of the imagination. Does it follow, however,

that we are in no sense here dealing with history? Wiles quotes
J. S. Whale: 'The Fall relates not to some datable aboriginal
calamity in the historic past of humanity but to a dimension of
human experience, which is always present – namely, that we who
have been created for fellowship with God repudiate it continually; and that the whole of mankind does this along with us.'
Wiles points to the fact that belief in an actual primordial sin
committed by an actual single ancestor of the human race has
sometimes been defended on the theological grounds that it is
required by the doctrine of original sin, and suggests that any
doctrine of the fall which so stresses the historicity of Adam's
transgression gives rise to 'certain embarrassments (e.g. concerning
the manner of the transmission of original sin)'.

We may certainly agree that the fall is not datable, if all that is
meant by that is that we cannot in fact put a date to it. We lack
the necessary evidence. It may be, however, that more is intended
by this assertion, namely, that the fall does not refer to the kind of
thing to which it is appropriate to ascribe a date. In that case it
would be a logical mistake to try to date it. We may also agree
that repudiations of God, whether in the past or in the present, are
not the proper subject for historians. Historical explanations are
not given in such terms. Finally, we may agree that the doctrine
of the fall is grounded in our present experience of estrangement.
In that sense it has reference to a present 'dimension of human
experience'. Traditionally, however, the doctrine has set out
not simply to describe an aspect of our present experience but also
in some sense to explain it. Why was an explanation required?
Possibly in order to protect the goodness of God against any view
that held that the world, as world, was essentially and inevitably
evil; possibly because the affirmation that all men everywhere
and at all times, past, present and future, are estranged from God
and are in need of a divine saviour was felt to need some justification. If they were all the descendants of a single ancestor, and
if they could not but inherit the stain of original sin which resulted
from his transgression, then such an explanation of the universality of original sin was to hand.

Clearly this will not do. Sin is not the sort of thing that can be transmitted physically. Might it not, however, be transmitted socially and culturally? Any worthwhile discussion of this point would involve consideration of the distinction between actual sin, for which one may properly be held responsible, and original sin, a human condition into which one has entered but for which one cannot be held responsible. It would be necessary to analyse the concept of freedom, as used in theological discourse, and to ask in what sense, if any, it is proper to ask for an explanation of an act that was free, and to try to reach some understanding, however inadequate, of the relation between an individual's own action for which he is himself responsible and the actions of the community in which he is reared which condition and bear upon his own free choices. It might then be possible to suggest how the alienations from God of the society into which he is born and in which he is reared renders practically inevitable his own deliberate repudiation of God.

The point that I wish to make here is this. The doctrine of the fall seems to me an attempt to do justice to the subtle interweaving of human action and the human condition. To speak of man's sin is at one and the same time to speak of man's responsibility and of sin's inevitability. Sin is not simply a natural condition; nor is it simply a lack of education or of intelligence; it is spiritual defection. Nevertheless, it is a spiritual defection that has penetrated the whole structure of human life and relationships. Certainly the languages of human responsibility and of human condition must be distinguished. It is tempting to think that it is a logical mistake to weave them together. On the other hand the facts themselves may be such that greater error is involved in keeping them utterly apart.

If it is true that men in the present repudiate God and that they are in a measure responsible for this repudiation, then their action in so doing is in a very real sense part of the historical order – language of natural causation will not do justice to the facts – even though historians will not describe their action in these terms and will probably be unconcerned even with questions of moral responsibility. Again, if it is true that men's present repudiation of God is not adequately described in terms of individual decision and responsibility but demands consideration of man's co-humanity, of an individual's interdependence with other individuals, and of generations' interdependence with earlier generations, then the doctrine of the fall may relate not only to the many present repudiations of God but also to the many past repudiations and the historical bond between them all. Action and reaction form the warp and woof of a single web of human life. The measure of responsibility that a man has for his actions is known only to God. The doctrine of the fall sets man's sin within the total context of human history without at the same time withdrawing the charge of human responsibility. Historical and existential languages interpenetrate.

Nothing that I have said answers the question whether there was one 'Adam' or whether there were several 'Adams'. So far as I can see it need make no difference to the doctrine of the fall whether monogenism is true or not. No doubt the doctrine will need reformulation, and Augustinian and Irenaean tendencies will lead to its reformulation in different ways. But I suspect that any adequate doctrine will include a reference to the past as well as to the present, that in the history of man there has been a rejection of God that deserves to be called deliberate – there may have been many such independent 'falls' – and that our present fallenness is what it is at least in part because of the heritage into which we have entered. Thus, although I am not concerned to defend the historicity of a single human ancestor, I am concerned to retain an historical dimension in the doctrine of the fall. The Genesis story may not be a satisfactory interweaving of history and theological anthropology. The knots may have to be unpicked. But the threads must not be left unconnected. New, though perhaps looser, knots will have to be tied.

III

In what I have so far said I have more than once indicated that I accept the fundamental importance of distinguishing between different languages, each with its own function and logic. However, I have also insisted that it is a mistake to believe that they

are utterly divorced from each other, or that there are no relations
of a logical kind existing between them. I wish now to expand
these remarks with especial reference to the language of
creation.

We use religious language for a number of purposes. We use
it to pray, to praise, to preach, to commend, and so on. In so
doing we are expressing certain feelings, attitudes, hopes and
evaluations. But we also use it to say things about God. That is,
we use theological language. We tell a story about God's being
and activity. The story we tell may be called mythological, since
it frequently speaks of God's activity in a pictorial and poetic
way and the categories which it uses are often categories which
we recognize as being more obviously appropriate to human
beings. Clearly much of what we say has to be taken symbolically.
We realize that God is other than man, other than any object
in the world, and this places severe limitations on what we can
properly assert of him. It is inevitable that we should exercise
some reflective and rational control on our story-telling. We
must refine what we say if we wish to achieve a better theological
understanding. We must demythologize in some way or other.

When we undertake this task, what comes out at the other end?
At one extreme there are those who maintain that nothing is left,
not even God himself. Certainly we can tell our mythological
stories. Certainly they have a religious function. But there is no
God to whom these stories actually refer. He exists within the
religious language; but, then, Jupiter exists within the mythological language of the Greeks. The use of such language may express
a religious attitude to the world. There is no need, indeed there
is no sense, in asking whether God exists 'outside' the world.
Questions concerning the relation of God to the world are logically misleading.

If this extreme view is rejected, there is another view which
maintains that we can intelligibly affirm that everything depends
on God, that the world is, therefore, the object of his 'creative
act', but that we can say little or nothing more about him. We
can travel only by the *via negationis*. Religiously speaking, we
may have to tell some quite complex mythological stories about

B

God's doings; but theologically speaking, in order to preserve the transcendence of God, we must negate everything that we have said. Anthropomorphism must yield to agnosticism.

Now there is an important – and, I should add, still living – tradition in Christian theology which seeks to avoid the dilemma of anthropomorphism or agnosticism by treading a kind of middle way. There is, it is claimed, an analogical use of language by which we can say certain things about God and say them intelligibly, even though we cannot fully grasp what it is that we are saying. Whether such a position can in the end be maintained is certainly debatable. I cannot help thinking, however, that the Christian faith is committed to making some such attempt. The Christian does not believe that God is creator in some unspecified sense. In affirming that certain attitudes of love, obedience, adoration and thanksgiving are appropriate on the part of man towards his creator, he is at the same time affirming that God is such as rightly to merit such a human response. God is love. This may mean more than that God is loving, but it cannot mean less. Love expresses itself in activity, care and concern. Love seeks a response from the beloved. Love is personal. In using such language we are not simply using an anthropomorphic and mythological language without any control. We use it analogically, seeking to refine it of those characteristics which belong solely to finite human beings.

Furthermore, Christian faith is committed to the belief that God's activity is somehow expressed within the world. It is not enough to restrict one's speaking to the doctrine of creation in 'its full transcendent reality', to use Wiles' expression. In following this road we may find ourselves more at home with some quasi-Platonic theory of forms than with a doctrine of a creator God. We must also attempt to do justice to God's immanence. Somehow or other we must speak of his activity within the world. Nor is it enough to say that such talk is religiously necessary but theologically mythological. To speak of God's immanent activity is for the Christian as theologically necessary and as theologically respectable as to speak of his transcendent activity. We must view nature and history theologically. Certainly it would be a mistake to introduce theological concepts into any story which sets out to be straightforwardly scientific or historical. Nevertheless, if the world is in fact the sphere of God's activity, then the languages of theology and history must in some way be correlated. There must be room for both kinds of story to be true. We are speaking of one world, the actual world. If our history is true, then the actual world must be such as to substantiate our historical story. But if our theology is also true, then the actual world must also be such as to substantiate our theological story. To speak of the theological story as 'mythological' is, to say the least, dangerously ambiguous. Even if it does not suggest that such a story is untrue, it certainly suggests that the 'actual' world is to be defined, and not merely described, in terms of the historical story. It is possible to see something of a similar ambiguity when Wiles, wanting to hold together the evolutionary and the mythological stories as he undoubtedly does, suggests that we should regard 'that aspect of the evolutionary story – the emergence of the distinctively human – as part of the whole story which has special significance for the doctrine of creation', since it 'sheds a particular light on the significance of the story as a whole'. What is this significance and for whom is it significant? Is the coming of human life nothing but an evolutionary process, to which we ascribe human significance by telling a divine, mythological story? Or is it also an instance of the activity of God, with a significance for God himself as well as for man? Is there a sense in which we may properly speak of God's 'working his purpose out', or does the divine transcendence rule such language out as nothing but anthropomorphism?

It is possible to call the language of God's doings mythological but to interpret this language in a number of different ways. It is not immediately clear what the function of such language is. Thus, if we consider the doctrine of creation in general, a doctrine which is at least in part distilled from the mythological language of the Bible, we discover that theologians offer us a variety of very different doctrines. We may refer at this point to the penetrating discussion of this matter by Professor I. G. Barbour in his book *Issues in Science and Religion*. At the end of his chapter on 'Evolution and Creation' he accepts the insights of linguistic analysis which insist that the evolutionary theory of science serves one purpose and the theological doctrine of creation another, but he refuses to see these distinctions as absolute and argues that there are points of overlap. The problem then is how we are to conceive this overlap. 'Having recognized the basic differences between the ideas of creation and evolution, we must go on to deal with the problem of the relation of God and man to nature, and especially the idea of God's activity in the world'.[1] To do this we require metaphysical categories which must be drawn both from religion and from science.

Barbour proceeds to classify a number of differing approaches. First, there are dualistic views. A metaphysical dualism of body and soul 'involves an absolute discontinuity between man and all other forms of life, and requires a special act of divine intervention in evolutionary history'. He himself suggests 'that it is this view of the soul together with the doctrine of the inheritance of original sin, rather than biblical literalism, which motivates the Catholic insistence on a historical Adam'. (Perhaps I might add here to the comments that I made earlier the observation that such metaphysical dualism is by no means a dead duck – it is stoutly and forcefully defended, for example, in Professor H. D. Lewis' Gifford Lectures, *The Elusive Mind* – and that it is not necessarily overthrown by pointing to the undoubted continuities which exist between man and other animals, continuities even of intelligent behaviour and of language. Furthermore, those philosophers and theologians who wish to avoid such a dualism while at the same time doing justice to the distinctiveness of mental and spiritual characteristics are often found introducing the concepts of a mental pole and even of something analogous to choice at all stages of the world's development, and from the strictly scientific point of view such language is as bizarre as that of the dualists.)

Second, there are the reductionist views, such as those of Julian Huxley, who 'sees man as essentially continuous with nature', espouses a monistic and naturalistic metaphysic, but 'claims to

---

[1] I. G. Barbour, *Issues in Science and Religion* (1966), p. 415.

have avoided materialism "by ascribing to the world stuff a potentiality for mind" '. (Empirically speaking, the world stuff certainly has a potentiality for mind, since mind has in fact appeared out of the world stuff. If, however, there is admitted to be a metaphysical problem here, then to speak of 'a potentiality for mind' is little more than a restatement of the problem.)

Third, there are the 'two-language' views. These take various forms. Some will assert that creation language is no more than the reflection of a human attitude to the world of man and nature. Others will hold that God is active in the realm of human existence but not in the impersonal world of nature. Others may speak of the 'vertical' dimension of divine activity and contrast this with the 'horizontal' direction of human activity. All distrust metaphysics, take a positivistic view of science and often a mechanistic view of nature. They all 'see creation and evolution as two unrelated languages that have nothing to do with each other'.[1]

Finally, there is a metaphysic of levels, which seeks to do justice both to the continuity and the discontinuity between various stages of the world's development, and not merely between the animal and the human. This may be developed in different ways; but there will be an insistence on God's continuing creativity in the world and an attempt to think together, however falteringly, the processes of nature, the actions of men and the equally real activity of God.

I agree with Barbour in thinking that this last approach is the most immediately consonant with Christian faith. I also accept the theological propriety, of this view, of insisting on God's *continuous* creativity. But it remains an open question whether there may not be good reasons for speaking of God's 'special' creative acts in relation to certain events in the world. At least I see no compelling case for ruling such language out *a priori* as the result of a logical mistake. It all depends on the way in which this language is to be employed. Furthermore, such language need not be 'mythological' in any loose and reductive sense of that much-abused word.

[1] Barbour, *Issues in Science and Religion*, p. 416.

IV

What is the bearing of all this on christology?

The thesis of complementary languages, helpful as it un-doubtedly is, calls for careful consideration of the relations between the two languages thus distinguished and leaves open the possibility of 'overlap'. It is necessary to specify the logical structure of the 'mythological' language concerning God, since Christian talk of God, whether mythological or not, generates its own rules of what may and what may not be properly said of the divine activity. It cannot be assumed that the precise logical characteristics of the doctrines of creation, the fall and redemption are all identical, even though they all belong to the same funda-mental language. Furthermore, in so far as statements in both languages claim to be true statements about man and the world, ontological questions concerning the relation of God and his creation can scarcely be side-tracked. To speak of 'mythological' language and to leave it at that all too readily suggests that they can.

When we turn to christology, we find that the heart of Wiles' thesis is contained in the suggestion that 'The theological convic-tion of the reality of the divine redemption was felt to require the underpinning of a distinct divine presence in Jesus; but in the light of the comparison with other related doctrines it seems reasonable to suggest that that very natural feeling rests on a mistake.' And further on Wiles writes:

There are many things to be said which give grounds for seeing the life and death of Jesus as a part of the human story which is of unique significance in relation to seeing the human story as a whole as a true story of divine redemption at work. To ask for some further ontological justification of that vision would be to succumb to the category mistake of confusing the human historical story with the divine mythological story.

On the basis of our earlier discussion I would suggest that no category mistake is necessarily involved in speaking of a special act of God in the life and death of Jesus or even in speaking of a distinct divine presence. There is nothing necessarily mistaken in relating the human and divine stories in this way when speaking of Jesus. Human and divine stories have to be related in general if we are to speak of God's activity on and in the world, and there may be sound historical and theological reasons for relating them specifically. There would indeed be a logical mistake if it were forgotten that there were two languages in use and if it were thought that they could be amalgamated into a single homogeneous language. This would be to suppose that the two stories were, to use Wiles' own expression, 'literally united with one another'. Such a confusion of logics would be parallel to the confusion of the divine and human natures of Jesus against which Chalcedon so vehemently protested. Traditional theology has been well aware of the perils of such a confusion. But this mistake is not necessarily involved in speaking of one and the same person in the two distinct but related languages unless the logic of either or of both precludes it. Somewhat similar problems arise when we insist on using the two languages of freedom and causality to describe one and the same human action despite the logical difficulties which such a double usage generates. So here the underlying issue concerns the over-all logic of our theological language, the specific meaning and validity of speaking of a special act of God and a distinct divine presence in the person of Jesus, and the bearing on these problems of what we wish to assert in our historical language. We need to examine carefully the meaning, validity and implications of what we affirm of Jesus theologically.

Let us agree that we wish to speak of the human story as a true story of divine redemption and to affirm that the life and death of Jesus are a part of the human story which has unique significance for our seeing the human story as a whole in this way. How are we to understand such language? Different answers can and will be given. Some may think of divine redemption in terms of an ever-present dimension of human experience, as adjectival to man, and argue that the story of divine redemption is 'true' in some extended sense of 'truth'. Others may think of it as a reserve of healing power on which they can draw by a proper discipline of the spirit. Others, again, may want to say that God is continuously redeeming as he is continuously creating, but that there

is no specific act of redemption. Some will think of the human
story as an on-going process to which succeeding men and generations contribute. Others will see it as a collection of individual
biographies which find their completion and fulfilment 'beyond'
this world of space and time. There are varieties of vision and each
will construe the divine language in its own way. According to
the significance which we attribute to the whole story, so we
shall differently interpret the activity of God.

The same holds true for the significance which we ascribe to
Jesus. Indeed, for Christians it is the significance which they
ascribe to Jesus which largely controls the significance which
they ascribe to the human story as a whole and to the creative and
redemptive activity of God. Was he a supreme teacher, an example of self-giving love, an inspiration to others to commit themselves to his way of life? Or was he all these things – and more?
Did he evince in both his teaching and his actions an authority
which marked out his relation to God from that of other men?
Did he mediate God's presence in a way in which no prophet
before him had mediated it? Is he present to succeeding generations of believers as no other figure of history is present to those
who live after him? Does he dwell in them, and they in him, in
any deeper sense than the most blatantly metaphorical? Are those
who begin by following him, and end in worshipping him, guilty
of idolatry as well as of a category mistake?

There is no quick answer to these questions. Some of them,
indeed, may be misleadingly phrased. Others may be capable of
more than one answer. The evidence of history, experience
and reflection will all have to be taken into account. But the
questions themselves should be sufficient to suggest the possibility that it was Jesus himself, in his earthly life and in his
risen presence, that compelled his disciples to modify the logic
of their theological language, rather than any misconceived
attempt to speak about him in a mythological language which
already lay to hand. Was it the logical ambiguities in the word
Kyrios which eventually led to the worship of Jesus and the puzzles
of Chalcedon, or was it something dimly but compellingly
apprehended in Jesus himself? When the author of the fourth

gospel wrote that the Word became flesh, was he speaking religiously but not theologically, or was he speaking theologically and truly? Was the ultimate and transcendent manifested in the contingencies of space and time, or do those who speak thus forget their grammar?

Should it appear that I have lapsed into the language of rhetoric, let me add at once that I do not claim to know the answers to these questions. Nor do I know how they might be conclusively answered. Perhaps eternity will tell! Certainly no present demonstration is available to us. I accept Wiles' view that 'there comes a point at which we reach a limit question, where we have to say "I can give no further reasons for seeing the thing as I do; this is my vision; do you not feel drawn to share it too?"' What I wish to suggest is that there is involved here a difference of vision, calling for differing attitudes, hopes and expectations, although these should not be exaggerated. There is, I repeat, a difference of vision. It is not the case that traditional theologians want an ontological backing for the same vision which is expressed in a reductive theology. The 'ontological backing' is a constituent part of their vision. If their vision is veridical, then the logic of their language must be adapted to meet the demands of their vision. If their vision is illusory or misunderstood, then no such adaptation will be necessary, and if any takes place it will be a logical mistake.

Certainly historical language must be given its due place in our account of Jesus. His life and death are a part of the human story and are to be located in the course of history. They can be connected with what preceded them and with what came after them, and in this way they are capable of historical explanation. Continuities exist. Furthermore, we can ascribe to the life and death of Jesus a special, even a unique, historical significance in relation to later historical events: for example, he was the founder of the Christian church – without him there would have been no Christianity. But this unique significance remains relative to the existence of the church. Similarly Mohammed was uniquely significant for the rise of Islam. Historical significance of this kind is essentially a relative significance.

While looking for continuities the historian must also do

justice to discontinuities. He must allow for the possibility of real novelty in the life of Jesus. Novelty of teaching presents him with no special problems. There is no obvious limit to what human beings may claim to be the case. Even if Jesus claimed to be Son of God the historian could accept the fact that Jesus made such a claim, even though he might assume that it was a false or meaningless claim. But difficulties arise when it is a matter of novelty of events. What of reports of Jesus' apparently miraculous acts? What of the claim that he was raised from the dead? The historian is here approaching the limits of his historical understanding. Should he simply reject such reports as fabrications? Should he say that they belong to another language-game, which speaks mythologically of the activity of God? And if the latter, can he rest content with the view that such language indicates a 'true' account of the human story as a whole, but not a 'true' account of the story of Jesus?

When we move on to speak of the significance of Jesus for the human story as a whole, we are no longer speaking historically. First, it does not seem to be the case that the historical past has any real unity which might justify the use of the phrase 'the human story' in anything but the loosest sense. *Il n'y a pas de l'histoire, mais seulement des histoires.* Second, this phrase embraces the future as well as the past, and the future is no concern of the historian. The concept of a universal history is a religious or a philosophical concept. It posits an underlying unity of history and an end towards which history is moving. From this point of view a particular part of human history may acquire special significance in so far as it forwards the movement of the whole and contributes to the end to which history is moving, but it remains a part of history and it is difficult to see how it might determine or define the significance of history as a whole. How, then, can the life and death of Jesus determine the significance of the human story as a whole unless they are in some sense the 'end' of history? Christians have indeed found themselves using this kind of language when speaking of the significance of Jesus, but to speak thus is to go beyond history. The life and death of Jesus belong to the past, while history moves on.

If we wish to affirm the unique significance of Jesus for the whole human story, we must make use of other than simply historical categories. If the language which seems to us to be most adequate and appropriate for doing justice to the whole of our experience is that of divine activity, then in this language-story Jesus becomes the decisive and determinative act of God. He defines and integrates the human and the divine stories. He is uniquely significant for the human story because he is uniquely significant for the divine story. In him we acknowledge simultaneously the perfection of humanity and the perfection of the divine creativity. How we are to understand the relation between these two perfections is the christological problem, but it would appear that the perfection of divinity must be counted both logically and ontologically prior.

To relate the human and divine stories in this way when we speak of the person of Jesus is one thing, to opt for a traditional christology is another. Even those who wish to speak in terms of a 'difference of degree' rather than a 'difference of kind' may speak of a special act of God and also, after a manner, of a distinct divine presence. For example, Jesus may be said to be the *classic* instance of the divine self-giving. The final choice between these two types of christology will depend on a variety of considerations, including the evidence which we have of the sort of person Jesus was and the authority that he claimed, the response that we believe to be appropriate to him, our understanding of the relation of God to the world which he has created and the sense which may be given to the idea that God has interpenetrated human life in the person of Jesus in a way which marks him out from all other human beings. Certainly we shall wish to affirm a continuity between Jesus and those who preceded him. In that sense he was no 'bolt from the blue'. He experienced the human condition. His life was a human life. His obedience was human obedience. But is there also a striking discontinuity? Does Jesus exercise a judgment on man as well as participate in the life and sufferings of men? Is he the agent of man's reconciliation to God rather than the first of the redeemed? Does his finished work transcend that which can be described in simply historical language? If so, may we not here be confronted with a special and unrepeatable act of God and a distinct divine presence of such a kind as Chalcedonian categories sought to express?

It is undoubtedly true that some of the arguments used to defend a traditional christology no longer convince. It may also be true that among such arguments should be included a naive use of the biblical story of the creation and the fall and an unwary application of the idea of salvation-history. What I have tried to show, however, is that logic, as such, does not rule out the notion of a unique divine act and a unique divine presence. God's activity in the world, whether in creation or redemption, remains in an important sense mysterious. How we should speak of it is an exceedingly difficult question. But if we speak of it at all we must expect our logic to be complex and intricate. The decision between logical truth and error must not be prejudged.

A REPLY TO MR BAELZ

PROFESSOR WILES

The editors have kindly invited me to write a short 'reply to Mr Baelz', which I am happy to attempt if it can be treated as a further small contribution to a continuing and, I hope, constructive conversation. My article was intended to be the starting-point for futher discussion and Mr Baelz's paper embodies precisely the kind of comment I had hoped to elicit. The main body of his paper is a careful discussion of the philosophical implications of the questions being raised. In particular he draws attention to the need for clarifying what we mean by the idea of divine activity in general. This was the issue which I myself felt it most incumbent upon me to try to take further after the writing of the paper and I have attempted to do so in a further article in *Religious Studies* (vɪɪ (March 1971), 1–12), entitled 'Religious Authority and Divine Action'. I will not repeat what I have said there. Baelz makes some valuable points about the approach to this topic, but in the end I am not clear just what he wants to affirm at this point. What is meant by speaking of divine activity as 'equally real' with the activity of men? This is not to complain about what has been said but to ask for something more. This is perhaps a somewhat unfair request, especially as his own *Prayer and Providence* is one of the most worthwhile attempts to tackle this problem in recent theological writing. Yet it is a more that does seem to be needed; for if we are to speak of a special activity or special presence of God, our understanding of it must be set against the background of our understanding of his general activity or general presence. Our difficulties on this wider score are a major factor in our contemporary difficulty with christology.

In general I find myself in substantial agreement with the philosophical points that he makes. In particular I would like to stress my complete agreement with him on two fundamental issues. I fully endorse his affirmation that 'if both languages are about one and the same world, what is said in one cannot be irrelevant to what is said in the other'; and I concur with his preference for 'a metaphysic of levels, which seeks to do justice both to the continuity and the discontinuity between various stages of the world's development'. But within such agreement there is clearly room for considerable variety of judgment about the ways in which the two languages are relevant to one another or about the nature of the partial continuity between different levels. How should we understand the relationship between freedom and causality, between a biological and a psychological account of the same entity? This seems to me to be a problem of the utmost importance for theology with which we have to go on struggling. All I want to claim at the moment is that it seems perfectly possible to relate such pairs to one another in general ways, which do not involve specific points of relationship of a distinct kind, without thereby weakening our hold on the fact that they both refer to the same entity and that therefore as wholes they are of great significance to one another.

Baelz argues that, in view of the fact of evil, divine activity cannot be thought of as something that applies uniformly to everything that happens in the world. Therefore the idea of 'special' creative acts in relation to certain events in the world ought not to be ruled out *a priori* as something that could only arise as the result of a logical mistake. I fully agree that there must be room for the idea of special activity in some sense. Baelz, however, is equally ready to acknowledge that some ways of understanding such cases of special creative activity (for example, a Eutychian christology) can justly be accused of an illogical confusion of categories. My question (and it is still for me a genuinely open question) is whether or not the christology of Chalcedon is guilty of that same failing. It is not always self-evident whether or not there is a category mistake even when one has been alerted to the possibility. It is possible to be aware of the distinction between two languages or two metaphysical levels (as Chalcedon clearly was in its own terms), but none the less, in one's attempt to give expression to the important fact that they both refer to the same reality, to relate them to one another in logically unacceptable ways.

I am fully prepared to accept that there is a flexibility about the logic by which one realm of discourse can be related to another. I accept Baelz's claim that in such cases the logic of our language may have to be adapted to meet the demands of our vision. But I would differ from him in the extent to which the 'ontological backing' can be properly spoken of in this case as 'a constituent part of their vision'. When he asks whether it was 'the logical ambiguities in the word *Kyrios* which eventually led to the worship of Jesus and the puzzles of Chalcedon, or was it something dimly but compellingly apprehended in Jesus', is this not a false dichotomy? Certainly there was something of profound and mysterious depth apprehended in Jesus, but I want to suggest that the particular way in which that something came to be articulated was dependent on a number of concomitant factors and not wholly implicit in the nature of the vision itself. No account of that vision fully satisfied them; nor indeed do I anticipate that any account we may give will fully satisfy us. They tried to understand their vision in the only way we can understand things, by relating it to associated beliefs of their own time. Those beliefs were not treated as fixed and immoveable. They too were certainly open to modification in the light of the new vision. There was a two-way influence. The historical judgment on which my paper was based was that a major influence on the way in which the person of Jesus came to be understood was a particular (and now very largely discarded) way of understanding the creation and the fall. That judgment is of course open to challenge on historical grounds, but I have not yet seen good reason to abandon it. It is important to my case to recognise that, as I see it, this relation to a particular understanding of creation and fall was not simply an argument 'used to *defend* the traditional christology', as Baelz puts it (my italics), but an important factor in bringing it into being in the first instance.

In the light of Baelz's discussion, I can perhaps restate the main thrust of my paper in a more careful way. The traditional christological statements are logically very odd. They relate God and man in a way which certainly appears at first sight to offend against the grammar of our normal speech about both God and man. But that does not mean that they can be declared nonsensical *a priori*. The logic of relating language about God and language about man is far too unclear and mysterious a thing for so high-handed a judgment to be justified. But it does seem to me to put the burden of proof on the shoulders of those who wish to insist that only the traditional christological statements are adequate, that the anticipated logic of our language has to be broken at this point. That burden they have in general been very ready to accept. But a number of the old arguments, as Baelz says, no longer convince. One oft-repeated argument has been the challenge: how could men with their intellectual and religious background have come to such a conclusion unless the nature of the vision itself absolutely compelled them to do so? It is primarily in relation to that argument that my paper was intended. It sought to show that one very important factor in leading them to their conclusion was the relation of Christ's work to creation and the fall, understood in ways which we no longer hold. Even if that influence be admitted it does not prove that the traditional way of understanding God's activity in Christ is false, but it does seem to me to be a factor weighing against acceptance of it. Nor certainly does it imply that complexity and mystery have been or can be removed from our understanding of Christ, any more than they have been from our understanding of creation or of sin – only that they may have to take other forms.

3

NEED JESUS HAVE BEEN PERFECT?

JOHN A. T. ROBINSON

The doctrine of the two natures has been one, classic way of saying how Jesus Christ could be both the self-expression of God and at the same time a completely normal human being – in the words of the Chalcedonian definition, 'of one substance with the Father' and 'of one substance with us'. It is a way that today is subject to formidable objections. Not only does it use categories that almost inevitably suggest that the human centre of consciousness in Christ was replaced or displaced by the divine, but it gives the impression to a modern man that Jesus was a hybrid: the very idea of a God-man, with two natures in the same person, evokes the picture of a sort of bat-man or centaur, an unnatural conjunction of two strange species. And at best it reinforces the popular image of the incarnation as a bolt from the blue, a dip of the divine into the human on the arc of a parabola receding as unrepeatedly as it came.

But, of course, originally no such isolating effect was intended or felt. The incarnation was part of a continuous drama in which the two worlds of the natural and the supernatural constantly interpenetrated. Irenaeus gave classic expression to the conviction that the revelation of Christ represented the recapitulation of the entire cosmic process. The trouble is that men of the twentieth century, unlike those of earlier centuries, do not naturally see the cosmic process in these dualistic, or two-natured, terms. Hence the incarnation so presented strikes them as an anomalous exception, not as the supreme exemplification.

If then we are to use the traditional categories in relation to the incarnation it is essential that we extend to it the re-valuation of them to which we have now become accustomed elsewhere. For we have come to see the natural and the supernatural not as two co-existent orders of being that have to be joined together, so much as two sets of language, man-language and God-language, in which it is possible to speak of the one cosmic process. In other words, as Professor Maurice Wiles has said,[1] what we are talking about are not two storeys but two stories. The one is natural, scientific, descriptive. The other is supernatural, mythological and interpretative. The former views the course of events in the categories of an evolutionary cosmology, the latter in terms of 'moments' like the creation, the fall, the incarnation, the parousia.

Thanks to the agonizing wrestlings of the past two hundred years (and particularly the past hundred), there is now a substantial measure of agreement about how these two ways of speaking are to be related to each other. The 'events' in the latter series are not to be slotted into the former, as and when the supernatural penetrates or perforates the natural by special creations, interventions, or acts of God. The supernatural is not a parallel, superior causal sequence, but an interpretation, a *re-velatio* or turning back of the veil, in terms of myth or a 'second' story, of the same process studied by science and history. The creation and the fall are not single acts of God or particular events in the historical past but ways of giving theological interpretation to processes and experiences that are going on all the time. Similarly, we are beginning to recognize that the parousia is not a once and for all event in the historical future, whether near or remote, but part of a myth designed to clarify what it means – as well as what it will mean – to see all things 'made new' in the kingdom of God. It is the affirmation by way of a single dramatic picture of Christ coming into everything and beginning to reign 'from now on' (Matt. xxvi. 64 = Luke xxii. 69). It asserts that the reality depicted by the fall, the truth of all things 'in Adam', is not the only or the final truth about the cosmic scene. What in each case the myth does is to focus and clarify in a single dramatized picture of black and white the realities obscured in the greys, the relativities and continuities, of the on-going process.

In order to affirm these truths of interpretation previous generations have felt it necessary to assert that there must be some

---

[1] See above pp. 3–12. It will be obvious how indebted I am to his contribution, which indeed supplied the stimulus for mine.

decisive events in the natural sequence to correspond to the moments in the supernatural, some day of creation, some special introduction of the soul of man, some datable fall, some predictable end of the world. If there were not this correspondence, then the reality of the theological affirmation seemed to be weakened or imperilled. We now see, however, that the demand for such 1 : 1 correspondence stems from a category confusion. Indeed, the events in the two series or stories are strictly incomparable. In the historico-scientific series we are dealing with a continuum, where all things are relative and interconnected, shading into each other by differences of degree, confused and 'grey'. In the mythological series we are concerned with discrete acts of God, with the unique in kind and not merely in degree, with the perfect, once and for all, absolute and final. These latter categories are not those of 'the flesh', or mere history, and to predicate them of that order is to deny the flesh as flesh. They are there to interpret the continuities and ambiguities of the flesh as the carrier of the Logos or meaning of God.

This is already to introduce christological language, which indeed the New Testament insists cannot be excluded from any part of the cosmic process. But before turning to the incarnation proper we may pause to watch this principle exemplified in the other so-called 'acts of God' in history, of which the exodus is viewed by the Bible writers as paradigmatic. To see the exodus as decisive for the interpretation of God's meaning for history it is not necessary to affirm that this event in the historical series is anything but confused, protracted, blurred at the edges, and generally uneventful. It need not have had even the relative decisiveness, say, of Creasy's 'fifteen decisive battles of the world'. To expect that it must be more 'eventful' if it is to be divine in significance is to confuse the categories of *chronos* and *kairos* (just as it would be, later, to say that that particular birth at Bethlehem – if indeed it even occurred at Bethlehem – *must* have been more 'eventful' than the rest).

Nevertheless, there is a point to be made on the other side which is of equal importance. The fact of continuity in the processes of nature and history does not mean that there are no climacterics, no genuinely new mutations, no moments which are not of more 'importance', to use Whitehead's term, than any others. To deny the need for 'special creations' to explain them does not mean that the first appearance of life and the emergence of *homo sapiens* are not points of determinative significance in the evolutionary process – however non-discrete, blurred and unremarkable these events may still in themselves have been.

Similarly, in history there are climacterics. There are Rubicons – however insignificant the stream. The 'sea of reeds', which has become for us the Red Sea, may have been another such ditch or swamp. Yet if the exodus proved to be a pure 'myth' in the popular sense, a non-event, that never happened or never changed anything, then it would be difficult, to say the least, to celebrate it as the supreme example of the mighty acts of God as Lord of history. That of which the interpretation is the interpretation must have sufficient validity in the man-language series if the God-talk is to be credible. And this applies not only to its historical 'status' but to its moral quality.

With these criteria I come to the heart of the matter, the incarnation. The word of course belongs to the mythological story, but it is of the essence of this story that the happening it interprets belongs equally to the purely historical series. Indeed, it is at this point above all that Christian theology has felt it necessary to insist on the 1:1 correspondence. There must also be within the latter sequence a once and for all event, unique in kind, discontinuous with the past, perfect, absolute and final. Anything less would be a denial of the decisive act of God.

Yet we must, it seems to me, be very careful here, much more careful than we have hitherto needed to be. All these categories belong to the 'second' language group. Can we assert them of the flesh and not destroy the flesh as flesh? This of course in another form is the question that dogged the whole Alexandria school of christology and represented its perennial temptation – to allow the divine to swamp the human and to end up in crypto-docetism. Yet we must ask it again, much more seriously – and that because of what we now know both about nature and about history.

Up till a hundred years ago or so it did not really matter in regard to the first man whether the anthropological story was confused with the mythological. Then it became vitally important to distinguish (though not to separate). If this had not been done the theological interpretation would have been discredited – whereas in fact it has been greatly enhanced: the Adam myth has much wider and profounder applicability than ever it did as describing something that happened only to our remotest ancestor.

Similarly today in regard to Jesus it has become vitally important to discriminate between what we can say 'according to the flesh' and what we can say 'according to the spirit' (though again without dividing or severing the two). 'Of the seed [or sperm] of David according to the flesh, Son of God according to the spirit', says Paul in Rom. i.4, perhaps citing an early formula, and the birth narratives of Matthew and Luke amplify this balanced statement with their genealogies on the one hand and their accounts of his conception by the Spirit on the other. The two may appear to us incompatible and the genealogies holed below water if Joseph was not the physical father of Jesus. But they are not in fact statements in the same series, any more than Darwinian statements on the origin of species belong to the same series as the statements of Genesis on the origin of Adam. Previous generations may not have needed to distinguish, but it is, I believe, imperative today to insist that the virgin birth story is *not* primarily intended to assert discontinuity in the biological series (an interpretation deliberately exploited in later church theology, though not in the New Testament, to break the entail of original sin) – thus setting it directly against the genealogies that accompany it – but is intended to affirm the entire process as the act and initiative of God. In other words, it is not told in order to make a negative statement about the flesh but a positive affirmation about the spirit. The minute and often murky continuities of heredity and environment are not abrogated, as the genealogies with their dubious liaisons are seeking to insist – though, of course, they are also making the theological interpretation of Jesus as son of David and son of God. That these continuities should be intact is of the essential nature of flesh. To deny the solidarities and relativities is to deny (as the New Testament never does) that, whatever *more* may need to be said of him, Jesus was completely one of us, *totus in nostris* (to use the phrase of Pope Leo), going back in his biological plasm to the first life on this planet and behind that to the elements of which the stars are made.

But the necessity for acknowledging more than we have done the relativistic, non-absolute character of the flesh, with its differences of degree rather than of kind, relates also to the rigour with which we must take historical criticism today, both in regard to what we can honestly say of the Jesus of history and in regard to the relationship of Christianity to other religions. I think we must freely admit that terms that we have used like sinlessness, perfection, uniqueness and finality do not and cannot belong to the 'flesh'. To assert them of Jesus is to make a theological not a historical judgment. This is *not* to say that Jesus was sinful, imperfect and without any uniqueness or finality. It *is* to say that from a historical point of view, according to the flesh, we cannot make such absolute pronoucements. For one thing we do not know. We simply cannot say, for instance, that Jesus was *always* loving. And we should be careful to avoid theological judgments that imply historical statements we cannot substantiate. (There is a cluster of such in the classic challenge that if Jesus claimed to be God – surely in itself very doubtful – then he must either *be* God or be mad or bad – the implication being that the latter two can self-evidently be ruled out. But the evidence is not so unambiguous.) We must boldly say nothing finally depends on the 1 : 1 correspondence.

Yet between the theological judgment and the statement of history the credibility gap cannot be too great. Jesus must have been sufficient to have evoked and sustained the response, 'Thou art the Christ, the Son of the living God' (Matt. xvi.16). The relative must have been such as to point through to the absolute, so that men could conclude that to have seen him *was* to have seen the Father. And for this the occasion must have been adequate, alike in moral quality and in what I called 'stature'.

The attribution of sinlessness to Jesus, as I said, is a theological judgment rather than an extrapolation from the historical evidence. Yet it is made remarkably early and by a variety of New

Testament writers. In II Cor. v.21 Paul says explicitly that Jesus 'knew no sin'; I Pet. ii.22 applies to him the words of Isa. liii that 'he committed no sin'; and Heb. iv.15, which Hugh Montefiore has argued is earlier than either of them, says that he was tempted at all points like us yet 'without sin'. These judgments, though made for doctrinal reasons, to present Christ as the perfect sacrifice for sin, could scarcely have been made, let alone sustained, within the lifetime of many who had known Jesus if the facts of history had blatantly contradicted them. The summary of the memory of him was that he 'went about doing good' (Acts x.38), and if that had not been true Christianity would not have survived its detractors for long. It is remarkable that not only do the gospels portray Jesus as having no consciousness of sin or guilt (that perhaps could be attributed to the theological position from which they are written) but they never seem to feel any obligation to defend the moral character of Jesus from Jewish attacks – his sitting light to the law (especially the sabbath and ritual laws) yes, but not his morals. And this is more remarkable considering the freedom with which they represent him as living and the company they represent him as keeping. The gospels report Jesus as referring to his own reputation as a gluttonous man and a wine-bibber, but never think it necessary to refute the charge. It would not have taken much to twist the Zacchaeus episode into living it up with the exploiting classes instead of identifying with the dispossessed. Nor would many a clergyman today be able to survive three circumstantial reports (Mark xiv. 3–9; Luke vii.36–50; John xii.1–8) in the local paper that he had had his feet (or head) kissed, scented and wiped with the hair of a woman of doubtful repute. The lack of defensiveness with which such compromising stories are told says a great deal.

Yet no sweeping historical claims are made for his perfection. In fact, Jesus specifically says (in a saying hardly likely to have been invented), 'Why do you call me good? No one is good except God alone' (Mark x.18; contrast the amendment in Matt. xix.17, 'Good? Why do you ask me about that?'). Moreover no attempt is made in the earliest tradition to cover up the fact that Jesus was, in the phrase of the Epistle to the Hebrews, '*made* perfect' in his obedience by having to learn from painful experience (Heb. v. 8–9). The incident of the Syrophoenician woman (Mark vii. 24–30 = Matt. xv.21–8), where Jesus is prevailed upon to do something which he had evidently no intention of doing at the start, is a classic instance of Newman's dictum (which he of course did not apply to Jesus) that 'here below to live is to change, and to be perfect is to have changed often'.[1]

There is no automatic 1:1 correspondence. Indeed, there are incidents in all the gospels, not least in the fourth gospel (e.g., John ix.16; x.20f.), where the 'second' language appears so dominant, to suggest that both Jesus' goodness and mental balance were far from that of the plaster saint or even of Aristotle's perfectly rounded golden mean. Yet the correspondence must have been *sufficient* to have provoked and justified the response. 'To whom else should we go?' (John vi.68): if Jesus had really thought of himself as a poached egg or been a profligate or even just another Zealot, there are other candidates that come to mind. To that extent the judgment of faith is ultimately vulnerable to the conclusions of the historian. And this is a risk that the Christian faith can never escape if it is to take the flesh as seriously as the Logos.

But what about what I have called the 'status' of the history as well as its moral quality? Obviously again if it could really be shown that Jesus never lived or was so insignificant a character as to have originated nothing it would be difficult, if not impossible, to sustain the judgment of faith that in this man took place the decisive act of God in world history. But this is very different from saying that the historical events must have the absolute, all or nothing quality such as is ascribed to them in the interpretation of the other story. There is no question but that in Jesus men did sense what could be called a climacteric of the human spirit. Both in word and deed something seemed to them to break through: 'No man ever spoke as this man speaks' (John vii.46); 'What is this? A new kind of teaching! He speaks with authority' (Mark i.27). Clearly here was no ordinary man. But, whatever the judgment of faith as to what *God* might be doing through him

[1] *Essay on Development* (1845), p. 40.

(and there was no ceiling they could place upon that), there is nothing in the response of contemporaries, whether negative or positive, to suggest that the man or the events themselves were different *in kind* from those that they met around them elsewhere. Even his miracles were not such as others did not (Matt. xi.27 = Luke xi.19) or could not (Matt. x.8; Mark. ix.14–20; John xiv.12) do.

But what of the total event itself that faith calls under its different aspects *the* incarnation, *the* atonement, *the* resurrection? In the 'second' story these are seen as once and for all unique transactions which have changed irreversibly the course of history, so that, as in the case of the fall, the situation is now no longer what it was. They are not just occurrences among others of the same kind but divine acts of an utterly different order. How far is the Christian committed to seeing any such decisiveness or finality in the actual history? Let us concentrate on what on any reckoning is the hinge event – the resurrection.

The very term, *hē anastasis, the* resurrection, marks the uniqueness, the finality with which it is seen in the 'second' series. Originally this term is part of the myth of the end and refers to the resurrection at the last day, and it is always so used in the gospels (e.g. Matt. xxii.30; Luke xiv.14; John xi.24; cf. Mark ix.9–11 where the puzzled objection that Elijah must come first before the Son of man's 'rising from the dead' suggests that any ressurrection predictions there may have been in the teaching of Jesus would have been understood to refer to the last day). Its subsequent application to what *we* call 'the resurrection' on the third day (and to no other risings from the dead, which are never designated by the decisive noun 'resurrection') implies the theological conviction, found throughout the New Testament, that this was indeed 'the beginning of the end'. This was the new act of creation, the start of the new humanity, the birth of the second Adam. The question is whether this momentous act of God required on the other scale a 'special creation' comparable to that which traditionally was deemed necessary to mark the emergence of the first man.

In the historical series the most notable fact about the resurrection narratives in the canonical, as opposed to the apocryphal, gospels is that nothing is described as happening. This reticence should make us wary of demanding instant 1 : 1 correspondence. But there is no doubt that the consequences of the resurrection of Christ as recorded in the New Testament – the empty tomb, the appearances, the transformation of the disciples – suggest, and have been taken to imply, a unique divine intervention (extending to a total molecular transformation) still more discontinuous with the ordinary processes of nature than the biological break felt to be required to match the theological significance of his birth.

But if we are concerned, here as much as anywhere else, to discern what is really being said at the two levels we must be more discriminating. Or we shall be requiring of the historical series statements for which there is no evidence and which are in danger of destroying the flesh as flesh. Equally, however, we must be aware of the other credibility gap – that of failing to provide sufficient historical cause to account for the theological judgment.

Let us start from this latter end. Any reconstruction of the history of the first century must stand condemned that fails to account not only for the initial transformation of the original disciples but for the continuing and all-controlling conviction of Christ as a life-giving presence in the Spirit indwelling those who had never 'seen the Lord', let alone viewed the tomb. That there was no such new spiritual reality, that nothing was changed, that it all rested on self-delusion or deceit, is to say that the unprecedented step of taking an element from the myth of the last things and transferring its 'finality' to a moment *within* history was purely arbitrary. Christianity would never have got started, let alone survived, if the credibility gap had been that wide.

Equally, it seems to me, if the so-called 'appearances' had been merely subjective hallucinations (the equivalent of seeing pink rats) or purely private it is incredible that Paul and others could have rested so much on them, especially when he sits so light to his own 'visions' (II Cor. xii.1–10). That there were in the period immediately following Jesus' death genuine, shared psychic experiences, with whatever degree of materialization (and the accounts vary), which were at least *thought* to be veridical, seems a necessary occasion of the first dawning of the spiritual conviction that was subsequently independent of them.

What of the empty tomb? Again the credibility gap seems to me to rule out deliberate deceit by the disciples (as suggested by the Jews according to Matt. xxviii.13), or that the women had gone to the wrong tomb and no one bothered to check (especially in the light of Mark xv.47), or that Jesus never really died (denial of this appears to be behind the special stress on eye-witness in John xix.32–5), or that his body was not buried but thrown into a lime-pit (the burial is one of the earliest and best-attested facts about Jesus, being recorded in I Cor. xv.4 as well as in all four gospels and, for what it is worth, the Acts kerygma (Acts xiii.29)). More plausible is the oft-repeated thesis that the subsequent belief in the resurrection *created* the empty tomb story because this is what the Jewish hope pointed to. But what it pointed to was a rising at the last day for the final judgment. *No one* expected to find a grave empty in the middle of history, nor if they had would they have associated this with 'the resurrection'. They would have associated it with bewilderment and probably with foul play – which is precisely what we find in the gospels (especially Mark xvi.1–8 and John xx.1–2 and 10–15). Only in John xx.9 is one man, reading back in faith, represented as putting the two together. So far from the empty tomb story being created to convince doubters, I would agree with C. H. Dodd's latest assessment that 'it looks as if they [the Evangelists] had on their hands a solid piece of tradition, which they were bound to respect because it came down to them from the first witnesses, though it did not add much to the cogency of the message they wished to convey, and they hardly knew what use to make of it'.[1] The evidence suggests indeed that it was a very primitive piece of tradition. Paul's words in I Cor. xv.4, that Jesus 'was buried' and that 'he was raised to life on the third day', seem to presuppose some connexion between the resurrection and the tomb (and not merely the appearances) as part of what he received at his first instruction as a Christian. What is significant is that he makes

[1] *The Founder of Christianity* (1971), p. 167.

nothing of it – ignoring it completely in his subsequent discussion of the relation between the natural and the spiritual body (I Cor. xv.35–55). This scarcely suggests a strong motivation in the early church to invent or elaborate it.

But none of this compels a supernaturalistic explanation of why the tomb was empty. 'They' have taken him away (John xx. 2 and 13) is the first and obvious thought – perhaps grave-robbers; for, as Jeremias, who now thinks that John xx preserves the earliest form of the tradition (!), says, 'it was unusual for the governor to release the body of a man executed for high treason, and fanatics could have remedied this decision by taking the corpse under cover of night to one of the criminals' graves'.[1] But the vagueness of the 'they' is appropriate. For what precisely happened to the old body will never be cleared up. The mystery, still unexplained, is subsequently interpreted (and this is the recognized function of angelic messengers), not as the disaster it first appeared, but as a confirmatory sign of the action of God. But unless there had been the new transforming reality of life in the Spirit, combined with the psychic phenomena, the physical evidence could not have been so construed, let alone created. Every reconstruction of the history is a matter of weighing probabilities, and others will assess them differently. But I believe we must be *free* (as the late Ronald Gregor Smith insisted) to say that the bones of Jesus may still be lying around Palestine. Belief in the resurrection does not *depend on* – let alone consist of – the fact that they do not; for we cannot be sure. We can make the affirmation of faith without being committed to a 'spill-over' from the absoluteness of the interpretative language into statements about the history which would remove the ambiguity and the 'greyness' which properly pertain to it.

Another way of putting this is to say that if we are to take the flesh of the incarnation seriously we must at all costs retain the possibility of 'offence'. The offence of Jesus to his contemporaries was that he came 'out of Nazareth' (John i.46), that men could truthfully say, 'Is not this the son of Mary, the brother of James and Joseph and Judas and Simon? And are not his sisters with

---

[1] *New Testament Theology*, I (1971), 305.

us?' (Mark vi.3); in other words, that the relativities, the continuities, the ordinariness, had *not* been broken. If to assert the
absoluteness, the Christ, the Son of God, the seamless robe of
history *has* to be torn, something has gone wrong. Yet Christian
theology has not been happy to live with the 'offence' of insisting
on the inviolability of *both* languages. There has been a constant
temptation to believe that if Jesus had a human father, that if
he was an ordinary fallible human being, that if his bones do lie
around somewhere in Palestine, then he could not be the Son of
God and vice versa. Yet the highest christology must be compatible with the dense mesh of history, retaining all its baffling
opacity.

As a test of our presuppositions, let me end with a rather
remarkable passage from the book of Wisdom (vii.1–6). The
speaker is Solomon.

> I too am a mortal man like all the rest, descended from the first man, who was
> made of dust, and in my mother's womb I was wrought into flesh during a
> ten-months space, compacted in blood from the seed of her husband and the
> pleasure that is joined with sleep. When I was born, I breathed the common
> air and was laid on the earth that all men tread, and the first sound I uttered, as
> all do, was a cry; they wrapped me up and nursed me and cared for me. No
> king begins life in any other way; for all come into life by a single path, and
> by a single path go out again.

The question I would ask is this: what do we need to affirm to say
that 'a greater than Solomon is here' (Matt. xii.42 = Luke xi.31)?
In the middle section there is clearly nothing that any Christian
would wish to deny of Jesus. 'When I was born, I breathed the
common air and was laid on the earth that all men tread': the
manger story (Luke ii.7) and Jesus' own words about the Son of
man having nowhere to lay his head (Matt. viii.20 = Luke ix.58)
fully bear that out. Clearly too, as he himself understood it, to
'exceed Solomon in all his glory' (Matt. vi.28–9 = Luke xii.27)
meant not having more splendid, supernatural robes but the
unsurpassable beauty of nature. It is however at the beginning and
end of the story that the pressures to modification have been felt.
All Christians have wanted to say of Jesus with St John that 'he
came from God and went to God' (John xiii.3). In other words, his

birth was due not simply to the forces of heredity and environment but to the purpose and initiative of God, and his life ran out not into nothingness and defeat but into God's resurrection order. That is not at issue. All that is in question is whether in order to affirm these things we *have* to say that the *way* he came into this world and went out again was *not* the path of any other king. I am simply not persuaded that the earliest witness of the scripture story commits us to saying that. It does not prevent us saying it. But we can have as high a christology without it, *both* in relation to the divinity *and* to the humanity of Christ – indeed, I believe, a higher.

4

THE THEOLOGY OF THE HUMANITY OF CHRIST

S. W. SYKES

J. F. Bethune-Baker in addressing the notorious Modern Church-men's conference of 1921 on the subject of 'Jesus as both human and divine' spoke as follows: 'To clear the ground I would start with two or three premises, and the first of them is that "ortho-doxy", in beginning with God, began at the wrong end.'[1] Warming to his theme he added:

Today, when in every department of investigation we begin with the relatively known and reason from what we find there to the unknown, it is Jesus as Man in His life in the world that we want to take as our starting point once again – as at the outset He was. That is what gives our modern study of the Gospels and Gospel history its interest and importance. We know He was human, we believe He was also divine. It is by finding out how He was man – what He was in His place in the historic process – that we may come to understand in what sense He was and is also God.[2]

The position of Bethune-Baker and some of his fellow modern-ists at the conference was not without its difficulties, since by 1921 confidence in the ability of historical enquiry to portray a Jesus of history who was 'also' credible as a divine figure had been severely shaken. Some words from Foakes-Jackson's paper acutely portray the modernists' dilemma:

They have lost the historical Christ, and have not regained Him by converting Him into a social reformer, a moral legislator, a revealer of a new conception of God . . . They ask us [the historians of the first century A.D.] to give them Christ as they want Him to be, and when we lay the facts before them, they declare them to be stones presented to hungry folk who are clamouring for bread.[3]

---

[1] *The Modern Churchman* XI, 287.
[2] *Ibid.* pp. 287-8.
[3] *Ibid.* p. 231. This paper, which was not given at the conference, was included in the conference number as a reply, since Foakes-Jackson's position had been criticised.

Notwithstanding Foakes-Jackson, Bethune-Baker believed that a modern approach to the person of Christ was bound to begin with the affirmation of his humanity. Since then this point has been repeated frequently enough by theologians of the most widely differing persuasions.[1]

Dr Robinson's essay, 'Need Jesus Have Been Perfect?', raises many similar sets of considerations. Like Bethune-Baker, he insists that the 'natural sequence' requires that nothing be allowed to qualify our statements about Jesus' flesh. Again like Bethune-Baker, he urges that we do not speak of Jesus' humanity with the same kind of language as that we use of his divinity. The differences between their work reflect the passage of fifty years of theological debate, but I believe there to be a consistency of fundamental assumption which requires careful investigation.

I

I wish to focus initially on Bethune-Baker's contrast between *knowing* that Jesus was human and *believing* that he was also divine. How do we *know* that Jesus was human? This is, on the face of it, a very odd question. A question about a person's humanity would normally be interpreted to refer to his humaneness; we simply do not enquire whether people belong to the human race or not. We *know* that they are human by simple inspection. Possession of two legs and a larynx is enough evidence. To know that a person walked and talked implies that he is human. For all ordinary purposes we need enquire no further.

It is when we ask about the basis of our confidence that the real oddness of the question begins to emerge. Knowledge of the facts of human generation lies at the roots of the matter. To belong to the human race means to have been begotten by two human parents. If we ask how we *know* that any figure of the past was human, the answer must be because of the strength of the assumption that those who look like human beings are conceived and

---

1 See the discussion of D. M. Baillie in *God Was in Christ* (1948), chs. I–III.

born in the normal way. To call this an assumption is not in any way to diminish the massive weight of evidence for it derived from all other known instances of this same process.

Applied to Jesus the argument is exactly similar. We *know* that a man called Jesus walked and talked; we would *assume* from this evidence that he was conceived in the normal way. On this account what we may say that we certainly *know* is that it would have been possible to have a conversation with a man called Jesus of Nazareth. What I shall call his *aspective humanity* – a humanity which one can look at, feel, and converse with – is a matter of indubitable knowledge.

But what is the status, in Jesus' case, of those normal assumptions we make on the basis of certainty about aspective humanity? In all other cases of the human species, to establish aspective humanity is to make permissible a whole series of reasonably certain generalisations. We assume, for example, that at a certain point in time that individual was conceived after sexual intercourse, that he conforms organically to either male or female body structure, that organs and limbs work in a certain way, that he goes through a process of maturation and disintegration until he dies, and that at death his body will decompose. These constitute the content of Dr Robinson's closing quotation from the book of Wisdom. Such generalisations are subject to the variations of particularity, and some are not as well founded as others. But it is important to notice that our concept of humanity is founded on such generalisations about normality. We create this concept by analogy; when we know of a person that he is a male adult of thirty years of age, by analogy we envisage him with all the general characteristics of men of his age. These characteristics I shall refer to as *empirical humanity*, since it is a picture composed on the basis of countless examples of known human beings in their varying ages.

The question is, of course, whether in the case of Jesus we can proceed from his aspective humanity, which is not to be doubted, to envisage, by analogy, his empirical humanity. In the history of theology, as Dr Robinson makes clear, this has been by no means a simple question. Some patristic writers would most emphatically have denied it. Despite the evidence of the gospels,

Clement of Alexandria did not see how Christ could be said to have had real physical needs of hunger. Many of the Fathers denied that he was ignorant of anything or needed to ask questions. In modern times the question, vexed enough in principle began to be aggravated by the widening gap between the New Testament and the developing modern world view. The question of whether Jesus did not share the mistaken views of his times in regard to demon possession was hotly debated from the eighteenth century onwards; even Gore, who was prepared to accept limitation of knowledge in Christ, felt that the issue was decided by Jesus' divine authority.[1] So used have we become to accepting the limitations imposed on Jesus by his environment that Bultmann's assertion that Jesus taught a false eschatology is generally debated on historical, not on doctrinal grounds.

It is, however, one of those historical questions with mainly negative consequences for doctrine. That is to say, if *historically* we can be certain that Jesus did or taught certain things which we consider sin or error, then *doctrinally* we cannot assert his sinlessness or inerrancy. It is this which constitutes what Dr Robinson refers to as 'the risk' of theology. On the other hand we cannot discover by historical study that Jesus was as a matter of fact sinless or inerrant, any more than we can establish by history alone what constitutes sin or error. The preoccupation of modern post-enlightenment theology with the threat of the historical disproof of its propositions has led to a certain overlooking of the fact that, in the absence of historical disproof, a doctrinal argument may carry considerable weight. Whereas Dr Robinson asserts that we 'should be careful to avoid theological judgments that imply historical statements we cannot substantiate', I am inclined to think that the consequences of a doctrinal argument could well be applicable to history. Thus, for example, the idea of Jesus' sinlessness is clearly intended to survive Dr Robinson's discussion of those New Testament passages which qualify the way in which we construe the notion.

My basic contention is that the question about the humanity of Jesus is a doctrinal one, with far-reaching doctrinal implications,

---

[1] *Dissertations on Subjects Connected with the Incarnation* (1895), p. 26.

and not in the least to be presented as conclusively decided by the mere statement that Jesus was a man.

This can be shown by examining the consequences for assuming that because the aspective humanity of Jesus is not to be doubted we may, by analogy, proceed to attribute to Jesus all the characteristics of empirical humanity. If this assumption is made we are explicitly allowing the weight of evidence for those generalisations about normal human nature, derived from countless millions of examples, to count fully in our interpretation of Jesus' human existence. We are providing this interpretation with unanswerable objections to numerous features of the biblical narratives. For empirical humanity is not born of a virgin mother, does not walk on the water, raise dead men to life, cure disease at a distance by word of command, nor yet rise from the dead. These are all examples of that 'spill-over' which Dr Robinson might well prefer to jettison. They are the crudest sort of break in our everyday continuities, and if we take the assumptions of empirical humanity seriously, critical reduction of the New Testament evidence to more sober dimensions would be the accepted task of the historian.

But can we stop here? Could there be *any* acceptable grounds, if the empirical humanity of Jesus was said to be a matter of firm *knowledge*, for not envisaging Jesus as simply the normal human mixture of strength and weaknesses, good points and bad points? We unhesitatingly discuss the merits and demerits of Peter and Paul in this way; what makes us hesitate with Jesus?

In practice the christology of those who most vehemently insist on what they call the 'full humanity' of Jesus hesitates at one point or another in drawing the full conclusions. John Knox provides a clear example in his discussion of Jesus' sanity, with its repeated use of the question, Could so eminently sane a person have thought of himself and taught about his death in the manner presented in the gospels?[1] What is clear is that, despite the apparent radicality of the questions Knox is asking, the 'sanity' of Jesus is being guarded as a christological presupposition, despite

[1] *The Death of Christ* (1959), ch. 3.

all the empirical evidence that human nature is liable to obsessive self-delusions. Doctrinal considerations invariably enter discussion of the humanity of Jesus; the issues are not simply those of unambiguous fact.

That the dilemma is an ancient one is shown by the role which docetism, or 'crypto-docetism', plays in the history of doctrine. Like many other terms used in theological controversy this has a highly ambiguous penumbra of meaning, and its imprecision has made it of very questionable value. The clearest meaning is when it refers to the insubstantiality of Jesus' flesh, the assertion that what I have called the aspective humanity of Jesus was an illusion. But from quite early times it was also used, polemically, to refer to christologies in which the humanity of Jesus was denied or diminished in one way or another. The significance of the existence of a 'heresy' called docetism is that it draws attention to the dangers in language like, 'He came down to earth from heaven'. The relating of Jesus to mankind, and the relating of the Jesus-event to God's saving work, has always called for great sensitivity and care. In the pre-Chalcedonian period theologies of the incarnation which were determined to avoid docetism in its gnostic form insisted on the reality of Jesus' humanity and his sufferings. But there was no precision or certainty about whether Christ has assumed fallen or unfallen human nature, tainted or untainted by human sinfulness. The confident belief that God had sent his son into the world was presented side by side with the insistence on the reality of Jesus' life experience.

However it is equally clear, if the two kinds of assertion are supposed to refer to the one and same being, that not merely must the 'credibility gap' not be too great, they must be in some kind of actual relation to each other. In the history of doctrine the bald statement that the divine word took our flesh is open to a number of interpretations. It could mean any one of the following: 'our flesh', in whatever condition it was at the moment of assumption, was at that moment instantly transformed to be henceforward a new type of humanity; 'our flesh', weakened by sin but not 'naturally' tainted by it, was assumed and remained as Christ's humanity until being raised in power; or, 'our flesh' was, and remained in the incarnate one, our sinful flesh, *natura vitiata*.[1] A fourth solution also presented itself as a possibility to some of the Fathers. This was that Christ's humanity was original humanity, that is, humanity as it was before the fall. Thus Leo I in his Tome wrote of his formula, *totus in suis, totus in nostris* (complete in what belonged to him, complete in what belonged to us): 'by "what belonged to us" we mean what the Creator put in us from the beginning ... For that which the Deceiver brought in, and man being deceived admitted, had no trace in the Saviour.'[2] If this solution is clearly ruled out by our Darwinian attitude towards the historical fall, it is surely clear that the other options remain as serious possibilities.

They are serious, however, only if theology remains willing to attempt to speak with some precision of the activity of God. Of this it will be necessary to say more at a later stage. But one must admit that there is a particularly perplexing aspect in the modern setting of this ancient christological question. This is the fact that we are now capable of pursuing our descriptive analysis of man much further than were the Fathers or even the theologians of the last century. We can particularise about genetic inheritance where they could only guess. Thus contemporary theology is faced with an apparently new dilemma; can it precisely say at what point the divine 'entered' the human?

This dilemma, however, is not confined to the doctrine of the incarnation, but occurs wherever the activity of God is spoken of in areas subject in principle to close observation and experiment (e.g. creation or free will). In these cases too, we ask, does God's activity result in some observable consequences? Is God actively engaged at this point in a way in which he is not engaged at some other point? It would seem to me that christology cannot function at all unless some statements are made which indicate a *special* activity of God in Christ; results, that is, which are *not* observable

---

[1] On these differing views see the following respectively: the argument of J. H. Srawley, 'St Gregory of Nyssa on the Sinlessness of Christ', *Journal of Theological Studies*, VII (1906), 434–41; R. L. Ottley, *The Doctrine of the Incarnation* (1902), p. 604 and K. Barth, *Church Dogmatics*, I/2 (1956), 151–5. But with this latter statement one must compare IV/2, 27–8.

[2] *Tomus ad Flavianum*, 3 (tr. C. A. Heurtley, *On Faith and the Creed* (Oxford, 1889), p. 198).

in mankind as a whole. To speak with Dr Robinson of 'climacterics' in our understanding of God implies, unless we are content to be in danger of delusion, believing that such an effect is integral to self-revelatory purpose.

If this is the case then the dilemma of locating the point at which the special activity of God is manifest is both ancient and, in fact, unavoidable. Our ability to describe the human phenomenon with greater accuracy merely sharpens a difficulty which has always existed. If Dr Robinson claims by the theory of two languages to have conjured this difficulty away, he may not unreasonably be suspected of having merely moved it to another place.

My conclusion is that consideration of the humanity of Jesus is not to be treated as *merely* a question of fact. It is a matter in which we may expect to find theological issues requiring patient elucidation. The most important of these is the soteriological argument which is frequently implied or employed in the discussion, and to this we must now turn.

II

In the case made for some revisions of the 'full humanity' of Christ one can find a strong, but occasionally covert, appeal to soteriology. Dr Robinson's defence of *totus in nostris* (without Pope Leo's qualification) and his insistence on not denying the flesh as flesh is an example of this argument. But contemporary theology contains numerous other illustrations. The statement that a Christ who is not 'fully human' is of no interest to contemporary man is soteriological in character. This is sometimes expanded to include an explicit refutation of certain gospel stories; thus it is said that if Jesus was 'fully human', he could not have been born of a virgin, walked on the water, or healed men at a distance. The same tradition of contemporary theology is frequently prepared to designate the whole patristic tradition of christology as docetic.

As we have seen, this position occasionally presents itself as a commonsense statement of fact, that Jesus was a man. In reality the force of the statement derives from the specific soteriology implied in it, namely, the sense that Jesus is identified with our human condition. But some care is needed in deploying the argument. The mere statement that Jesus was 'a man' does not yield an unambiguous meaning. It might amount to no more than the assertion of particular masculinity; it does not necessarily embrace femininity. Further traps exist in thoughtless, and sometimes sentimental, talk about Jesus' suffering or status as an outcast. It would not be difficult to imagine a birth of greater indignity and discomfort (in a ditch, for example) nor a career much less prestigious (as a tax gatherer), nor a life-experience more rejected (as a leper) than that which the stories reveal. The attempt to connect Jesus with homosexuality seems a product of this kind of sentimentally motivated argument.[1]

The theme of identification is theologically effective only if what Jesus was and did can in some sense be shown to be typical or representative of the human condition and human experience. Some strands at least of New Testament soteriology bridge this gap by speaking of corporate solidarity 'in Christ'.[2] However, it is precisely this language to which other writers object, as involving concepts foreign to the modern western way of thought.[3] We have then a dilemma. The more a theologian insists on the particular humanity of Christ, the more need he has of a concept of its representative status. For those who argue within the structures of Johannine and Pauline christology this presents no particular problem.[4] But in that case the humanity of Christ is not simply a particular humanity; and one has set out on the road of beginning to specify what distinguishes Christ's humanity from ours.

[1] H. W. Montefiore, 'Jesus, The Revelation of God', in N. Pittenger (ed.), *Christ for Us Today* (1968), pp. 101–16: 'If Jesus were homosexual in nature (and if this is a true explanation of his celibate state) then this would be further evidence of God's self-identification with those who are unacceptable to the upholders of "The Establishment" and social conventions.' Professor Nineham's objection that this amounts to trading on the fact that such speculations are insoluble by our available evidence seems fully justified.
[2] See Professor Moule's essay in this volume, and, in particular, the quotation from C. H. Dodd, pp. 108–9.
[3] This is the assertion of Professor M. F. Wiles in 'The Unassumed is the Unhealed', *Religious Studies*, IV (1968), 53. But it is not clear to me, even if this is in fact the case, that modern western theologians have simply to acquiesce.
[4] It is very far from clear in Professor Wiles' essay how the salvation, to which Christ is said to be the way, is communicated to contemporary believers, if there is no sense of relationship between Christ's humanity and ours beyond the highly vapid contemporary notion of 'human nature'.

We must step back for a moment from the closer pursuit of individual arguments to notice one important dispute which has far-reaching implications in determining the eventual form of a christology. This concerns the method of approach. As Bethune-Baker rightly observed, there are two basic approaches, starting at different ends. The anthropological approach defines man and his needs and finds in Jesus a saviour. From anthropology is constructed a soteriology and from there a christology. Its advantages are obvious; it is 'relevant' and it starts with the known. The other approach is the theological, which starts with God and his sovereign activity. Christology is possible because God acted. Man is saved because God acted to save him. Its drawbacks are notorious; it is said to be 'irrelevant' since it starts with the unknown.

In this section I am not proposing to insist that, despite its drawbacks, only the theological approach does justice to its subject matter; I am concerned with a more limited aim, that of refuting the suggestion that, somehow, only the anthropological approach is valid in christology, and that the theological considerations have no force or less force.

As we saw, Bethune-Baker's premiss that whereas the divinity of Christ is a matter of *belief*, his humanity is a matter of *knowledge* is open to serious doubt, if by humanity is meant anything more than aspective humanity. A further objection may be urged against his statement that we ought in christology, as in all other subjects, to begin with the relatively known. It is true, of course, that the structure of theological discourse is built upon human speech and human experience. To give content to the term 'divine' we are obliged to speak of situations which fall within the bounds of human experience, however we may wish to qualify features of that experience and to point beyond it. The epistemology of theology roots it in human speech. In this sense, whatever we may say about the divinity of Christ or of God acting in Christ is bound to be interpreted initially by reference to some human state of affairs.

However, when we give reasons why we feel bound to talk of Christ in that way at all, instead of using the more immediately intelligible terms of prophet, teacher and healer, it may be that we are forced to speak of *God's* initiative (however difficult that language may be) as distinct from man's initiative. In this language we want to emphasise, as we would when speaking of why there should be a world of experience at all, that something contingent is the case because it is a result of God's plan and foreknowledge. Needless to say this sort of language is everywhere evident in scripture. Not so unnecessary to emphasise is the fact that this sort of language must be allowed its own logic. To treat it as a mythological, poetical or otherwise fancy way of saying something whose *real* meaning is readily intelligible in more straightforward human terms about human initiative and intentions is to miss its point. The function of a theologically-based christology is to relate all that is known of Jesus to the questions of time and eternity, natural and supernatural which are the subject matter of theology.

And here one must simply dissent from the suggestion that there exists a 'substantial measure of agreement', of the kind Dr Robinson suggests, regarding God-talk. There are surely not one, but many, ways of speaking about God. If some sentences using the term God are mythological in character, then other sentences may not be. There is no necessity for them to be all of one sort. But to regard *all* talk of God's activity as mythological in character would be, even if it were agreed (which it is not), a most serious step in theology. Could one speak, as Dr Robinson does, of 'the purpose and initiative of God'? Of what is theological, interpretative language supposed to be a *re-velatio*? If one takes a view of nature and human nature such as that of Bertrand Russell or Alex Comfort, would a theological interpretation speak of realities or processes in nature other than those of which they speak?

It is at this point that it becomes clear that the interpretation of the significance of Jesus and attitudes towards Jesus' astonishing powers as recorded in the gospels are crucially linked. Once again the wholly sceptical position on the life of Jesus is an intelligible and consistent one. If we are proposing to apply to Jesus all the assumptions we make about empirical humanity, then we will be bound to read the stories of his supernatural power in the gospels

in the light of Hume's convenient principle that only testimony
whose falsehood would be more miraculous is sufficient to establish an alleged miracle. To the sceptic the presence of miraculous
stories in the gospels is easily their most important feature;
apologetic attempts by Christians to turn them into incidental
adjuncts create a misleading imbalance in the total framework of
interpretation.[1] It is not that we are required by the New Testament to accept an either-or alternative on the miraculous as a
whole, nor to neglect the question of testimony by which we may
properly distinguish between the differing stories. Nor do I believe
that we are forced to accept as a means of understanding the New
Testament language about God's activity in Jesus the 1:1 correlation between divine 'events' and human events which Dr Robinson regards as the chief characteristic of myth. My point is
rather that the whole event of Christ raises at a particular time in
history the question of a power not to be explained in terms of
mere nature. Christology cannot in the end avoid the significance
of the *difference* between the story of Jesus and the lives of other
men; and it would seem to be at least open to theologians to take
a less embarrassed attitude towards those factual reasons offered
from the first for singling out Jesus from other prophets or leaders.

It must be admitted that the way we handle or even consider
the appeal is affected by our understanding of time and of nature
as it changes with increasing knowledge. That cannot be denied.
We are not required to think ourselves into a first-century world
picture, and to present it as if it were or could be contemporary
theology.

At the same time it seems to me necessary to protest against the
theological scholarship which simply accepts whatever may be
said to be offered by the natural sciences as an account of reality,
and then uses that account as a criterion for ruling out of court the
stories of the New Testament. In this respect a further parallel

---

[1] David Cairns is still worth quoting on this point. 'These signs, therefore, are integral
parts of the revelation, and not adjuncts to it. They are revelations of the ideal purpose
of God for mankind, and therefore of his character. They therefore necessarily influence
our idea of God. Inasmuch also as they imply the coming into the order of nature of
powers that cannot be explained in terms of mere nature, they must inevitably affect
our whole conception of the world.' *A Faith that Rebels* (1928), p. 93.

between Bethune-Baker and Dr Robinson is revealing. Speaking of the virgin birth story as myth, Bethune-Baker asserts that 'we know enough of the order of Nature now to discredit the ancient idea that the new can only come about by a break in the continuity of Nature'.[1] To this statement he adds the following note: 'Whereas it would be rational in ancient times to believe the story, it would be irrational today because it could not be related to the generally accepted *Welt-anschauung* of the period.'[2] But it seems to me neither that our natural knowledge is of the kind that seems to be suggested, nor that it is the function of the 'generally accepted *Welt-anschauung*' to determine the rationality of theological statements. In particular we must question whether, so long as highly competent scientists disagree concerning the significance of man's moral and spiritual capacities, any precise sense can be given to the notion of a 'generally accepted *Welt-anschauung*'. It is one thing to admit that aspects of natural science raise questions in theology and affect our understanding of the relations of time and eternity; it is quite another to insist that the alleged ideology of science as a whole provides the sole criterion for testing theological statements.

In particular the insistence that there cannot be a break in the continuity of nature needs to be questioned in relation to christology. Christ is not the *absolutely* supernatural, nor the *absolutely* novel, and traditional christology does not attempt to assert this. The humanity of Christ, however conceived, contains elements of continuity with all other human beings. But I can see no *a priori* reason for supposing that the humanity of Christ may not itself contain genuine elements of novelty; and it is these novel elements which provide us with the factual reasons for embarking upon christology at all.

But this is the exact point of greatest difficulty. If we deny that there is anything remarkable about Jesus, if Jesus really was an ordinary, fallible human being and no more, then our christology has no basis in fact; if, however, we desire our christology to be based in fact and begin to specify *in what respects* Jesus is remarkable, then the question arises whether these attributes begin to remove

[1] *Loc. cit.* p. 288.   [2] *Ibid.* note 2, p. 289.

him from empirical humanity. Traditional christology used Jesus' miraculous powers as evidence of his divinity; to the modern mind for various reasons this is unattractive. But can Jesus *both* be ordinary *and* a climacteric? Can one assert *both* that there is nothing remarkable about his history *and* yet that it points through to the absolute so that man could conclude that to have seen Jesus was to have seen the Father? To bear the weight of such a statement something more explicit needs to be provided than Dr Robinson's bare reference to the 'adequacy' of Jesus' moral quality and stature.

Other modern christologies are less inhibited, though scarcely in a less vulnerable position. They speak of Jesus' openness to God or perfect love or true obedience to the Father, oblivious of the fact that these raised precisely the same questions (as well as difficulties of their own). For such 'openness' is, in all empirical human experience, vitiated and corrupted by self-centredness. Are we then to say that Jesus was not self-centred? Not only would such a statement set him at a remove from all the rest of humanity, it would not even have as much empirical evidence for it as would a direct appeal to the miracles! As Apollinaris discovered to his cost, any anthropologically precise christology runs the immediate risk of being accused of compromising the 'true humanity' of Christ.

It is precisely this dilemma which I believe to be inescapable. We can therefore prescribe a simple test to apply to those theologians who insist most strongly on the 'full humanity' of Christ, and who inveigh most vehemently against what they claim to be ancient and modern docetisms. What account do they give of the human excellences of Christ? Does this account distinguish Christ from the rest of humanity? Any account which does not distinguish him from the rest of humanity is not credible as christology; and any account which does so distinguish him is clearly not merely 'normal' or 'empirical' humanity. Nor will it do to insist on precision in the theology one criticises, while concealing the dilemma under vague terminology in one's own. Rather than mislead ourselves into believing that these christologies have given us an exciting new account of Christ's humanity,

I prefer to return to explore the traditional doctrine of sinless perfection.

III

It will be observed that I am content to speak separately of the 'divinity' and of the 'humanity' of Christ, in the terms of traditional christology. These words should be treated as theological shorthand, rather than reified abstractions. They refer respectively to the relationship of Jesus Christ to man, and to the significance of this relationship for an account of God's activity in his world. The separable problems with which talking about 'humanity' and 'divinity' deal do not disappear if we decline to use what Dr Robinson refers to as 'dualistic' language; and by raising the issue of the 'sinless perfection' of Christ's 'humanity' I am abbreviating what is bound to be discussed if it is said that a life of which we have concrete historical testimony is somehow a paradigm of God's activity in the world. The conditions of that life, and God's activity in the world are separate issues; but the associating of them has clear consequences for both. To speak of 'sinless perfection' in relation to 'humanity' is to speak of the consequences of the latter for the former.

The idea of perfection has many problems, the chief of which is the problem of learning and of knowledge. The nature of Christ's knowledge has perplexed theologians deeply. Not only are we encouraged to think in the gospel of Luke that Jesus' youth and young adulthood was a period of intense learning and progress in knowledge, there is also rather little suggestion of radical novelty in his teaching. It has been frequently observed how strangely this contrasts with the picture of deep fellowship with God painted especially in the gospel of John. Theologians have consequently wrestled to depict two sorts of knowledge in Christ in order to do justice both to the divinity and to the humanity, and have then had the further problem of trying to relate them to each other. The result of such attempts is, inevitably, a formidable sense of unreality, which it is all too easy to depict as meaningless.

But to speak of Christ's perfection cannot mean, if the New

Testament evidence counts for anything, that learning was no part of the experience of Jesus. He was certainly to that extent at least psychologically 'normal'. But how far may we press our conception of 'normality' when it comes to Jesus' sense of fellowship with God? The problem is whether our 'normality' continues to be a criterion. There appear to be only two courses open; either to compromise Christ's likeness to our 'normality' by admitting in him a special knowledge of God (in effect a divine centre of consciousness) whether we specify its consequences in great detail or not; or, to assert a 'normality' totally within our own range, but crowned by another sort of gift in no way expending or altering the limits of normal human consciousness. The problem, is whether, if there is anything special about Christ's knowledge, it has to be brought closely into relation with our own awareness of our limitations.

Another aspect of this same problem concerns emotional maturation. A 'normal' human boy evidently passes through certain stages of development, long before they are the subject of his powers of self-control, by which his basic attitudes are formed, and in which his future masculinity very largely consists. The difficulty of envisaging such 'normality' in Jesus' development in the terms of our knowledge of it is the precise twist it gives to the traditional 'scandal of particularity' in terms of sexual differentiation. The more particularity one admits in christology (limitation to a particular age, country, town, religion, family and so on), the more one is in need of a transcending category. This category had traditionally been the notion of 'man' or 'humanity'; and all particularities of time and place could be seen to be necessarily part of being human. To have a mother and father, to live in a society, and to be part of a particular world order is acceptable on this principle. But to be either male or female, though also necessarily part of being human, seems to be a much more radically divisive alternative lying at the basis of personality.

I see no way, in fact, of deciding the issue. Either one continues to speak of 'human nature' as a category transcending masculinity, and femininity, and asserts that, though Jesus was in every respect a human male, this is in no essential way different from any of the other drastic limitations of time and place imposed by the act of incarnation; or, one strives for an idea of bisexuality and is prepared to speak of Christ as a pioneer of such experience. In either case one is involved in postulating a category which corresponds to nothing precisely in our world of experience. The assumption that one can slide easily from 'man' to 'Man' contains more than an element of andocentric arrogance; and there are obvious objections to a theory of bisexuality. The important corollary of either course is that christology in any case requires transcending categories in order to surmount the limitations of Christ's human experience as a male; and it seems to me at least an open question whether these transcending categories should not at least *arise out of* the evidence for the event of Christ. The story of the virgin birth of Christ is such evidence, and Christian tradition has unhesitatingly regarded it as coherent with its view of the character of Christ. Although I would hesitate to argue that the virgin birth narratives prove that Christ's humanity transcends ours, I regard them as congruous with that doctrine and would be inclined to inquire carefully about the precise nature of the objections to them.

The second difficulty concerns the 'perfection through suffering' spoken of in the letter to the Hebrews. In this highly sophisticated theological essay, explicitly designed to reassure and confirm the faith of those undergoing suffering, such references have by no means solely or even primarily the psychological or biographical force which some modern theologians have wished to see in them; or if they have, it would be legitimate to demand equal attention to the psychological implications of the author's conception of the vocation of Christ as high priest.

At the same time a serious theological question lies at the heart of the contentions of the letter. The risen Christ, who through suffering had entered into his glory, is 'perfected' in a sense in which the infant Jesus is not. The problem here is of speaking intelligibly of the humanity of the risen and ascended Lord in relation to the humanity of the incarnate Lord. This is not a problem created by the over-zealous prosecution of theological speculation in the patristic era, since it is parallel to the problem of identity and the survival of death in any theology which speaks of hopes beyond the grave. Of any person who has passed through the experiences of life it is possible to ask: what is that person *sub specie aeternitatis*? Is it him as an 'innocent' babe; or as a young man at the height of his power; or in mature middle age; or in his declining years; or at the moment of death? Psychology gives us no clues, and if we are to speak at all it is in the language of theology that we must do so.

Hence to say that Christ's humanity is at each stage a perfect development of that stage (i.e. not to insist on adult psychology or knowledge at the stage of childhood) may well be compatible with saying that the risen Christ is perfected through suffering and death. The former is the *sub specie aeternitatis* view of Christ's manhood at any particular moment; the latter is a manner of saying that in no other way than through suffering and death could the redemption of man have been achieved. The latter is, in other words, the theological imperative – it had to happen thus and not otherwise – which lies at the root of any human statement about creation or redemption.

It would have to be admitted, however, that even with proper explanation the concept of perfection seems unattractive to us, basically because of its association with a dull conformism. Thus for contemporary apologetics and preaching the term may well be avoided. But in the context of Christian doctrine it continues to be useful in pointing to two important affirmations of christology.

In the first place it stresses the 'ideality' of Christ. Here Schleiermacher was perfectly correct in pointing out that the true alternative to postulating the 'ideality' of Christ is to look forward to a further and more perfect revelation of God.[1] This, as Schleiermacher realised, is the great divide in post-enlightenment theology. Indeed it is a good deal easier to see that it *is* a divide than to know precisely on what grounds the decision might be taken either way. The enlightenment sponsored, and still sponsors, the view that in the end the historical relativity of the Christ-event will prove fatal to its attempt to claim finality; that the future requires a Christ-principle loosed from its historical

[1] *The Christian Faith* (1928), p. 378.

shackles. Schweitzer's christology was an explicit attempt to achieve precisely that. This view emerges, however, as a clean break with the biblically dominated traditional christology, which (to quote Schleiermacher again) 'knows no other way to a pure conception of the ideal than an ever-deepening understanding of Christ'[1] – a Christ, that is, given to us and known by us through human history.

The second affirmation linked with the perfection of Christ's humanity concerns its relation to our own understanding of our humanity. The true position in christology can never be that we 'approve of' Christ; awarding him by our own moral insight high, or even full, marks as a human being. Granted that in the assertion of Christ's perfection there is an element of such response, by which our own human values recognise their true goal. But the final position of Christian discipleship goes far beyond this, in recognising that in Christ our own values are set a transcending criterion. To confess the perfection of Christ's humanity is thus to recognise God's presence within the compass of human capabilities. The true order of christology is to say: Christ reveals that perfection of which humanity is capable. To associate the idea of an historically given revelation with that of perfection is to raise all the problems we have mentioned, but not to do so, that is, explicitly to avoid the idea of perfection, is to facilitate the covert transposition of christology into another type of doctrine altogether. If such a transposition needs to be effected, and I do not believe that it does, then it ought not to be effected covertly. In the history of doctrine the alternative view has been named unitarianism, with which historians of doctrine in the last two centuries are fully familiar. The proper alternative to affirming the perfection of Christ's humanity is to be prepared to affirm, with much unitarian thought, its imperfection, and to accept the full consequences of such a view for the traditional structure of Christian doctrine.[2]

---

[1] *Ibid.*, p. 378.
[2] See especially Joseph Priestley's *History of Early Opinions concerning Jesus Christ* (1786) and Thomas Belsham's *A Calm Inquiry into the Scripture Doctrine concerning the Person of Christ* (1811).

APPENDIX

ON PANNENBERG'S CHRISTOLOGY 'FROM BELOW'

In *Jesus – God and Man* (London, 1968), Wolfhart Pannenberg asserts that, in contrast to the christologies of early Brunner and Barth, the correct method in christology is 'from below', from the historical man Jesus to the recognition of his divinity. At the same time he retains a 'relative justification' for the method 'from above', and does not wish to argue that the whole tradition of incarnational theology was a mistake (p. 35). His intention is to enable him, against a substantial amount of previous German theology, to place the fullest weight on the actions and fate of the historical Jesus and especially on the resurrection, as the 'from below' basis for the grounding of Jesus' divinity.

Many of the themes of the above essay (for example, the consciousness of Jesus, his 'sinlessness', and the universal significance of his manhood) are treated by Pannenberg in his exceptionally wide-range work, but there are problems with the intelligibility of its fundamental thesis which limit its usefulness for the purpose of the above discussion. Thus it is questionable whether the standpoint of the resurrection is theology 'from below'. More fundamentally the meaning of the distinction, 'below' – 'above', is cast into doubt by Pannenberg's explicit attempt to reformulate Christian theism by speaking of 'God' as 'the power of the future' (especially in 'The God of Hope', *Basic Questions in Theology*, vol. II (London, 1971), pp. 234–49). Moreover the status of the 'modern anthropology' on which Pannenberg relies to provide him with knowledge of 'the essence of humanity' is certainly vulnerable to far-reaching criticism. All these problems and many more require a sustained analysis and critique which it would not have been possible to give in the course of the above discussion, but which I hope to be able to offer elsewhere in due course.

A REPLY TO MR SYKES

DR ROBINSON

I am grateful for the attention Mr Sykes paid to my essay and the opportunity to reply to it. I confess that I am not altogether sure whether the references to myself, added to what was originally an independent argument, have not confused the issues. His basic thesis, as I understand it, is to query Bethune-Baker's approach (and I make no judgment as to whether he has been fair to him) that the way into christology must necessarily be through the manhood of Christ, which is then made normative of what we can say of his divinity. On this basis some things – e.g., virginal conception – are then ruled out as incompatible with what science or a modern world-view will allow. I would entirely agree that this is a dogmatic and presumptuous procedure. I have never said that anything – historical or doctrinal – *rules out* virgin birth, empty tomb, or indeed the possibility of radical discontinuity or novelty in the historical process.

My thesis was to argue for the *freedom* to suspend judgment on these things, on the grounds that the doctrinal affirmation of God's initiative or presence in Christ (from which I should be perfectly happy to *start*, if that were the appropriate way in) does not of itself *require* affirmations of the history that remove the ambiguities or destroy the continuities that pertain to it as 'flesh'. And part at any rate of my reason for stressing this is that we have not the evidence historically to assert what Schleiemacher called the 'ideality'. We cannot, as I said, even affirm that Jesus was *always* loving.

To be sure, Mr Sykes is claiming to uphold the same freedom. 'I am not proposing', he writes, 'to insist that, despite its drawbacks, only the theological approach does justice to its subject matter, I am concerned with a more limited aim, that of refuting the suggestion that somehow, only the anthropological approach is valid in theology, and that the theological considerations have no force or less force.' (I have said that *this* contrast does not really fit my position – but let us leave that aside.) By the end, however, he seems to me to be insisting *not only* that 'to confess the perfection of Christ's humanity' is 'to recognise God's presence within the compass of human capabilities' but that this is a necessary way of doing so. Not to confess it is to opt for his imperfection and for unitarianism and 'to facilitate the covert transposition of christology into another kind of doctrine altogether'. But this is precisely the antithesis that I wish to avoid. I want to affirm God's presence in Christ – to the hilt – without necessarily being committed to asserting of the history, the flesh, an absoluteness which would require it to be different in kind and not merely in degree from all other flesh – and for which we have not empirical evidence anyway.

It is not a question of theological considerations having no force or less force. It is a question of what kind of force they should have. I would still insist that the doctrine of Jesus' sinlessness, for instance, cannot be made to deliver or substantiate any historical statement about him. What is relevant (as I said) is the fact that this doctrinal affirmation was made so early and so widely in the Christian church. But this is an historical statement, and is indeed evidence that the gap between that affirmation and his actual character could not have been that wide. Again, we cannot say that he *could* not have been mad. He may have had what in anyone else would be classed as illusions of grandeur. The fourth gospel seems in many passages to depict him thus. The theological issue is not whether 'sonship of God' rules this out (and so settles the historical facts), but whether a man with that sort of ambiguity can still be for us 'son of God'. Obviously there comes a point where credibility is so strained that we look elsewhere. But this is a matter of degree, and the point will be assessed differently by different people.

By speaking of two languages rather than two natures, two stories rather than two storeys, I am not trying to 'conjure away' any difficulty. Nor did I mean by the 'substantial measure of agreement' that there is only one way (a mythological way) of speaking about God. I was referring to the relationship of the so-called 'events' of myth and history. Of course, the relationship between the theology and the history remains as baffling and ambiguous as it ever was – indeed I should say that the ambiguity was endemic. We shall never know, for instance, what happened to the body of Jesus. I would wish to rule out nothing – except what is excessively improbable on historical or psychological grounds. I certainly would not exclude the possibility of total molecular transformation. But equally I do not think the *doctrine* requires it, let alone substantiates it.

Of course, Jesus was not an ordinary man in the sense that he was in no way extraordinary. The whole gospel shouts aloud that here was a new development, a break-through, which could not be contained within the skin of the old. Yet grace need not destroy nature. The reaction, for instance, to one of the most remarkable stories told about him – the raising of the widow's son at Nain (Luke vii.11–17) – indicates that God could be seen to be in this (and in all that Jesus was and did) without the relativities necessarily being abrogated: ' "A great prophet has arisen among us", they said, and again, "God has shown his care for his people".' Of course, from the other side, a view of nature or of human nature that is closed to exclude the possibility of grace or revelation must be incompatible with a 'second' story. I am not saying that 'Jesus was an ordinary fallible human being *and no more*'. But I am saying that he *could* be 'both ordinary and a climacteric'. As far as we can judge, he *was* 'self-centred' like any other man, in that he did not simply look at things automatically with the outlook of God. Yet his obedience was such that he was able to say, '*Nevertheless* not what I will but what thou wilt' (Mark xiv.36). He was fallible, but when the sticking point came he did not fail. The alternatives are not 'absolute ideality' *or* imperfection.

PART II
PRIMITIVE CHRISTOLOGIES AGAIN

5

THE SEARCH FOR THE BEGINNING

SEBASTIAN MOORE

I

Implicit in Christian belief are the following two propositions:

1. That the assertion of an eschatological judgment on the whole of human existence has cash-value: in other words, that it is not just an attitude, a way of looking at life, an exalting myth, but refers to something that has happened, is happening and will be totally achieved. The gospel constitutes a deeply exploded crack in human existence. It constitutes significantly more of a judgment on all achievement and culture than is come upon by a developing understanding of the human sciences.

2. That this coming of judgment on the world, this totally new way of thinking about ourselves which even the vaguely Christian vaguely take for granted, finds support in the man Jesus of Nazareth and the events in which his life culminated.

It is this latter proposition that I am concerned with in the following essay. Everything hinges on the nature of this 'support'. Before I embark on the essay, let me eliminate, as clearly too weak, a meaning of this term that is suggested by the French *support*. According to this, some unknown Spanish knight is the presumed 'support' for the myth of El Cid. Or some unknown Galilean rabbi is the presumed 'support' for the grand Christ-myth. In this meaning, 'support' means more or less the same as 'pretext'.

It is when we come on to ask what is the *positive* support that Jesus must be for the Christ-myth, that we get into the midst of what I deem to be *the* christological problem. In the following essay I seek a description of the man Jesus. But what demands, dictates and directs my search is not the curiosity of a female novelist. It is the requirement in being a Christian. We do not and we cannot, whether our approach is that of the female novelist or that of the scientific historian, know what Jesus was like. I am asking rather: 'what must he have been like, whether we like it or not, to support what we believers believe about the world, its judgment and consummation? What *sort* of thing are we saying about an individual who preached, healed and got crucified, when we say with Paul 'upon us the ends of the earth have come'?

I am increasingly unclear as to how this theologically directed curiosity proceeds. Since it is curiosity about an historical event, it cannot avoid the methods of the historian and the novelist. The theological motivation of my curiosity does not alter the fact that it is curiosity about a particular man. And so it might appear that, theology having once given me my motive, it retires from the scene and leaves me in the field with Trevor-Roper and Elizabeth Goudge. But this is not so. For it is not that, holding as I do the Christian belief, I am 'naturally' very interested in what sort of a man Jesus was. I am more nearly pressed by theology than that. I think really what I'm asking is: '*Can there have been such a man as there must have been for Christian belief to work?*' In the toils of this kind of question, I exercise myself in a dialectic of Jesus of Nazareth with his social, spiritual and political context. I consider that the above question springs irreversibly from Christian belief itself, and that some such exercise as I engage in is demanded, equally inescapably, by the question.

Can there have been such a man? This question of its nature refers to the contemporaries of Jesus as well as to Jesus himself. There is a limit to what any society can recognise as a member of it however unconventional. A Martian or a mushroom is not sufficiently engaged in human society to be contestable or crucifiable. The question, then, is 'can any conceivable society have had to cope with such a man? Is there any conceivable socio-political crisis that can have had such a storm-centre? Is that conflict conceivable, whose resolution was the proclamation of the crucified in power?'

There are two ways of sliding off this question: in a dogmatic and in a reductionist direction. We might say, on the one hand, that Jesus claimed divinity and for this was crucified. But even a conventional apologetic has long conceded that a direct claim to divinity on the part of Jesus would not have been intelligible. On the other hand, we might say that that which brought on the fate of Jesus was no more than that which earned crucifixion for other trouble-makers. But this is to deny to the man called Jesus that impact on his contemporaries that is implicit in the man he must have been if Christian belief is valid. He then becomes a 'support', in the French sense, for the Christ-myth: the executed zealot on whom there happened to fasten the projections of an apocalyptically speculative age.

We cannot, then, slide off the question, either to the right, in the direction of dogmatic slumbers, or to the left, in the direction of a socio-historical reductionism.

The question about a man in history is always a question about his contemporaries. It is the question 'what did they see and hear, what did they have to deal with, what was the dent in their cultural expectations?' This is the sort of thing a man is. His life is a seen life, an experienced life, a reacted-to life, a crucified life. A placid liberal individualism has thought it possible to consider a genius, artist or saint simply in himself and apart from his extension into the lives of others. This tendency has been strongly reinforced in the case of Jesus by the uniqueness that Christian tradition claims for him. A man who is God is a tall order. He becomes less of a tall order if we don't have to worry about the people who took in his washing and who had to make up their minds about him. Only, what we are then talking about is an abstraction. An abstraction limpidly expressed by Hastings Rashdall: 'Christian theology is the result of thought or reflection on the life and teaching of Jesus Christ, or what at any time that life and that teaching were understood to be.'[1] So theology gets built on a Jesus distilled and made still, drawn aside from his world, whereas it is precisely and only in collision with that world that he has provoked theology into existence. 'The life and teaching of Jesus' either describes a bloody mess, or it is about nothing at all.

My question concerns the mess. Can there have been such a mess as there must have been if Christian belief is to work? More

---

[1] *Doctrine and Developments* (1898), p. viii.

specifically, can a human society have been, at this initial and crucial Christian moment, pushed as far beyond human tolerance – on the analogy of noise-tolerance – as must have been the men who gave the gospel to us if the gospel is what we believe it to be?

I cannot resist the impression that much Christian talk and writing about Christ shows signs of avoiding this question, of being uncontaminated by it. Hence its unreality. Hence its ability to sound quite reasonable, while at the same time proclaiming a madness. Hence its ability to proclaim a revolutionary event while remaining wedded to the powers that be. The original row over Jesus has gone silent in our theology of him which owes both its existence and its nature to that row. This makes our theology a most extraordinary performance. The disquiet it causes in those other scientists of the human who have been sufficiently interested to inspect it closely is only too understandable.

Can there have been such a man, can there have been such a mess, can there have been such an event, can there have been such a turn in the lives of people, as there must have been if Christian belief is true?

It is agreed on all hands, and without any prejudice to Christian faith, that the full and overt formulation of Jesus' divinity, as we find it in the fourth gospel and still more in the great councils, is the fruit of theological reflection and does not have to be projected back into the original confrontation of Jesus with his friends and enemies. Nevertheless, Christian belief does demand that there has been a certain confrontation of Jesus with those people, a confrontation wherein there is somehow at stake that break in human existence, that worldly judgment of God on this world, that conquest of unconquerable fate, that is serenely and clearly affirmed in the great christological formulas.

So the nagging question reappears in the form 'can there have been such a confrontation? Can the whole meaning of human existence have been at stake when an arrested Galilean teacher stood before his judge amid the shouts of an average crowd?' This is simultaneously a question as to the *nature* of the confrontation. For the question 'could X have happened?' is or at least contains the question 'is X conceivable?'. And the only way to attack *that* question is to try to conceive X. That is what I am doing in what follows.

The question 'can X have happened?' is a kinked one. But the attempt to believe, the attempt to test out my belief by asking what it demands to be the case in the world I experience, is a cognately peculiar operation, but one very close to our basic thoughts and doubts and needs. I find it sobering to look back, over decades of theological reflection, to a moment in the gun-room-bathroom of H.M.S. Rodney, long since scrapped, when one of my messmates said to me, 'God couldn't have sent his Son. It just isn't that kind of world.' Sobering to think that I'm still stuck with that problem.

II

To understand a thing, you have to set it in a context, to see it in context. No context, no understanding. Thus to understand the phenomenon of Jesus, we have to set it in a context, to relate it to a frame of reference.

Now there are here two possible frames of reference. One may interpret his behaviour by referring it to such concepts as 'man in need of redemption', 'the divine plan', 'the Father's will', etc. Or one may interpret his behaviour by referring it to such realities as 'the political situation at the time', 'the history of Israel' and, more broadly and deeply, to what we know, from history and our own and others' experience, of the sort of alternatives that offer themselves to people, in making up their minds to the effect that some people become politicians, some thinkers, some artists, some teachers, some mystics, some social reformers, some revolutionaries, etc.

As an example of Jesus' behaviour interpreted in the first reference-frame, we may give: 'Jesus laid down his life, on behalf of sinful man, in an act of loving obedience to the Father.' As an example of the second line of interpretation, we may give: 'Jesus realised that he could not be both the total witness to his belief in the Kingdom and the Founder of the Kingdom. He chose the former, and it brought him to the cross.'

It should be clear that these two lines of talk are dramatically different. We should *feel* this difference. Liberal Protestant writing – I think especially of Harnack – blurs it. The standpoint is human. Jesus is being considered as a teacher and influencer of men. We are not reading about what God was doing, but about what this man said about God and impressively lived by. But every so often 'the Father' slips in as a character in the drama. The writing goes Christian-pious, and our pious Christian ears do not hear the crashing gear-change. Conventional Catholic writing – I think of the authors I was brought up on – also blurs the distinction, from the other direction. The standpoint is the Christian Story with God as the chief character. But every so often there is a human touch, and for a moment we are allowed to see Jesus exposed just as we are to the ordinary logic of events. Again there is no evidence of consciousness of leaping a method-ological chasm. Of course we have had better than either of these schools. We have had for instance Barth. But 'the humanity of God' is a theological concept. It does not describe that piece of humanity that has so bewilderingly changed the question of God.

We must make this distinction between a Christian theological and a human description of the phenomenon of Jesus. And when we have made it, in the clear understanding of its urgent necessity, we suddenly see that far more has got to be said in the human description than, with the two lines of description confused, we would ever have supposed. This essay is an attempt to indicate this 'far more'.

If the life of Jesus does not, for me, put up any questions of the sort that the life of Napoleon, of J. F. Kennedy, of Gautama Buddha, of Hughie Long put up, then I am a docetist. My Christ has not a real humanity. He is a theological construct. He never existed. If you have never seen Jesus, in your mind's eye, as faced with inescapable political social and personal-integrity options, then you are a docetist. Your Christ never existed. He is a puppet in a theologians' puppet show.

In my unavoidably simplified but not I hope too distorted picture, the data with which Jesus was presented were as follows:

    1. The history and tradition of his people.

    2. The self-interpretation of his people as bearers of a divine mandate to promote in this world the knowledge of the Lord.

    3. A sense of personal involvement in that task (not uncommon among serious and pious Jews).

    4. A sense of unique involvement therein which was to give the whole meaning to his life.

    5. The possibility of interpreting the reign of God in different ways and acting accordingly – as an eschatological reality to be piously hoped for, as a political reality to be currently worked for, as an ethical reality to be achieved in one's own life and imparted to others by teaching and example, as a mystical reality to be equated with self-discovery.

Jesus had to compound all that lot. He had to interpret to himself, in the light of these various possible versions of the kingdom, his own sense of being uniquely involved in its achievement. All these different versions of what the kingdom was were reflections of the different human temperaments. He could go from rabbi to rabbi, and hear from each a different view. Rabbi X was notoriously pious. He had found in prayer the resolution of the aspiration of Israel with its present wretched state. Rabbi Y on the other hand was known to have strong political views, and to attend zealot meetings. Jesus could look in on these meetings and hear the sort of thing that was said there.

None of these interpretations spoke to his sense of a personal destiny. None of them went far enough. Each carried the kingdom off down this or that side-track. 'The kingdom suffers violence, and the violent bear it away.' But he couldn't opt out. On the contrary, he had to opt in. And what could 'in' mean? His daimon took him in to the heart of the confusion which is, in Newman's words shortly to be cited, 'absolutely beyond human solution'.

As I see the matter, whenever Jesus pressed a rabbi for the latter's ultimate stand on this kingdom business, he would in the end be met with a shrug of the shoulders – that pious shrug with which we express under pressure our spiritual fatigue and agnosticism. Jesus had to go beyond that shrug. He had to go all the way.

What was that way? It was completely uncharted. There was no precedent. The rabbis he passed on his meteoric course might look after him with admiration, but ultimately with incomprehension. He was alone. We find this difficult to grasp. Automatically and surreptitiously we build up around the historical Jesus the theological pattern that exploded out of his consummation, and think of him as living in that pattern, taking his bearings from its concepts, with 'sinful man' as his point of departure, 'the Father' as his point of arrival, in the same way that we take our bearings from our parents, the people we meet, the interests that emerge, the jobs that are offered. We must spot this tendency in ourselves and arrest it. Jesus was not following theology: he was making it. Jesus made theology in the sense in which men are said to make history. Jesus wasn't a Christian. Jesus wasn't a priest. Jesus was alone. In the world of man, in the thick of that world, Jesus was going on a way that no man had stepped. He expressed it sometimes in a way that we would regard as suicidal. 'We're going up to Jerusalem – where they kill prophets.' He was asking of God what no man had ever asked of him: that he would change the nature of things: that he would vindicate him in the assertion that the reign of God was not an idea but a fact, and a fact that knew no bounds and no distinction between the political world in which some men strive to realise the idea and the spiritual realm in which others pursue it. Jesus' life asked God: are you fact in this world, and not just something people talk about? Are you just a matter of culture?

What God (was it 'God'?) was requiring of Jesus was so unorthodox that he must have seemed to be no God at all. The phenomenological presence of God in this world – a presence in tradition, in rite, in teaching, in temple, indeed in all the languages available to a community – was blacked out by the power that led Jesus to Jerusalem for that Passover. The conditions in which Jesus lived for God were not those of a protective theological description of the world, but rather the conditions described by Newman in a celebrated passage of the *Apologia*:

To consider the world in its length and breadth, its various history, the many races of men, their starts, their fortunes, their mutual alienation, their conflicts: and then their ways, habits, governments, forms of worship: their enterprises, their aimless courses, their random achievements, the impotent conclusion of long-standing facts, the tokens so faint and broken of a superintending design, the blind evolution of what turn out to be great powers or truths, the progress of things, as if from unreasoning elements, not towards final causes, the greatness and littleness of man, his far-reaching aims, his short duration, the curtain hung over his futurity, the disappointments of life, the defeat of good, the success of evil, physical pain, mental anguish, the prevalence and intensity of sin, the pervading idolatries, the corruptions, the dreary hopeless irreligion, that condition of the whole race, so fearfully yet exactly described in the Apostle's words, 'having no hope and without God in the world', – all this is a vision to dizzy and appall: and inflicts upon the mind the sense of a profound mystery, which is absolutely beyond human solution.[1]

It is only by the powerful convention of a religion-culture that God is *fact* in the hopeless and directionless world described by Newman. Of course he is in it, in the meaningless disaster, *as problem*, as anguish, even sometimes as an unaccountable strength-for-life. But to protect themselves from meaninglessness, men have needed more than this. They have wanted to have God for fact. An honest inspection of our own religious experience will discern this need and the cultural strategy on which our spiritual sustainment has depended. We know the agnostic chill that settles upon us among the contemporary ruins of our temple, a chill that reductionist theology does little to alleviate. We know now only too well that this epiphany of God in advance of the facts is only achieved by screening off an area, psychological or spatial or temporal, in which it can go unquestioned by the mute and nearly meaningless world of man. What I am saying is that the option of Jesus to go up to Jerusalem demanded an epiphany at the cross-roads of life, unhedged by the protective screen of culture.

When I really look at this idea, I think that if you or I really understood what Jesus was about we should be horribly embarrassed. It is important to realise that what I am saying now is knocking against your private compromise on this God-in-this-world business and against my own. I am referring to a transformed human situation which neither of us really wants very much.

D

Jesus went all the way on this. He accepted a position at the centre of the human religious problematic as that problematic had been worked out by a uniquely God-pursuing and God-pursued people, and he allowed it to destroy him.

Staying strictly within the limits of my method, I have to say that his followers became convinced that he had been vindicated. Trying to be as honest as I can, and invoking all that I know of human psychology, I am more and more deeply convinced that the birth of this faith is unaccountable for in ordinary psychological terms. A prominent German Catholic theologian describes the birth of this faith in the following way: 'It seemed more and more unthinkable to them that this Jesus should be dead and gone like Abraham, David and Jeremiah.'[1] I have no doubt that the New Testament evidences an experience that is tougher than this piece of wishful thinking. To begin with, there is a difference between a Jesus who is 'still around' and a Jesus who is Lord of history and firstfruits from the dead. There's just none of the flavour of the New Testament, none of the newness of the New Testament, in this kind of explanation. The disproportion between the literary product and the imputed motivation of it is like what you'd get if you said that Shakespeare was moved to write *Macbeth* by a feeling that crime does not pay.

Out of the resurrection-faith came the assertion 'God has made both Lord and Christ this Jesus whom you crucified', an assertion that, with an ease that belongs only to power, leaps across the gap between theological and political discourse.

But once the vindication of Jesus has become dogma, the dogma easily stands between the believer and the fact, the human workout, that gave birth to it. We become hugely deaf to that original event, to its unmanageably problematic character, to the inconceivable *risk* that Jesus, in the limited terms we have to live by, took. Nothing it seems will penetrate this deafness. In vain does the scripture tell us that in a garden called Gethsemane the man sweated blood begging his 'Father' to let him off the hook. Oh no, we say, he was accepting the will of the Father, and we all know what that was. Do we hell. How can we talk in this

---

[1] Heinz Robert Schlette, *Epiphany as History* (1969), p. 68.

way about a passion that prized open this dark world with which we come to terms long before it brings us to this pass? In vain does the scripture tell us that he cried out on the cross 'why have you abandoned me?'[1] In vain does the scripture try to root the event in this world for us by recording the cynical colonial inscription over the cross. In vain does the scripture say, over and over again, and of all the classes of persons involved in the event, 'they did not understand'.

Not only am I concerned to understand the event in the human terms in which it had to be worked out. I am concerned also to understand the extraordinary reluctance of believers to seek such understanding – to the extent of saying, in answer to one who puts the most obvious question to the event, 'I don't see what you're getting at.' To me, it's like you say 'isn't the house on fire?' and someone answers 'how d'you mean?'. I suspect that there is a fear, deep in all of us, that there *may* be nothing human inside the great dogmatic assertion of the divinity of Christ. And to refuse to acknowledge that fear is to refuse to acknowledge that believing is bloody difficult.

Can we be clearer as to the nature of this difficulty? Yes, I think we can. First of all, it is the difficulty, is it not, of conceiving as a real possibility the human style that we have had to posit as 'support' for the Christ of faith. What is this human style? I came nearest to it, I think, when I said: 'The phenomenological presence of God in this world – a presence in tradition, in rite, in teaching, in temple, indeed in all the languages available to a community – was blacked out by the power that led Jesus to Jerusalem for that Passover.'

But is this so difficult to conceive? Surely history furnishes models for this: a certain type of prophet for instance, who in the midst of a people clutching their gods is led to his destiny by a daimon which they would not understand and – more important – which *he* cannot name to himself with their names. A man who, in the power of this daimon, can accept none of their

---

[1] This incident may, however, for all its apparent realism, be a literary device, setting Jesus in the 'ideal type' (in the Weberian sense) of the hardpressed man who speaks in one type of psalm.

alternative uses and directions for life. A man in whom we feel –
and who himself painfully feels – that human life is happening
in him for the first time, and has a goal that is calling for a new
single-mindedness. While we may have a very short list indeed of
men who seem really to have embodied this idea and suffered the
consequences of this embodiment, there are plenty of men who
have described and desired it. One thinks inevitably of Nietzsche.

If this were all we had to conceive of in the case of Jesus, there
would be no difficulty. But there is more. There is not only the
being an outsider to the common understandings of religion and
the direction of life. There is a reinterpretation of those understandings from this new standpoint. It seems that when he spoke,
something very odd happened. It is of the essence of a traditional
religious language that it is 'at second hand'. Yet here was the
familiar language coming over as known 'at first hand'. So that
instead of describing 'a world that we have heard about and
piously hope is real', the language is describing the world as it is.
It is as though life itself were being restored to its original meaning,
a meaning infinitely refracted into the world we know, the hugely
inconclusive world of Newman's terrible description. How this
kind of voice can ever have been heard on the earth is already the
beginning of the 'difficulty'.

But once we allow that this voice *has* been heard on the earth,
an important thought suggests itself. This position of Jesus, of
being impelled by a new and nameless power, a power which
people cannot live without naming, and of being thus authoritative, having as it were author-status, in respect of his religious
tradition, can be understood to justify the extraordinary option
he took in going up to Jerusalem and certain and evidently
fruitless death. For this was a bid beyond the options that our
fragmented and fitfully meaningful life legitimates. What that life
says is 'do what you can. It will be destroyed by death. Some of
it will survive you and be fruitful – perhaps. You do not know
how. I do not know how.' But the psychology that we have constructed for Jesus by taking a broad heuristic hint from the timbre
of his teaching made him significantly less passive than we are in
respect of that speech which I have put on to the lips of life. By

taking the witness of the gospels as a whole, we can just get a glimpse of a scale of values on which the option which, on our scale, is suicidal, is mysteriously legitimated. The decision to go up to Jerusalem was the enactment of that fuller claim on God which is implied in the whole style of Jesus. That claim, made within our limits, would be presumptuous, for God, in our fragmented world, is only presumptive.

It is in respect of the authoritative reinterpretation of life and the cognate new turning of a man's steps to death, that Jesus appears to us incredible. But not in respect of the daimon. Not in respect of that special solitude which consists in being closer than other men to the heart of life. This we have known in history. This we increasingly know we need for ourselves, as the supportative power of tradition caves in under us, as there opens up before us a frightening new vision, of the meaningfulness of man as something secured by a conspiracy, as a story we have been telling ourselves in our lighted corner of an indifferent universe. Blindly we seek for some quite other sustainment, as our numbered time turns to the dust of galaxies. As these thoughts crowd in on us, there stands more clearly to our vision the man who goes alone and directly along the way we take in bewilderment and in anxious dependence on received ideas. What we find difficult to believe is that one who took this way had the authority to do so and received in his final consummation the corroboration of the unknown power in which all things rest.

In other words, what we find difficult to believe is that the way we now see we have to take makes final sense. What is being asked of us by the gospel is to believe, just that significant bit more, in the original life that wells up inside us and demands a new pattern of relationships. So that what proves nearly incredible about a Jesus withdrawn from his protective dogmatic shell and exposed to life, is the point at which he converges on our own immanent crisis of faith and meaning.

What is this life that is in us? What is this crisis in our relationships that spells out 'faith' as the only way on? What does 'faith' here mean? That it has meaning, and the only meaning, becomes clear the more we see that its opposite is cowardice. For me at

least this questioning of life, this dark thrust forward, is mysteriously strengthened and corroborated by being allowed to work
in a dialectic with the question of Jesus. And so I conclude by
addressing these words *To God on the Resurrection*:

> Did you speak then once for all
> in that man's rising?
> Is that your nature unknown one
> to put a fist through history
> and leave it there
> a decaying church in the sun
> to turn once history's corner
> into the glare:
> is *that* you, a once for all turning out of twilight?
>
> We who would find you everywhere
> are too tender-minded for you
> too tender for the single orgasm
> you choose to be in our comedy
> sweeping up history's reject
> and mocking us there just once
> in the waking of the dead
> which is history's end:
> is *that* you, a dead end for the dead?
>
> And who am I to say we to you
> who say you to me
> and expose me as lonely we
> deprived of the fustian rhetoric
> which addresses you
> on the non-existent stage you darken
> switch on the auditorium lights
> while we shuffle with our belongings
> to the words I am the resurrection:
> is *that* you, a once for all non-event?

III

But what are we to make of the decision of Jesus to go up to
Jerusalem? Although the theologically motivated enquiry into the
behaviour and social impact of Jesus ranges over the whole
spectrum of his life and teaching, this decision is the point on
which the Jesus problem may be seen to converge.

Now if we take off the theological pressure, there is no great difficulty in conceiving a motive for this decision. It could have been like the action of the Buddhist monk who in protest sets fire to himself on the temple steps. It could have been the operation of a death-wish. It could have been a hardly rationalised gambler's throw. But if it was any of these things, then it seems to me that the character of Jesus falls below that level of uniqueness and significance that it must have to 'support' Christian belief. To afford this support, his fatal decision must be somehow of a piece with the proclamation of the crucified Jesus in the self-authenticating power of the Spirit. It must be the question to which that power was the answer. And this makes of the decision of Jesus something quite extraordinary, a step beyond the limits of proper human expectation. To attempt, albeit unsuccessfully, to conceive of such a step, is a task implicit in holding the Christian belief.

To try to take the weight off the decision of Jesus, and to rest it entirely on the empowering of the Spirit in the church, will not do. The rallying of a community of believers to believe something about a man whose own motivation need have been no more than that of the disillusioned or world-weary leader, does not serve as an adequate foundation for Christian belief. It was Jesus, and not just the flagging spirits of his followers, that was raised up on power.

If, that is, we wish to be Christians. It is perfectly reasonable to regard the man Jesus as a mere pretext for a myth whose power has been world-changing. But it is merely confusing, and indeed pointless, to equate this opinion with Christian belief.

The next question is this. Having forced upon us this enquiry and its hugely problematic result in this matter of the man Jesus, does the New Testament itself give us a push in the direction of accepting this result and saying 'yes I believe. There has been such a man'?

In this connection I am increasingly amazed by the order in which the New Testament got assembled. Broadly speaking the order is: first, the bare proclamation that God has raised up the crucified in power, secondly, a detailed account of the arrest, trial and execution, lastly, an account of the teachings and the miracles.

Of that teaching Goethe can say: 'Let intellectual and spiritual culture progress, and the human mind expand, as much as it will: beyond the grandeur and moral elevation of Christianity, as it sparkles and shines in the gospels, the human mind will not advance.'[1] And Harnack can say of Jesus that he refers to the deepest and most searching spiritual truths as though they grew on trees for anyone to pluck. Both judgments seem to me right, to catch something effortlessly magical in the gospels. Yet this body of teaching figures in the documentation of the Saviour almost as an afterthought. What an extraordinary religious movement this is, whose first and greatest promoter only mentions one saying of the Master, and that *en passant*. The teachings were not presented as standing in their own right – which they most certainly do – but as the veracity, directness and unambiguous direction of the man who, crucified, is raised up and proclaimed to the nations. This total eloquence of a piece of evidence produced by witnesses who are not leaning their case on it, gives a unique ring of truth. It is as though an admirer of Shakespeare the man, having gone on and on about special circumstances attendant on his death, added 'by the way, he also wrote plays' – and handed us for the first time the Shakespeare corpus.

But in the end there's no getting away from the fact that it all comes down to a dialectic between my own struggle with despair and the question of Jesus. There's a question-mark over Jesus, and there's a question-mark over my own life. As I hover between a whole network of received ideas and a dark way, which can look to them for no support, I am haunted by this man who made an option in defiance of religious good manners. At testing moments, my life asks him, 'did you rise from the dead?'. And sometimes I get an answer that sounds like 'mind your own business'. It's a salutary answer. It provokes life. It calls up that dark and love-impelled affirmation of life in terms of which alone we may grope towards a confession of the risen Christ.

[1] Quoted in the first lecture of Adolf Harnack's *What is Christianity?* (3rd ed., 1904), p. 4.

6

THE MANHOOD OF JESUS IN THE NEW TESTAMENT

C. F. D. MOULE

A modern Christian investigator necessarily comes to the study of the New Testament with certain questions in his mind which might not belong to a non-Christian, or even to a Christian if he lived in another period. It is impossible to disabuse oneself of such questions: one can only try to be aware of them, and to be ready to accept the possibility that, if they are not New Testament questions, there may be no New Testament answers, or, if they are essentially modern questions, there may be no answers from any period of antiquity. Conversely, it is possible to pay too little attention to antiquity. An investigator who, while tolerably proficient as a New Testament scholar, is not professionally expert in the subsequent history of Christian doctrine, may be insufficiently acquainted with certain important facts – not least the subtleties of ways in which his own questions may already have been asked (albeit probably in a different form), and answers may already have been given in the past. The manhood of Jesus is a subject in which such drawbacks may be particularly great, in view of the wide range of the answers that have been thrown up by the continual debate over this question. In any case, even a master of the entire story might well be disposed to ask whether human insight could ultimately improve on previous attempts, subtle and less subtle, to express the mystery in terms of various conceptions of Godhead and of human personality. Some of these attempts are reviewed in – to adduce just one example – J. McIntyre's *The Shape of Christology* (1966). If there is any new formulation over and above these classic attempts, it is likely to spring from some of the new insights of psychology, sociology, and anthropology: which only emphasizes the limitations of one who approaches the question from the modern world but with only the equipment of a New Testament specialist.

Thus, it is with modern questions inevitably in mind, and yet with a necessarily insufficient grasp of the entire story up to and including the modern era, that a New Testament investigator who is not professionally equipped in the history of Christian doctrine has to go to work: and it is necessary to emphasize this limitation and bring it out into the open, if this study is to take its proper place in the total investigation. This being said, we proceed as best we can. In any case, the manhood of Jesus is only one facet of christology; and this investigation touches on only a few arbitrarily selected aspects of New Testament thought about the manhood of Jesus. It takes three paradoxes in New Testament convictions about Jesus – his humiliation and exaltation, his continuity with and discontinuity from the rest of humanity, and the individuality and yet inclusiveness of his person – and shows that no christological statement that bypasses these or simplifies them away is true to New Testament ways of thinking. Also, an attempt is made to find some basis, not indeed for resolving these paradoxes, but at least for bringing their opposite poles into some mutual relationship.

I

Perhaps a suitable starting-point in the discussion of the paradox of humiliation and exaltation is the observation that Phil. ii.5–11 probably has nothing to do with so-called 'kenotic' theories of the incarnation, despite its frequent use as the key text for them. By 'kenotic' theories are meant attempts to explain the human limitations suffered by the divine Son of God in terms of a deliberate act of self-emptying, as though the pre-existent Son of God voluntarily emptied himself of divine prerogatives for a time, in order to share to the full the human lot, and resumed his full capacities only after the death on the cross. Against this, it has been widely recognized that it is none of the intention of Phil. ii. 5–11 to explain anything. Rather, it has come to be interpreted as simply a statement, an assertion in pictorial language, about the supreme humility of one whose pre-existent divine dignity enhances the greatness of his condescension. But for my part –

and this is my reason for starting from this passage – I am inclined to join the minority of interpreters who go still further and identify, rather than contrast, the so-called condescension with the so-called dignity, thus underlining a divine paradox which stands every human scale of values on its head. I agree[1] with those who interpret *harpagmos* not, concretely, as 'something worth snatching', but, abstractly, as 'the act of snatching' (i.e., virtually, 'acquisitiveness'), and who render the phrase in which it occurs in some such way as: 'Jesus did not reckon that equality with God meant snatching: on the contrary, he emptied himself. . .'. This would mean that, whereas ordinary human valuation reckons that God-likeness means having your own way, getting what you want, Jesus saw God-likeness essentially as giving and spending oneself out. If this is really the intention of the passage, then the participial phrase usually rendered, in a concessive sense, as '*though* he was in the form of God' might even, perhaps, have been intended, rather, in a causative sense: precisely *because* he was in the form of God he recognized equality with God as a matter not of getting but of giving. Of course there is no denying that the 'pattern' of Phil. ii.5–11 as a whole is the pattern of descent followed by ascent, humiliation followed by exaltation: it is, as it were, a V-pattern – from heaven to the depths and up again (or, as some aver, up to an even higher status than before – which would require a pattern more like a square-root symbol $\sqrt{\ }$!). But that, I believe, need not prevent our seeing, at the same time, a straight line pattern in it, by which height is *equated* with depth, humiliation is *identified* with exaltation. Indeed, the very paradox of the truth lies in the fact that what, in ordinary human estimation, is a V-pattern of descent followed by ascent is, in the eyes of God, a straight line of equation: the two diagrams, therefore, positively need to be there together, if the paradox is to be expressed. 'He was rich, yet for your sake he became poor' (II Cor. viii.9) can be glossed by 'penniless, we own the world' (II Cor. vi.10). And, whether or not this is a true exegesis of the Philippians passage, the para-

---

[1] See my essay, 'Further Reflexions on Philippians 2: 5–11', in *Apostolic History and the Gospel, Biblical and Historical Essays Presented to F. F. Bruce*, eds W. W. Gasque and R. P. Martin (1970), pp. 264ff.

dox of the conflicting diagrams is demonstrably present in St John's famous 'exaltation' (*hupsoun*), which is, at one and the same time, an uplifting in shame on the cross and an uplifting in the glory of accomplishing God's will; and, indeed, this motif informs a great deal of New Testament thinking, as we shall see.

If, then, this is genuinely an insight of the New Testament, we may state at least one finding of supreme importance for the understanding of its estimate of the manhood of Jesus, namely, that (at least in certain passages) it recognizes what is ordinarily called 'emptying' as really 'fulfilling': *kenōsis* actually *is plērōsis*; which means that the human limitations of Jesus are seen as a positive expression of his divinity rather than as a curtailment of it:

'Jesus divinest when thou most art man!'[1]

This is a principle which is undoubtedly borne out in aesthetic experience. Anybody will recognize, for instance, that creative art involves an acceptance, and a positive use, of limitation. A craftsman in wood has to know all about the grain and the capacities of the wood he is working with, and, by accepting them and working within them, he exploits them in such a way as to express himself to the full as a craftsman in wood-carving.[2] So God the creator, when working in humanity, may be expected to express himself most fully, so far as the idiom of that medium goes, by accepting the human range of capacity and exploiting the human medium to the full. This is no more self-emptying than it is complete self-fulfilment in a given medium. It would be positively inartistic, it would be limiting and less than creative, to go contrary to the nature of the chosen medium. Fulfilment in any given medium and on any given level of expression involves acceptance and full affirmation of the medium and the level. On that showing, it is arguable that 'emptying' is a positively misleading description of the activity.

But, if the artistic quality of craftsmanship is fulfilled and en-

[1] F. W. H. Myers, *Saint Paul* (1902), p. 16.
[2] Cf. a description of Schroeder's art, in a concert programme (King's College Chapel, 11 July 1970), which refers to the texture of a partita composed by him as 'notable for that artistic economy of means which is the hallmark of a composer who understands the instrument's strengths as well as its limitations'.

hanced by acceptance of the characteristics of the chosen medium, it is, admittedly, true that this does also mean foregoing the scope that some other medium might offer (though *any* 'medium' must, by definition, offer *some* limitation). There is, it must be granted, an 'emptying', a *kenōsis*, in respect of *scope*, even if this is in the interests of the 'fulfilment', the *plērōsis*, of artistic *skill*. It is possible to recognize a change of 'status', even if not of character. It is thus legitimate if the kenoticists speak of incarnation as limitation in this sense, while insisting on the continuity of undiminished moral attributes – as it were absolutely divine artistry, in a miniature. Besides, since the human imagination likes to work in spatial metaphors, it is only natural if, from time to time, this creative fulfilment-by-self-limitation, this complete fulfilment of the creator's nature by the positive affirmation of a given element, is spoken of in terms of the creator's condescending 'descent' into a 'lower' sphere and his abandonment of 'lofty' status, and if fulfilment in a given medium is described as 'emptying', as though qualities belonging to a higher region had to be jettisoned. But it would be a mistake if it were imagined that such language implied a deliberate renunciation of possibilities, as in so-called kenotic theories. Anything so contrived or artificial would simply be inappropriate to the Christian conviction that, as God expresses himself through every medium and fills everything, so the incarnation is God's natural filling of this particular area, as natural as the filling of a cavity by water which pours into it, following its contours until it is full. Viewed in this way, the incarnation is a positive filling, not a negative emptying; and, as such, it should, strictly speaking, constitute nothing for surprise, as though it were something incongruous with God's majesty, however much it may be a theme for adoring wonder, as congruous with God's eternal, generous self-giving. However, when God is conceived of as omnipotent, it is easily forgotten that the omnipotence of a personal God is exhibited (to quote the collect) 'most chiefly in showing mercy and pity', and that the omnipotence of a creator God is shown precisely in creative self-limitation. Consequently, religious writing often expresses surprise that so lofty a being can stoop so low. There is, no doubt, an intended paradox in the prophet's utterance:

> Thus speaks the high and exalted one,
> whose name is holy, who lives for ever:
> I dwell in a high and holy place
>   with him who is broken and humble in spirit,
>   to revive the spirit of the humble,
>   to revive the courage of the broken (Isa. lvii.15)

And the same paradox runs through St John's gospel. E. Käsemann, it is true, has brilliantly put the case for virtually eliminating the paradox, and regarding St John's gospel as a docetic document.[1] The dominant theme, he maintains, is the glory of Jesus: he is the glorious, pre-existent Son of God who bestrides the world like a colossus. To be sure, the phrase 'the Word became flesh' does occur; but what sets the tone is the phrase which follows hard on its heels: 'we saw his glory'. The unquenchable glory of the divine is what dominates. Despite the passion narrative and the occasional bow to a conventional gospel of humiliation, this is not really a *theologia crucis* but an only thinly disguised *theologia gloriae*. In a vigorous reply,[2] G. Bornkamm is able to show that this selection of what is to be deemed the dominant note does not do full justice to the gospel's dialectic. It is impossible simply to ignore the paradox without doing violence to the gospel as a whole. There is no denying that the fourth evangelist allows himself sometimes to draw a very docetic picture; but then he also contradicts it. The truth seems to be that he simply states both facts – Jesus is the pre-existent Son of God, the unique Son who shares God's glory; yet also, Jesus is the one who accepts human limitations; and he does not bring them into anything like a unified system. If Jesus asks a question not for information but to test a disciple (John vi.6) – a very docetic portrait – yet also he has to escape and hide, like any mortal, when his life is prematurely threatened (viii.59, xii.36). The gospel simply has it both ways and does not make any very obvious reconciling gesture. But, while the human mind needs the paradoxical form to express the truth, it does also crave a recon-

---

[1] *The Testament of Jesus* (1968).
[2] 'Zur Interpretation des Johannes-Evangeliums' in *Geschichte und Glaube* I (*Gesammelte Aufsätze* III) (1968), 104ff.

ciling factor; and if there is any factor at all that makes for something like a unifying and organizing of the two extremes, it is the filial relationship. The Son's absolute and unique oneness with the Father is shown precisely in his submitting to the Father's will: 'I and the Father are one' (x.30) precisely because 'the Father is greater than I' (xiv.28). That is, Jesus exhibits the nature and character of God in the only way in which they can be absolutely and perfectly exhibited in the context of human behaviour, namely in such a relationship as properly belongs to man over against God, the relationship of glad and willing filial obedience. To this extent the paradox of glory and humiliation, of equality and subordination, is resolved in that relationship of perfect intimacy and identity of purpose which expresses itself in perfect obedience. Oneness of will is expressed in subordination of will, freedom in constraint.

Perhaps this may be said to be true – if only by implication – of the Epistle to the Hebrews also, which is equally notorious for its violent juxtaposition of the paradoxical extremes. If, in the prologue, Jesus is 'the Son who is the effulgence of God's splendour and the stamp of God's very being' (i.3), yet it is equally true that 'son though he was, he learned obedience in the school of suffering' (v.8). One would need to alter that last phrase, 'though he was', into 'precisely *because* he was',[1] in order to bring it into line with the insight which belongs to Phil. ii.5–11 if it is interpreted in the manner proposed; and this the Epistle to the Hebrews never does. Nevertheless, the underlying theme of Sonship might, if it were explicitly exploited in this way, provide a unifying principle.

Thus, Professor John Knox is probably right when he maintains[2] that the New Testament writers believed firmly in the humanity of Jesus but never properly reconciled this conviction with the twin conviction of his divinity; but possibly he might give more credit than he does to the filial relationship as a clue to the understanding of this conflict.

---

[1] Curiously, Hebrews itself, at xii : 7, uses a line of argument in which suffering is associated with sonship; but even there, the point is not quite the one here in question.

[2] *The Humanity and Divinity of Christ* (1967), *passim*.

II

But the crux of the incarnational question is perhaps more precisely identified in another paradox, namely, the paradox of continuity and discontinuity. According to New Testament writers, the humanity of Jesus is both continuous with and discontinuous from that of the rest of mankind. By 'the humanity of Jesus' in this context we mean (if we follow a line of thought which is specially clear in the Pauline writings but is not unrepresented elsewhere) his 'generic' humanity, his being the entire human race – Jesus as 'Adam'.[1] It is evident that the New Testament writers firmly believed that Jesus' humanity in this sense – Jesus as inclusive of humanity – was continuous with our humanity. If Jesus did not 'belong' to humankind, men and women would not find new life in him. The principle later formulated by Gregory of Nazianzus in the much-quoted phrase 'what Christ has not assumed he has not healed'[2] is certainly implied in such phrases as the following:

For if the wrongdoing of that one man brought death upon so many, its effect is vastly exceeded by the grace of God and the gift that came to so many by the grace of the one man, Jesus Christ. (Rom. v.15*b*)

. . . by sending his own Son in a form like that of our own sinful nature, and as a sacrifice for sin, he has passed judgement against sin within that very nature. (Rom. viii.3*b*)

. . . that he might be the eldest among a large family of brothers. (Rom. viii.29*b*)

For since it was a man who brought death into the world, a man also brought resurrection of the dead. As in Adam all men die, so in Christ all will be brought to life. (I Cor. xv.21f.)

. . . one man died for all and therefore all mankind has died. His purpose in dying for all was that men, while still in life, should cease to live for themselves, and should live for him who for their sake died and was raised to life. (II Cor. v.14*b*f.)

It was clearly fitting that God for whom and through whom all things exist should, in bringing many sons to glory, make the leader who delivers them perfect through sufferings. For a consecrating priest and those whom he

---

[1] This leaves unasked (at least in so many words) such thorny questions as whether the humanity assumed by Christ was sinful before the assumption.

[2] *Epistola* 101.7 (P.G. 37, 181), *to gar aproslēpton, atherapeuton*.

consecrates are all of one stock; and that is why the Son does not shrink from calling men his brothers, when he says, 'I will proclaim thy name to my brothers; in full assembly I will sing thy praise'; and again, 'I will keep my trust fixed on him'; and again, 'Here am I, and the children whom God has given me.' The children of a family share (*kekoinōnēken*) the same flesh and blood; and so he too shared (*meteschen*) ours, so that through death he might break the power of him who had death at his command, that is, the devil; and might liberate those who, through fear of death, had all their lifetime been in servitude. It is not angels, mark you, that he takes to himself, but the sons of Abraham. And therefore he had to be made like (*homoiōthēnai*) these brothers of his in every way, so that he might be merciful and faithful as their high priest before God, to expiate the sins of the people. For since he himself has passed through the test of suffering, he is able to help those who are meeting their test now. (Heb. ii.10ff.)

But on the other side of the paradox is an affirmation of a new-ness and sinlessness which mark a distinction between Christ's humanity and ours.[1] It is true that sinlessness is a negative quality for which there could be no direct evidence, and that, in any case, the explicit affirmations of Christ's sinlessness in the New Testa-ment are all part of the expression of a belief, reached, no doubt, through experience, in his Saviourhood rather than being part of a discussion of the quality of his manhood as such: his sinlessness is an aspect of his proved ability, whether as an unblemished sacrifice or under some other figure, to rescue us from sin. But it nevertheless constitutes a New Testament conviction about the character of his manhood. Here are the chief passages:

Christ was innocent of sin, and yet for our sake God made him one with the sinfulness of men, so that in him we might be made one with the goodness of God himself. (II Cor. v.21)

. . . tested every way, only without sin. (Heb. iv.15*b*)

The price was paid in precious blood, as it were of a lamb without mark or blemish – the blood of Christ. (I Pet. i.19)

But perhaps even more significant is the association of newness and the idea of new creation or new birth or a new beginning with Jesus. Here are the chief passages:

[1] The other half of Gregory's terse epigram (see above) was: 'but what has been united with God is saved', *ho de hēnōtai tō(i) theō(i), touto kai sōzetai.*

The old leaven of corruption is working among you. Purge it out, and then you will be bread of a new baking. As Christians you are unleavened Passover bread, for indeed our Passover has begun; the sacrifice is offered – Christ himself. (I Cor. v.7)

When anyone is united to Christ, there is a new world (*ktisis*); the old order has gone, and a new order has already begun. (II Cor. v.17)

Circumcision is nothing; uncircumcision is nothing; the only thing that counts is a new creation (*ktisis*)! (Gal. vi.15)

. . . his is the primacy over all created things. In him everything in heaven and on earth was created . . . He is, moreover, the head of the body, the church. He is its origin, the first to return from the dead (*prōtotokos ek tōn nekrōn*) . . . (Col. i.15*b*,16*a*,18*a*)

He it is who sacrificed himself for us, to set us free from all wickedness and to make us a pure people marked out for his own. (Tit. ii.14)

. . . the first-born from the dead (*ho prōtotokos tōn nekrōn*) . . . (Rev. i.5)

. . . the prime source of all God's creation (*hē archē tēs ktiseōs tou Theou*). (Rev. iii.14*b*)

All these phrases in different ways bear witness to a conviction that with Jesus a new humanity had begun – as human as the old, but not sinful like the old.[1] And it is possibly this distinctiveness and newness, coupled with a conviction about the continuity, that led Paul to use the ambiguous word *homoiōma* which is capable of implying both identity and also resemblance without identity. In Rom. viii.3 the phrase *en homoiōmati sarkos hamartias* might

---

[1] Cf. Iren. *adv. Haer.* III. 21.10 (Harvey, p. 120), where the question is asked why, if God wanted to make a new beginning, he did not again take dust from the ground, but, instead, caused the fashioning to be made from Mary; and the answer given is *hina mē allē hē plasis genētai, mēde allo to sōzomenon ē(i), all' autos ekeinos anakephalaiōthē(i), tēroumenēs tēs homoiotētos;* i.e. (apparently) 'in order that the fashioning [in question – that is, the making of the new humanity in Christ] should not be different [from the original fashioning of the first Adam], and that what was saved should not be different, but that he himself [i.e. the original Adam] should be recapitulated, with the likeness [to the original Adam] preserved'. In F. Sagnard's edition, in *Sources Chrétiennes* (1952), p. 373, the Latin text is: Vt non 'alia' plasmatio fieret neque 'alia' esset plasmatio quae saluaretur, sed eadem ipsa *recapitularetur*, seruata similitudine; and his translation (p. 374), taking *plasis* as concrete: 'C'est pour que cette oeuvre ainsi façonnée ne fût pas autre que la première et qu'il n'y en eût pas une autre à être sauvée, mais que ce fût exactement "la même", "*recapitulée*", en respectant la *ressemblance*.'

mean 'in what was exactly like sinful flesh' or 'in what only resembled sinful flesh'. The English Jerusalem Bible adroitly renders 'in a body as physical as any sinful body' but the French seems to reproduce the ambiguity of the Greek: 'dans une chair semblable à celle du peché'. Similar doubt attaches to *homoiōma* in Phil. ii.7.[1] At any rate, it is this conviction of newness and a fresh start that, no doubt, is involved also in the idea of virgin birth. Without discussing the historicity of the virgin birth, or the objection that it does for the modern mind precisely what it was intended by the New Testament writers not to do, it is evident that, to the ancient mind at least, it meant that Jesus, if truly man, was yet, as truly, a new kind of man, free from the entail of human sinfulness. It bears witness to the same end of the paradox in Christian conviction as that for which the 'newness' passages stand.

But if both ends of the paradox are there – both the continuity and the discontinuity – we ask (exactly as we did in relation to the paradox of humiliation and exaltation) whether there is anything that brings them together inside an intelligible system. One point at which any tentative answer to this question may be reasonably tested is the attitude of New Testament writers to Christ's temptation. One widely agreed characteristic of real humanity is that it has genuinely free will, and that the temptation to use that will contrary to God's will should (at least at some stage) have exercised a genuine attraction. Therefore, if Christ's humanity was real and continuous with ours, then there must have been something in him which consented to temptation,[2] in which case was he not sinful? Alternatively, if there was nothing in him that consented to temptation, then the temptation cannot have been real: he was incapable of sin and not genuinely human. Now Heb. iv.15 asserts that Christ was indeed tempted, yet without sin. In view of our notions of temptation, is this simply a bleak affirmation of an insoluble paradox, without the shadow of an attempt to bring it into a plausible unity? I wonder whether, once more, it may not

1 The other occurrences of *homoiōma* in the New Testament are Rom. i.23, v.14, vi.5, Rev. ix.7. Relevant also is *homoiotēs* in Heb. iv.15, vii.15; but none is quite conclusive for our purpose.
2 See e.g., Knox, *op. cit.* p. 47.

be to the filial relation and the quality of loyalty which it implies that we must look for some sort of an answer. Filial obedience means loyalty. The perfect Son is undeviatingly loyal to the Father's purposes. But what does loyalty mean, in human personality? Does it not mean a steady and undeviating 'set' of the will's current? In a desperately long battle, a soldier may yearn with every muscle in his weary body to gain the relief of desertion; but it is possible for him, at the same time, never to deviate a hair's breadth from the steady 'set' of the current of his loyalty to his country or his cause. Physically – even mentally – he may consent to the relief he longs for; but the 'set' of his will remains constant in its direction. In another context, and by way of another example, one might say that this 'set' of the will will negate what might otherwise have been 'looking lustfully on a woman' (Matt. v.28).

So, perhaps, it may be with the humanity of Jesus. He is involved in all the circumstances of normal humanity: whether by heredity or not, at least by reason of belonging to a sinful society, he is involved in extreme temptations to 'desert'. He is involved also in circumstances where to choose any course is necessarily to do harm to somebody (for instance, by breaking his mother's heart or precipitating the downfall of a disciple). But that does not necessarily mean (does it?) that the 'set' of his loyalty was not undeviatingly in the direction of God's will, nor that he could not make, with absolute perfection, the right response to those particular circumstances. This conception of response makes it seem to me incorrect to suggest that, because Jesus' physical and mental constitution must have been particular and not general or 'average', therefore he cannot have been perfect. Perfection of response is, in any human situation, necessarily quite particular. But the 'scandal of particularity' does not prevent a new perfection coming into existence – a perfection of response in given circumstances: for a Jew, of Jesus' constitution, in the social and political circumstances of his day and country, his reponse (so the New Testament writers seem to say) was absolutely in line with God's will. And this absoluteness, though within the narrow limits of the particular, represents a newness of relationship within the old, spoilt humanity. To respond to him is, therefore, to be brought inside a new creation.[1]

But of course the questions arise: Is this a newness of degree only or also of kind? And is it possible thus to speak of absolute perfection within the relative? One can only reply, to the first, that the newness is something which Christians believed they could not have by their own efforts. It was 'given', and no amount of striving could achieve it. In that sense, the perfection of Christ's response was an 'intrusion', if you like, from outside. It did not simply 'emerge', as by evolution: it was a gift from 'above', a new 'creation'. And yet it was achieved within the circumstances of humanity at that time and in that place. It was genuinely from within, in man, in flesh like ours. And, secondly, while of course it is impossible to demonstrate that such absolute perfection existed, the point is that to conceive it in terms of response does offer a way of relating the absolute to the particular and the relative, if the evidence of Christian experience seems to require such a postulate. I doubt if we can get much further than simply the recognition that both the perfection and the relativity have to be affirmed if we are to do justice to Christian experience. But if there is any unifying factor, it will be in terms of personal relationship and filial loyalty and 'the paradox of grace'.[2]

III

But the relation between the divine and the human is not the only major paradox created by the interpretation of Christian experience in the New Testament. Another concerns the relation, in the manhood of Jesus, between the individual and the corporate. Later christological thought has formulated the problem in terms

---

[1] Cf. a brilliant passage about Christ's temptations in Austin Farrer's *Lord I Believe* (1962), pp. 44ff., including the following: 'The essential point here is that we should see in what the impossibility of his sinning lay. If it lay in the virtual fixing of his choices before he made them, then indeed he had no temptations, nor was his life a human life at all. But suppose it lay in a perfect trust reposed by him in his Father, assuring him that in all the unseen possibilities and sudden temptations of the coming time, his Father's power and Spirit would not fail him? . . . Certainly there was something fixed and inflexible about him, but it was not a pattern of moral choice forestalling all surprises, it was divine Sonship, filial love, absolute dependence, entire derivation' (pp. 46f.).

[2] D. M. Baillie, *God was in Christ* (1948), ch. v.

of the question, Was Jesus a man or was he Man?, and the late
D. M. Baillie is among the writers who have come down decisively in favour of the view that, since Jesus was undoubtedly a man,
it is impossible to identify him, as is done by such as R. C. Mober-
ly, with Mankind.[1] But it is clear that at any rate Paul recognized
Christ as 'Adam', that is, as Man, in some collective sense, as well
as knowing him as an individual figure of history. I have attempted elsewhere[2] to present a summary analysis of Paul's subtle use
of the preposition *en* followed by a designation of Jesus. I have
also tried to show that, although Luke and John, with their much
more individualistic tendency, do not share Paul's language in
this respect (despite John's striking use of *en*), the recognition of
Christ as an inclusive personality seems to be implied, for Christians of the New Testament period generally, by their sacramental
practice. There is not space here for a repetition of these studies
in detail; but it seems difficult to escape the conclusion that the
New Testament reflects a conviction that Jesus was both an individual of history and a corporate, inclusive personality – a body,
in whom Christians found themselves limbs. And it seems,
therefore, that experience of Jesus Christ, from the first days until
now, confronts us with a paradox that has to be accepted, whether
or not it is capable of any sort of resolution. C. H. Dodd states
the matter clearly as follows (his references are to St John's
gospel):

He was the true self of the human race, standing in that perfect union with
God to which others can attain only as they are incorporate in Him; the mind,
whose thought is truth absolute (xiv.6), which other men think after Him; the
true life of man, which other men live by sharing it with Him (xiv.6,20, vi.
57).

It is clear that this conception raises a new problem. It challenges the mind to
discover a doctrine of personality, which will make conceivable this combination of the universal and the particular in a single person. A naïve individualism
regarding man, or a naïve anthropomorphism regarding God, makes nonsense
of the Johannine Christology. Ancient thought, when it left the ground of such
naïve conceptions, lost hold upon the concrete actuality of the person. It denied
personality in man by making the human individual no more than an unreal
'imitation' of the abstract universal Man, and it denied personality in God by

[1] *Op. cit.* ch. IV.   [2] *The Phenomenon of the New Testament* (1967), ch. II.

making Him no more than the abstract unity of being. A Christian philosophy starting from the Johannine doctrine of Jesus as Son of Man should be able to escape the *impasse* into which all ancient thought fell, and to give an account of personality in God and in ourselves.[1]

It may be questioned whether the Johannine use of that particular term, 'the Son of Man', is itself so characteristic of the doctrine to which reference is here made; but that is a detail. The main point stands – that in Jesus a new problem is presented, and a new hope arises. The problem is constituted by one who, although a vividly portrayed individual, yet turns out also to be more than individual – an inclusive personality, the species *novus homo*. The hope is that this opens up new possibilities of (as C. H. Dodd puts it) giving an account of personality in God and in ourselves – and of entering into the resulting experience. And it is relevant both to the problem and to the hope that in the New Testament there is reflected a new way of experiencing the Spirit of God. For Christians, 'the Holy Spirit' (their most usual description of the Spirit of God) was the Spirit of God's unique Son reproducing in them the intimate trust and obedience which Jesus himself had shown (Mark xiv.36, Rom. viii.15, Gal. iv.6). This means that the attitude of the individual, Jesus, is multiplied by as many times as there are Christians: it becomes available in plurality; so that whereas Christians find themselves 'in' Jesus Christ (as their more-than-individual environment, as the body of which they are limbs), yet each one, individually, finds himself indwelt by the Holy Spirit and thus possessed of (and possessed by) the individuality of Jesus. Somewhere in the Christian experience of the Holy Spirit through Jesus Christ lies the new synthesis of individuality and corporeity: the paradox of the incarnation, while it remains intellectually insoluble, is thus put into effect in experience.

IV

To conclude: the New Testament states paradoxes about the manhood of Jesus without successfully reconciling them into a

[1] *The Interpretation of the Fourth Gospel* (1953), p. 249.

rationally coherent system; and it seems probable that the incarnation has to be recognized as of such a character as to impose this insoluble tension on the human mind. If there are any pointers towards a unification and a resolution of the paradox of continuity and discontinuity, they seem to be in the direction of something in terms of will and of personal relationship, and of a perfection of response on the part of Jesus to particular circumstances – a perfection such that the result is seen and experienced as a new and creative event, rather than merely a better example than anything that had gone before.

And, as for that other paradox, of the individual and the corporate, it may be that the resolution is in the experience of the Holy Spirit. According to the predominant usage in the Pauline epistles, Christians are in Christ but the Holy Spirit is in Christians.[1] And the Holy Spirit in Christians enables them to utter the cry of intimacy and obedience, 'Abba, your will be done!' which the individual, Jesus of Nazareth, uttered in his lifetime. Somewhere here, perhaps, lie the roots of that subtle relation between the individual and the corporate which, whether it can be explained or not, is certainly one of the phenomena of christology.

As was said at the beginning, the topics of this sketch have been arbitrarily selected out of an endless range of problems; but there is no doubt that the manhood of Jesus is among the most pressing of christological questions; and, within that area, the paradoxes here briefly considered are of decisive importance in New Testament thought.

[1] See *The Phenomenon of the New Testament, loc. cit.* and references there to M. Bouttier.

7

THE HOLY SPIRIT AND THE PERSON OF CHRIST

G. W. H. LAMPE

The resurrection is the starting-point for christology. The first Christians were convinced that 'the Jesus we speak of has been raised by God', and that 'God has made this Jesus...both Lord and Messiah' (Acts ii.32, 36). Their belief gave rise to a double question: What are the implications of the Easter faith concerning the relationship of Jesus to God, on the one hand, and, on the other, to those who have faith in him as Lord and Messiah? In the first instance an interpretation of his person was required which would justify both the worship as Lord of a man who had been crucified, and also the two-way assertion implied by the credal confession, 'Jesus Christ is Lord': that Jesus is the Messiah and the Messiah is none other than the man Jesus, that Jesus is Lord and the Lord is the same Jesus who was known before his death. The christological problem was to explain this twofold affirmation; but it also involved the question of the relation of the risen Lord to believers. The disciples' Easter experience attested the Lordship of Jesus; but it was not simply a theophany. Whatever Paul precisely meant when he said that God 'revealed his Son *en emoi*'[1], he intended to say more than that he had seen an apocalyptic vision of Christ in glory. It involved the transformation of his whole life through faith that Jesus had not only been exalted to heaven but was a present spiritual reality 'in whom' Paul now lived and who lived in him. Christology had to do justice not only to Thomas' confession, 'My Lord and my God' (John xx.28), but also to Paul's experience that 'the life I now live is not my life, but the life which Christ lives in me' (Gal. ii.20).

The relationship of Jesus to God, revealed through the resurrec-

[1] *NEB*: 'to me and through me'; Gal. i.16.

tion and confirmed by the tradition of his life and death, itself illuminated and transfigured by the resurrection, could be interpreted through a wide range of theological concepts and images, serving to indicate, with various shades of emphasis, God's 'outreach' towards men, his self-disclosure, and the communication and imparting of himself to them. Some of these, derived from Hebraic theology and in certain cases modified under Hellenistic influence, emphasised the uniqueness of Jesus' relationship to God. The title 'Lord' signified the exaltation of Jesus to God's throne (Ps. cx.1). Against the background of its application to the patron and saviour deities of Hellenistic personal religion, on the one hand, and its reference in the Hebraic tradition to the Lord God, on the other, 'Lord' expressed the conviction that Jesus uniquely mediated God's authority, that he transcended the category of ordinary humanity, and that he stood, as it were, on the side of God over against all other men, as one who exercised God's sovereignty over them.

Other images, though not lending themselves to the same extent as 'Lord' to the actual identification of Jesus with God, expressed the singularity of his relationship to God and his role as bearer and agent of God's self-communication to the world. He could be seen as God's holy one, his chosen, sent into the world by God and thus his 'apostle' or his 'angel of great counsel', predestined and thus pre-existing in God's eternal purpose, or, by an extension of this idea, actually pre-existent as Son of God, a designation which, when so applied, begins to take on the overtones of the later and very different theological concept of God the Son. At a still more highly developed level of theology his significance was interpreted through the concept of Wisdom, the image of the invisible God, the effulgence of God's splendour (Col. i.15; Heb. i.13), the projection, as it were, of God's essence in creative action, and through the parallel concept of the Word, God's self-communication in creation, revelation and salvation, Hellenised as the divine mediator coming from God and immanent in the cosmos.

Some of these concepts could also interpret the relationship of Christ to his followers, as an immanent presence in the community and in the individual believer, a Lord in whose life and character his people could in some measure participate. They could share derivatively in his 'sending': 'As the Father sent me, so I send you' (John xx.21). Christ is God's Elect: Christians are God's chosen, in and through him. Much more adequate for the expression of the possibility of participation in the living spiritual reality of the Word and Wisdom of God was the concept of sonship. Like 'Lord', 'Son of God' could span a wide range of meaning. It could express the conviction that in Jesus the messianic expectations had been fulfilled. What had been said of the Davidic king was true of him: 'Thou art my son, this day have I begotten thee' (Ps. ii.7). It implied that Jesus, in a far fuller sense than the Israelite king, was God's elect agent towards men and the focus of their response of obedience towards God. The sonship of the Davidic or messianic king was representative of a relationship established by God with Israel as a whole; the community itself is the son of God (Hos. xi.1, etc.). In Christian thought the sonship of Jesus the Messiah passes over, through him, to the community of believers, so that, as St Paul expressed it, 'he might be the eldest among a large family of brothers' (Rom. viii.29). Sonship thus interprets both aspects of christology: the relationship of Jesus himself to God, and of believers to the immanent presence of the risen Lord. This is also true even of that more profound awareness of sonship which seems to have made it possible for Jesus to address God, in a special and unprecedently familiar way, as 'Abba'. Through him believers can themselves participate in this closer sonship: 'To prove that you are sons, God has sent into our hearts the Spirit of his Son, crying "Abba! Father!" ' (Gal. iv.6).

The concept of sonship could thus express both the belief that in his relationship to God Jesus transcended the normal boundaries of human experience, and also the conviction that in his relationship to believers he is at the same time the transcendent Lord and the immanent presence who 'dwells within' them (Rom. viii.10). Matthew and Luke use the concrete pictorial imagery of the miraculous birth (which Matthew, at any rate, read out of Isa. vii.14 in the LXX) in order to express the transcendent 'otherness'

of Jesus. Unlike Marcion's christology, these Matthaean and
Lucan traditions retain a genuine human birth for Jesus, but it is of
such a nature as to single him out as one who has come into the
human race, by a new creative act of God, from outside the chain
of human generation. Yet even this imagery of miraculous
birth, so striking a symbol of Jesus' otherness, is transferred by the
fourth evangelist to the immanent relationship of Christ to
believers. They are miraculously born by a new act of God, to be
'the offspring of God himself' (John i.12–13).

The Logos concept lent itself least readily to this double
reference. It was well suited to express Christ's relationship to
God. He is the incarnation of God's creative self-utterance, the
embodiment of his self-communication to the world. It was less
fitted to express Christ's immanence in his people. Only when the
idea of 'Logos' had acquired a new and dominant role in Hellenistic philosophical theology could it be applied both to the 'putting
forth' or 'generation' of God's immanent Reason for the 'economy' of creation and redemption, and also to the rationality which
unites the rational creation, by an innate kinship, to the Reason
or Logos of God: men are *logikoi* because they participate in the
Logos. The Logos theology of the second and third centuries, however, represents a transposition into philosophical and cosmological terms of the idea that Christ is the human embodiment of God's
self-revelatory communication to men. It was required by the presupposition of Hellenistic theology that there must be a mediator
between God, who is simple unity, unchangeable and perfect being,
and the sphere of multiplicity, change and temporality – that, indeed, there cannot be divine creation without a mediator. If God
was present and active in Christ, involved in the world of time and
space, this was not God the Father but the mediating Logos of God.
Hence the great problem for patristic theology was the relation between the Logos and the Father: how far and in what sense the Logos
mediates God to the world; to what degree the Logos communicates
the divine essence itself. The question was less often asked why God
should need a cosmic mediator at all. It was not often asked, because of the ease with which the Father addressed by Jesus as Abba
had come to be identified with the Father of the Universe of the

Timaeus, and the idea of the Logos, adopted to interpret the relation of Christ's Lordship to God and to the world, had been assimilated to the divine Mind of Neoplatonism.

In the New Testament period 'Word' and 'Wisdom' language expressed the conviction that Christ encountered men from the side of God; that he had been 'sent' or had 'come down' from heaven where he pre-existed with or in the Father. A different image was required for the corresponding interpretation of the relation between Christ and believers, the immanent presence of Christ as the source of their new life. The enigmatic term 'Son of man', with a stronger claim than other christological titles to have been used by Jesus himself, could point to an individual figure who represents, symbolises, and in some way embodies in himself a faithful people of God, and also to his vindication at God's hands and his exaltation to Lordship as the agent of God's judgment. For fairly obvious reasons, however, this term was used by the early church only with reference to Jesus himself, and then retrospectively, and not as a self-designation of the community which lived in the consciousness of his continuing spiritual presence. For the post-Easter relationship of Jesus to his followers Matthew was content to speak of the assurance that he is with them, in sovereign majesty, to the end of time (Matt. xxviii.20). Luke presented a different picture. The risen Jesus has ascended to heaven, and is no longer with his followers (Luke xxiv.44). Although he will come again in person, the time for this is far off. In the meantime the promised Spirit that he has received from the Father and poured out on his disciples is the link between them, guiding their mission and enabling them to perform in his name works like his own. For the fourth gospel Jesus' 'departure' from the world is the necessary prelude to the coming of another 'paraclete' who will dwell with his disciples and be in them, witnessing to Jesus, glorifying him, and bringing to mind and interpreting the true meaning of his deeds and words. Paul had already used the concept of 'Spirit' interchangeably with that of the immanent presence of Christ. It would be difficult to demonstrate that Paul makes no distinction whatever between the Spirit and the risen and present Christ, but functionally he

equates them. The Spirit is the mode of the immanent 'indwelling' of the pre-existent and exalted Son of God as the directing
and motive principle of the life of the believer and of the church.
This life is 'sonship' towards God, constituted by the exaltation of
Jesus as Lord and his immanent presence in the mode of the
Holy Spirit, the Spirit of God, who reproduces in the Christian
society the essential quality of the character of Jesus: the 'fruit of
the Spirit' which is pre-eminently love. Pauline theology points
towards the possibility of understanding Easter, Ascension and
Pentecost, which Luke presents as distinct events, as three aspects
of one and the same reality, or even as three ways of talking about
the same thing.

'Spirit' had been another of those concepts used by the Old
Testament in speaking of God's 'outreach' towards man. In the
context of God's creative and inspirational 'inbreathing' it can
serve, like 'Word', to indicate that God approaches man from
beyond; inspiration comes from outside a man's own personality.
But it is much better fitted than 'Word' to denote God's immanence. It had been used in the Old Testament to describe the
mysterious influence or power of God which may reach out and
touch a man, inspiring the ruler with wisdom and discernment
to judge righteously, the warrior with leadership and courage or
the power to perform great feats of strength, the artist to create
beauty, the prophet to hear and proclaim the word of the Lord.
Although the inspiration may be unpredictable and spasmodic
(though the ideal of kingship, with which the Spirit is especially
associated in the Old Testament, includes a more permanent
endowment), it is nevertheless an 'indwelling' or 'possession'. This
does not involve a suspension or supersession of the normal human
faculties, but their enhancement and intensification. At the more
advanced levels of Old Testament thought the Spirit can be conceived of as the personal presence of God with, or in, the human
personality, making it, for the time being, an agent of his own
purpose and activity. In Christian thought this immanent divine
influence becomes 'the Holy Spirit' (a rare phrase in the Old
Testament) whose mission is to make Christ present to and in his
people so as to become the principle of life 'in Christ'. Through,

or as, the Spirit the ascended Christ 'comes down' to be present in human life.

The category of Spirit-possession was used to some extent in early Christian thought to interpret not only Christ's present relationship to believers but also his relationship to God. If believers are sons of God through the indwelling of God's Spirit, possessing their souls and reshaping their lives according to the pattern of Christ, can Christ's own sonship be interpreted in the same terms? The gospels suggest this possibility. In the synoptists Spirit-possession and messianic sonship are linked together in the narrative of Christ's baptism. The Spirit descends upon him and he receives the divine assurance that he is Son of God. The fourth gospel alludes briefly to the Spirit 'coming down' and 'resting upon' him (John i.32), but it does not develop this theme. Luke, however, enlarges on it: Jesus is Messiah because he was anointed with the Holy Spirit and power (Acts x.38); he is the recipient of the Spirit and the mediator of the Spirit to his followers (Acts ii. 33); he is the Spirit-possessed prophet foretold by Moses;[1] his works are paralleled by those performed by the apostles in his name because he has poured out on his people the Spirit that possessed him wholly and permanently and not, as in the case of the Old Testament saints, occasionally and partially.

The early church felt constrained to interpret Jesus in terms of deity 'coming down' to the human sphere in his person. It might be expected that the most appropriate concept for the expression of this image would be Spirit-possession. God's Spirit is his own active presence: God himself reaching out to his creation. It also stands for the immanence of the presence of God within men's souls. The Spirit may possess a man and in some measure unite his personality to God. Yet this is without any diminution of his humanity; rather, it means the raising of his humanity to its full potentiality, the completion of the human creation by the recreating influence of the creator-Spirit. Through Spirit-possession a man may be divinely motivated and act divinely – he may be at one with God – and become at the same time, and because of this, fully and completely human.

---

[1] Deut. xviii.15; Acts iii.22, vii.37; cf. Luke ix.35.

Surprisingly, the early church made relatively little use of this idea in trying to give a rational account of the relation of Christ to God. Although the very title 'Christ' signified the 'anointing' of Jesus with the Spirit, this tended to be forgotten and 'Christ' became either simply a name or, in later theology, a way of emphasising that in the incarnation human nature was 'anointed' with deity. Some attempts were made to formulate christology in terms of 'Spirit'. In most of these 'Spirit' is used in a broad and somewhat vague sense to mean, not the Holy Spirit as the third Person of the Godhead, but Deity. God is 'Spirit'. If Christ is Son of God, rightly worshipped as divine, he, too, must be 'Spirit'; and since he lived and died as man in a fleshy body there must be in him a union or mixture of 'Spirit' and 'flesh' (human-ity). This union might be envisaged as 'indwelling',[1] or as the descent of 'Spirit' from heaven and its incarnation as man.[2] Had the church developed this concept it might have been able to work out a highly valuable christology. One of its merits is the use of the same term, 'Spirit', to denote both 'deity' as such, that is, God in his own being, and also God as present and manifested in the historical person of Jesus. This could have been a good foundation for the Nicene assertion that the deity that we recog-nise in Christ is the deity of God in his own being, and nothing less. A developed Spirit-christology lends itself readily, on the other hand, to a full appreciation of the truth that Christ is the 'proper man'. If the relation of Spirit to manhood in Christ is conceived of in terms of possession rather than incarnation it becomes possible to assert that Christ reveals both the nature of God and also the perfection of man. God's creative Spirit does not diminish the completeness of a human personality by taking total possession of it. On the contrary, it perfects its own creation, for it establishes a union with God which in no way abrogates the freedom of the human person. This is not an impersonal and quasi-mechanical process, but a relationship between persons. It consists, in its perfection, of the total response of the human spirit

[1] E.g., Herm. *Sim.* 5.6–7; *Barn.* 7.3.
[2] E.g., Ign. *Eph.* 7.2; Callistus according to Hipp. *haer.* 9.12, 17; Tert. *carn.* 18, *Prax.* 26; Cypr. *idol.* 11.

to the fully pervasive influence of the divine Spirit, so that the human attains its highest fulfilment in becoming the free and responsive agent of the divine. If the service of God is perfect freedom it cannot be the case that, if God takes complete possession of a man, his human personality becomes annihilated in deity.

On the other hand the belief that the perfection of manhood was realised in Christ as the 'proper man', the crown of creation, always proved difficult to reconcile with the Alexandrian formulation of the Logos/Son christology. This affirmed that the eternal Person of God the Son 'came down' and took human nature in such a way that there was one personal subject of the experience of Jesus Christ, and this subject was the divine Person. However strongly this christology may maintain that the human nature assumed by the Logos/Son was complete manhood ('flesh ensouled with a rational soul'), it cannot easily find room for the balancing Antiochene and Chalcedonian insistence that Christ is of one essence with ourselves in respect of his humanity. The manhood of the Logos/Son cannot but be radically different from the manhood of a man.

Even when Apollinarianism is formally avoided, and a genuinely human 'rational soul', as the seat of the will, is ascribed to the incarnate Son, this christology still asserts that the hypostasis or entity to which the human rational soul belongs is the Second Person of the Godhead. The difficulty does not lie merely in the use of concepts which are no longer meaningful, such as 'nature' conceived of as an entity, or a metaphysical 'centre' or 'core' of personality. It consists, rather, in the idea that human thoughts and feelings are thought and felt by a divine subject. Superficially this idea is attractive for soteriology: God decides to experience what it is like to be one of his own human creatures; he makes our human thoughts and emotions his own and knows from the inside what we are. But it implies an excessively anthromorphic picture of God – God who is limited in his own nature and can add to his experience. The great defect of this idea is that in the last resort it almost inevitably suggests that Christ's manhood is no more than an outward form, like a suit of clothes in which God the Son has dressed up as a man – the king disguised as a

E

beggar. The classical affirmation that the Word became man, but not a man, indicates that once Christian thought had *identified* the person of Jesus with the Logos/Son, and had transferred the image of 'Son of God' from the historical figure of Jesus to the pre-existent Logos as the Second Person of the Godhead, it was set on a course which was bound to lead to a reductionist doctrine of Christ's manhood and a weakening of the force of those insights which had found expression in the belief that Christ is the new Adam and 'the eldest among a large family of brothers'. Christology could then avoid this conclusion only by developing the idea of *kenōsis* to the point where, in order to become incarnate as true man, 'made like these brothers of his in every way' (Heb. ii.17), the divine Person has virtually divested himself of deity. The Logos/Son christology suffers from the great defect that it almost inevitably leads to a diminution of either Christ's humanity or his deity. Nevertheless, it was preferred by patristic theology to an interpretation of the person of Christ in terms of the 'possession' of a man by God, involving no diminution of either deity or humanity.

This was due to three major considerations. Orthodox belief was deeply suspicious of any theory which might seem to imply that Jesus was a 'mere' man. To describe his relationship to God as an indwelling of the Spirit suggested that he was a prophet: greater, no doubt, than all other prophets but nevertheless, like them, an inspired man. This appeared to contradict certain basic presuppositions of christology: that, as Athanasius, in particular, so strongly insisted, man cannot be saved by a man; the Saviour must be no less than God; that Christ is not the bearer of God's Word but the very Word incarnate, and hence that between him and the prophets and saints there is an essential difference and not merely a difference in degrees of inspiration; that Christ's saving work was unique, accomplished once for all, because it was carried out by a unique person; and that this person is the one eternal person of God the Son and not a duality of persons, human and divine, in dialogue with one another. The fear of asserting a duality of Sons, Jesus and God the Word, which has always made Nestorianism a bogey, was heightened by the tendency of those who, like Paul of Samosata, reacted against the Trinitarian pluralism of the Logos/Son concept to replace it by the idea of impersonal Logos rather than Spirit. They interpreted Christ in terms of 'Word', the uttered, revelatory, Word of God which came to the prophets, on the one hand, and 'man', the human person of Jesus, on the other. This imagery suggested, in a way which the concept of immanent divine Spirit need not, an external relationship only, in which Jesus the man is addressed, from without, by God.

On the other hand, Spirit christology was also prejudiced by the orthodox fear of patripassianism. The Logos/Son christology was developed in order to enable God-in-Christ to be distinguished from God-in-himself; God operative, and involved in creation and human history, from God absolute, unchangeable, impassible. It enabled Christian faith to be harmonised with the fundamental principles of Greek theology. The concept of the Logos provided for a mediator to bridge the gulf between God and the universe, himself belonging to, and coming from, God's side, and for an exact and eternal reflection of God to be received and transmitted to the world. In Platonist theology it enabled the archetypal ideas to be located in divine mind. The price paid by the pre-Nicene theology for this achievement was pluralism and subordinationism in the concept of the trinity; the Logos tended to be regarded as God at one remove or 'second God'. 'Monarchian' theology, on the other hand, interpreting Christ's divinity in terms of impersonal Word or indwelling Spirit, seemed to remove the apparent buffer provided by the Logos/Son concept and to open the way to the scandalous notion that God in his essential inner being, 'the Father', became incarnate, suffered and died.

Thirdly, to speak of Christ's deity as 'Spirit' made it difficult to distinguish, as orthodox theology required, between God-in-Christ, the divine being who pre-existed, was incarnate, and is exalted to the right hand of the Father, and God-in-Christ's-people, witnessing to the former and assuring them of sonship to the Father in him. Partly in order to give a theological account of Christian experience and partly because scripture seemed to demand it, the church wanted (though it found this very hard in practice) to maintain a threefold distinction between Father, Son and Holy Spirit and not to allow confusion or blurring between these last.

Trinitarian theology sought to give an account of the relationship of Christ to God and of Christians to God through Christ, making use of pre-Christian concepts which had distinguished God's transcendence from his outreach and his immanence. Its aim was to draw such theological distinctions as would explain why Christians worship Jesus Christ as God but yet refrain from saying that God is Jesus Christ; why they can affirm that in Christ God was reconciling the world to himself and yet maintain that God is impassible. Yet when Arius forced upon the church the question, 'Who or what was incarnate?', the answer could only be 'God'. The Logos who became incarnate can be no other than, nor less than, God; Logos and Father are of one and the same essence. At the same time, the alternative designation, 'Son', involved a constant tendency to project on to the eternal Logos the attributes of human personality. It is true that ancient theology used 'person' as a metaphysical and not a psychological term, and that it denoted an individually distinct mode of existence rather than a 'person' in the modern sense. Nevertheless, the tendency was, and is, to think of the Son as a heavenly 'person' on the analogy of a human person. It is seen, for instance, in christologies which have attempted to deduce the nature of the union of manhood to deity in Christ from a consideration of the being of the Son: to begin by thinking what the existence of the eternal Son is like (as though this were possible for created minds), and to infer from this what the condition of humanity must be when hypostatically united with deity in the person of the Son. At the level of popular theology an excessively anthropomorphic conception of the Son has sometimes produced a picture of a vacant place in heaven during his earthly sojourn. Among more sophisticated theologians it has lain at the root of certain objections to kenoticism, on the lines of the question, 'How could the universe have continued to function if the sustaining Logos had temporarily divested himself of his divine attributes?'. The combination of the Nicene *homoousion* with a mythological conception of the Son makes it almost impossible for a satisfactory christology to emerge. The pre-Nicene church's trinitarian difficulties came to be transferred to the problem of the union of man with God in the incarnate Person, while the doctrine of the consubstantiality of the three Persons brought trinitarian theology almost back to its starting-point. Those distinctions within deity which Christian faith had seemed to necessitate became reduced to tautologous abstractions: the Son is God, differing from the Father only in that he is God subsisting in the mode of filiation; the Holy Spirit is God, differing from the Father and the Son only in that he is God subsisting in the mode of procession.

The incarnational, Logos/Son, christology has presented grave difficulties both for trinitarian theology and for the doctrine of the true manhood of Christ. In ancient and modern theologies alike there has been an oscillation between two tendencies. Sometimes emphasis has been laid on the distinction between the Father and the Son, and the completeness of the assumed manhood has been minimised: Christ was the distinct Person of the Son walking this earth in human flesh. In reaction against this, stress has at other times been laid on the unity, and identity as God, of the Father and the Word, sometimes to the extent of denying to the Logos an eternally distinct hypostatic subsistence, and a radical distinction has been made between the Word and the 'assumed man', the human 'son of David'. A Spirit christology would seem to avoid this difficulty, for whereas the concept of incarnation seems to necessitate a pluralistic trinitarian doctrine, that of inspiration or possession is compatible with a monistic theology, a full recognition that Jesus was genuinely a man, and an equally full acknowledgment that his deeds and words were done and said divinely: that his Person mediates true God to man.

A primary question which confronts the advocates of such a christology is whether the assertion that in Jesus God encounters us claims as much as the classical affirmation that Jesus *is* God. At the cost of compromising the reality of Christ's manhood and of being forced to make artificial distinctions, such as Cyril's assertion that deity 'suffered impassibly' and Leo's apportionment of Christ's experiences to the divine and human natures respectively, the Logos/Son christology could ascribe everything predicated of Jesus Christ to the one personal subject, God the Word. Against this, Spirit christology must be content to acknowledge that the personal subject of the experience of Jesus Christ is a man. The hypostasis is not the Logos incarnate but a human being. Spirit christology cannot affirm that Jesus *is* 'substantivally' God. Since, however, it seems that this affirmation is in the last resort incompatible with the belief that Jesus truly and fully shares in our humanity, this need not be a fatal objection. It does not follow that Jesus is only 'adjectivally' God, that is to say, God-*like* or 'divine' in the sense of being a man who possessed to an excellent degree the qualities that we attribute to God. An interpretation of the union of Jesus with God in terms of his total possession by God's Spirit makes it possible, rather, to acknowledge him to be God 'adverbially'. By the mutual interaction of the Spirit's influence and the free response of the human spirit such a unity of will and operation was established that in all his actions the human Jesus acted divinely. In his teaching, healing, judging, forgiving, rebuking, God teaches, heals, judges, forgives and rebukes, without infringing the freedom and responsibility of the human subject. The unity of operation, 'without separation and without confusion', is such that although Jesus is a man his activity is, in the term which the Cyrilline tradition came to employ, 'one theandric energy'.

A christology of this kind has the advantage of enabling us to dispense with certain mythical concepts, such as a pre-existent Son (for it is the possessing and inspiring Spirit that is the eternally pre-existing deity which operates humanly in Christ), a descent from heaven of a personal being who chooses to be born and become an infant, a divine being who may either exercise or voluntarily suspend his omniscience. Apart from this, however, it is questionable whether, despite the ancient rejection of Nestorianism, more is needed for an adequate christology and soteriology than the total possession of a human Jesus by God's Spirit in such a way that he is, wholly and invariably, the human agent of God's operation. The strength of the doctrine of the hypostatic union lies in the fact that it enables us to say that God took human nature and made it 'his very own'. A reinterpretation of christ-ology in terms of inspiration, indwelling and possession allows us to make the same affirmation while avoiding the metaphysical difficulties, both christological and trinitarian, of the classical formulation.

An 'inspirational', as opposed to 'incarnational', christology has often incurred the charge of 'adoptionism'. Adoptionist christologies have been, and should be, rejected for two main reasons. First, because they suggest that at a given point in his life the man, that is, the 'mere' man, Jesus, who had not previously stood in any extraordinary relationship to God, came to be 'adopted' as God's Son, the recipient of the descent of the Word or of the indwelling of the Spirit. Secondly, because they also suggest that the reason why it was *Jesus* who was singled out from all other men for this unique 'adoption' was his human excellence. His spiritual and moral attainment was such that he became fitted and worthy to be raised to sonship, that his saintliness passed over into the closest partnership with God's Spirit, and that he merited the reward of elevation to actual divinity. Nothing of this need be implied by a christology of Spirit-possession. Adoptionist heresies in the early church tended to locate the adoption of Jesus at his baptism by John. Although there is no reliable historical information concerning his life before that event, it is more plausible, on grounds of historical and psychological probability, to believe that he grew up from infancy, and his character devel-oped, under the determining and controlling influence of the Spirit of God. There is no inherent improbability (quite the reverse) in the idea of a human soul growing to maturity in God, a soul of which God had taken possession from the first beginning of consciousness. Such a life would, of course, reach the perfection of manhood, this being understood as the perfection of the rational creature's relationship to the Father-Creator. There is, however, no question here of human attainment apart from God, of moral and spiritual achievement as a precondition for union with Deity, or of a divine reward for human merit. A christology of inspiration and possession states no less clearly than a christology of substance that in the person of Jesus Christ God

has taken human nature and from the moment of birth or before
has made it his own; but it envisages this as a personal taking
which involves a reciprocal relationship of inspiring and guiding
influence and trusting and obedient response, and not as the
hypostatic union was conceived of in ancient metaphysics.

The appropriate analogy for this union of man with God is, as
has often been pointed out, the experience of grace, summed up
in the Pauline 'not I, indeed, but the grace of God working with
me' (I Cor. xv.10), and, 'the life I now live is not my life, but the
life which Christ lives in me' (Gal. ii.20). This immediately
raises a major objection to a Spirit christology: that it is inadequate
to express the uniqueness of Christ's Person and work, and that it
reduces Christ to the status, not indeed, as in some adoptionist
christology, of a superior man, but of a saint or prophet living in
utter dependence on God's grace. Only the classical Logos/Son
christology, it is often said, can assure the believer of the authority
and finality of Christ as revealer and saviour. Uniqueness, however, cannot be predicated of Christ without qualification if
God's purpose is, as Paul believed, that his Son may be 'the eldest
among a large family of brothers' (Rom. viii.29), and if Christ
'had to be made like these brothers of his in every way' (Heb. ii.
17). The Christian saint is really 'Christlike', and a difference in
kind between Christ and all other men seems to be incompatible
either with his true humanity or with the faith and hope of
Christians that they are indwelt by his Spirit and may be progres-
sively conformed to the image of God revealed in him until they
come to be like him in the resurrection life. It may be enough to
acknowledge that Christ is unique in being wholly possessed and
inspired by God's Spirit and in being, therefore, the unique agent
of God's atoning or reconciling work. It is *through* him, by virtue
of the unique closeness of the union of God's Spirit with his human
personality, that all other men, including the most saintly, can be
brought into a union with God which is like, but not equal to, his
own. For this reason the Christian, while refusing to accord
worship to another man, however close to God that man may
be, knows himself to be under a compulsion to give divine
honour to God-in-man and man-in-God in Jesus Christ, since it

is through him as the 'fount of grace' that the saintliness of other men has been made possible.

Christ's uniqueness, on the other hand, must not be understood in such a way as to make it difficult to see in him the new Adam, the archetype and originator of a Spirit-possessed community whose ultimate vocation is collectively to reproduce and represent Christ. It must not impair the hope that in the end, when the 'possession' and 'indwelling' of man by God's Spirit has been brought to completion in that community, and God's people are manifested in the perfection of their relationship to the Father-Creator, Christ will, in this sense, have come again. This representation of Christ through the indwelling of the Spirit in the community may be the most intelligible way in which to understand the 'second advent' of Christ: as his glorious presence (*parousia*) *in*, rather than *with*, 'all those who are his own' (cf. I Thess. iii.13; II Thess. i.10).

What is meant by the 'finality' and the absolute authority of Christ may need to be analysed carefully in the light of Spirit christology. Absolute authority belongs to God alone. A revelation would possess infallible and final authority if it came immediately from God, as a self-disclosure which was not mediated through any non-divine mind and which was implanted by God in the consciousness of the human recipient in some miraculously direct fashion without being apprehended by the normal process of the human intellect. But in the nature of things divine revelation is not communicated like this; it can never be taken neat. It is always mediated through the human mind and its form and content are affected, and largely conditioned, by the ways in which men think and feel, by the limited extent of their knowledge and their inadequate sensitivity, and by their cultural and other presuppositions. Only on the basis of a christology which failed to acknowledge the reality and completeness of Christ's manhood could absolute finality and infallible authority be ascribed to the words and deeds of Jesus, even if there existed an entirely authentic and accurate record of them. Not only in respect of his ignorance of 'that day or that hour' (Mark xiii.32), that great problem for the Logos/Son christology in antiquity, but also as regards his ascription of Davidic authorship to Psalm cx (Mark xii.36) and, what is much more important, his endorsement of the demonology, apocalyptic eschatology and other religious beliefs of his time (assuming that the gospels preserve an authentic tradition in this matter), the authority of Jesus is not final. In certain respects God's communication of truth to man moves on and leaves the revelation to and through Jesus behind. Except to those whose christology is thoroughly monophysite, this is in no way startling. It is no more surprising than is the fact that the Spirit has communicated, and continues to communicate, God's self-disclosure in areas of man's social and individual life which were still unexplored or did not yet exist in the time of Jesus. The finality and authority of Christ does not arise from his absolute uniqueness and discontinuity from the rest of mankind but from the Christians' experience that it is through Christ, by reference to his disclosure of divine judgment and mercy and love as their norm and criterion, that they are able to recognise and evaluate the continuing communication to them of God's self-disclosure through the Spirit – the Spirit that fully possessed Christ and can be called the Spirit of Christ. Thus, for example, some sayings of Jesus (assuming them to be authentic and that we interpret them correctly) speak of divine retribution and eternal punishment. It is legitimate to claim that it is God's continuing self-disclosure through the Spirit that possessed Jesus, checked and verified by reference to the overall significance of God's revelation of himself in Jesus and to the total impression made upon us by the character of God as so revealed, which may persuade us to discard these elements in Jesus' own teaching. It is possible, though it is by no means a simple matter, to appeal from the words of Jesus to the Spirit in Jesus.

It is sometimes alleged that only a substance christology and the attribution to Christ of uniqueness in kind rather than in degree enables an answer to be given to the question why there has been only one incarnation and why it should be assumed that there will never be another. If Christ was a man indwelt by the Spirit, and if God's desire is that other men should come to be indwelt by the Spirit, why has it never been the case, and why should it not in future be the case, that the Spirit has indwelt, or may indwell, another man as fully and perfectly as Jesus? The problem is not a major one, and there could be several lines of reply. The uniqueness of Christ's possession by the Spirit does not consist only in the perfection of his unity with God but also in its being the source as well as the archetype of the indwelling of the Spirit in believers. Their faith and hope is that the Spirit may reproduce in them Christ's life and character, not that they may become agents of the Spirit independently of any reference to Christ and even, perhaps supersede Christ. It is the very fact that the more fully inspired a saint or prophet might be the more he would model himself on Christ's example, and, in doing so, become ever more conscious of his inferiority to Christ, that makes a second Christ-event inconceivable. If God has, as it appears, willed that his Spirit should communicate with men and inspire them through Christ, that is, by witnessing to Christ and referring to him as the archetype and norm, then this is a fact of God's dealings with men which it would be profitless to question. Like his election of Israel, it has to be accepted. It is such considerations as these, rather than classical christology in itself, that cause Christians to deny that Jesus could be superseded by another 'Christ'.

Spirit christology obviously has far-reaching implications for trinitarian theology, and to develop it would involve a considerable re-structuring of the trinitarian dogmatic formulations. The threefold distinction may be retained, God in his transcendence (or the being of God) being distinguished from God 'reaching out towards' and addressing (or God's Word) and from God operating immanently and influencing, inspiring and possessing (or God's Spirit). Or, on the other hand, it may be thought sufficient to distinguish between God as transcendent Spirit and God as immanent Spirit. In either case the concept of the pre-existent personal Son, or pre-existent Christ, would have to be re-expressed in terms of the eternal Spirit who was manifested at a particular point in history operating humanly in the person of Jesus Christ. A major question arising from this would be what Christians mean when they claim to 'encounter Jesus Christ', and to worship

Jesus Christ here and now as contemporary. Would they be satisfied to give an account of their experience in different terms from these: that they encounter here and now, or are encountered by, God, the Spirit who was in Jesus, meeting them with the identical judgment, mercy, forgiveness and love which were at work in Jesus, inspiring them and recreating them according to the pattern of Jesus; and that they worship God, the Spirit who was in Jesus and who now re-presents to them, and makes real and contemporary, Jesus' Lordship? Or would they, rather, assert that in their experience Jesus of Nazareth, the man fully possessed by the Spirit and thus united with God, meets them from the other side of death? Or must Spirit christology after all give way at this point to the concept of the incarnation of the pre-existent divine being, the Logos/Son?

8

ONE JESUS, MANY CHRISTS?

DON CUPITT

Among men of religion the prophet Mohammed is one of the most clearly remembered. He was a man who, after considerable spiritual struggles, emerged as a passionate and eloquent prophet of the one God in his middle age. He had great practical gifts as warrior, organizer and statesman, but above all he was a man of God. We have this fairly distinct picture of Mohammed even though the first biography of him, by Ibn Ishaq, was not written till over a century after the prophet's death, and the various biographical traditions about him obviously stand in need of critical sifting. We have this distinct idea of Mohammed, even though the details of his biography are not central to the faith of Islam, but belong to the secondary material, the *hadith*. Through thirteen centuries Islam has been remarkably constant, and has always 'projected' a pretty constant picture of Mohammed. Critical sifting of the biographical traditions about him has not radically changed this picture, and there is considerable agreement about Mohammed among scholars. Perhaps it is just because it has never wished to worship him that Islam has never had any very strong interest in idealizing its picture of Mohammed.

The situation with Gautama, the Buddha, is rather different. The canon of sacred writings is very large and rather late. The tendency to make the Buddha himself the object of worship, or at least an instrument of contemplation, has distorted the picture of him. For example, it magnified his birth, changing his father from a minor chieftain into a great king: and in the familiar iconography his beatific expression bears no trace of the struggles of the historical man. Piety has idealized the Buddha; but nevertheless it can be said of him too that we have a fair idea of the kind of man he was, and of the issues which concerned him. He asked, what is man? What are the causes of suffering, and how can it be escaped?

What is the final good for man, and how can it be attained? We know fairly well what answers he gave, and Buddhism too, in spite of the idealization, has projected a fairly constant image of the Buddha.

With Jesus the position is much less clear. He has been more intensely and directly worshipped by more different kinds of people than any other man, and this worship has blurred him. As we can faintly distinguish the historical Buddha beneath the smiling benignant Buddha of piety, so Christians have distinguished the Jesus of history from the divine Saviour of the developed ecclesiastical faith. But the truth is much more complex. Buddhist iconography projects one dominant image of the Buddha, but Christian iconography has projected a great number of images of Jesus: there was the shepherd–teacher of the first few centuries; the *Christos pantocrator* of the period dominated by Byzantium; the twisted, naked crucified man of the later Christendom period; and there have been many others. From the very first the 'theologizing' of Jesus began to erase his human features, so that even though substantial, early and detailed books about him (which have the form of biographies) are at the centre of the canon of sacred writings, the figure of Jesus himself has remained enigmatic and capable of very diverse interpretations. He has been seen as moralist, prophet, apocalyptist, hero, redeemer, priest and king. Men of the highest ability who have read the gospels afresh very closely have reached conclusions about Jesus much more varied than we could find in the case of Gautama or Mohammed.

The fact of varied interpretations of Jesus is notorious, and it has been said that everyone who writes a life of Jesus sees his own face at the bottom of a deep well. This is too simple, for while there is undoubtedly distortion, it is of more than one kind. We should first distinguish *positive* from *negative* distortion. Positive distortion occurs when the reader projects upon Jesus an ideal self-image. George Bernard Shaw, in his Preface to *Androcles and the Lion* (1915) described Jesus as a 'highly-civilized, cultivated person', a Bohemian socialist. William Blake, in *The Everlasting Gospel* (1818) portrayed Jesus as proud, independent and mocking.

Tolstoy, in his later writings, saw Jesus as the same relentless moralist of altruistic love that he was himself. These are examples of positive distortion: negative distortion occurs when the reader discerns in Jesus all the qualities which he repudiates. Thus Nietzsche, in *The Antichrist* (written about 1888; published 1895) saw Jesus as something between an immature adolescent and a hypersensitive psychopath – Dostoyevsky's Idiot. The poet A. C. Swinburne in his *Hymn to Proserpine* (from *Poems and Ballads*, 1866) sees Jesus as a morbid ascetic who immolated himself before a cruel dying Father-God. Both men in a way projected upon Jesus their own traits: Nietzsche was inclined to be a solitary valetudinarian, and Swinburne had sado-masochistic inclinations, if one may be forgiven the vulgarity of so categorizing them. But the point is that if they projected upon Jesus traits which were present in themselves, it was not as ideals to be pursued but as vices to be spurned.

A second distinction, cutting across the first, must also be made between two other kinds of distortion. Some writers, like Seeley and Renan, *assimilate* Jesus to the spirit of their own time, making him exemplify and authenticate the ideals current in their own society. Other writers, of whom Kierkegaard and Schweitzer are examples, emphasize the strangeness of Jesus, and make of him a stick with which to beat their contemporaries. They see Jesus as a *corrective* to the spirit of their own time, emphasizing that he lived by values unknown or abhorrent to most people nowadays. Schweitzer attacked some of his predecessors for positive distortion very effectively and has had great influence. His own corrective distortion is perhaps associated with his decision to go to Africa. At any rate, he and such later writers as Rudolf Bultmann and R. H. Lightfoot have tended to disseminate the opinion that the truest account of Jesus is one which says that he was an eschatological prophet, that we do not know a great deal about him, and that what little we do know is very strange to our ears. A rough generalization has gained currency to the effect that nineteenth-century pictures of Jesus were assimilatory and suffered from positive distortion, whereas twentieth-century pictures of Jesus are corrective and much more soundly based on scholarly

study of the texts. I have already given sufficient reasons for thinking that generalization is too crude and question-begging. It would
be nearer the mark to say that in nineteenth-century religious
controversy all four kinds of distortion are richly in evidence;
whereas in the present century, a time when Christianity has been
on the defensive, and whose history has been ugly, corrective
distortion has been more popular in theological circles. But positive distortions can still be found, as when Jesus is portrayed as a
revolutionary nationalist leader.

Again, as we may contrast the historical Buddha with the Buddha
of piety, so we may contrast Jesus with the Christ of later Christian
piety. But since the French Revolution the climate of opinion has
tended to be critical, humanist, anti-authoritarian and anti-eccles-
iastical; so that the contrast between Jesus and the ecclesiastical
Christ has generally been made to the latter's disadvantage. It is
said that the Christ of Christian iconography – whether as represented in pictures or in theological formulae – is abstract, inhuman
and antipathetic. A good and unfamiliar example of this complaint
is to be found in H. G. Wells' *First and Last Things*.[1]

In reaction, many theologians (including Kähler, Tillich,
Bousset, Bultmann and Barth) have nevertheless asserted that the
Christ of Christianity, the preached and worshipped Christ, is
the 'real' Christ and that the historical Jesus is a figure of no
particular religious interest. The difficulty with this is that there
is no single preached Christ. More recently there has been a swing
back, and efforts have been made to define the relation between
Jesus the eschatological prophet and the Christ of the early
Christian preaching.

All this is an oft-told tale. My purpose in recalling it is simply to
point out a paradox. More than any other religion Christianity
has revolved obsessively around one particular man: it has loved
him, worshipped him, meditated upon him, portrayed him, and
sought to imitate him – but he slips away. Recently I heard someone essay the generalization that Islam is a religion of victory whereas Christianity's central imagery is of suffering and defeat. Yet the
crucifixion of Jesus has not always and everywhere been seen as of

---

[1] *First and Last Things* (1929), pp. 70ff.

central importance and even where the cross *has* been prominent it has been seen in many different ways. In the Anglo-Saxon poem *The Dream of the Rood* Jesus crucified is seen as an enthroned prince, and as a hero in battle: he is utterly different from the tortured hideous figure of Grünewald's altarpiece at Isenheim. It is true that for much of its history Christianity has been a religion of salvation from sin, especially in the West, and Jesus has been seen as the divine redeemer who procures for us the forgiveness of sins. But this has not always been so, and especially in recent times there has been a marked swing away from the ideas of God the almighty and reproachful Father, the guilty sinner, and Jesus as mediator. There is at present more emphasis on Jesus as the pioneer of faith.

This great diversity of Christianity is partly the result of its having flourished in so many different cultures. At least five may be distinguished. There was Jewish Christianity; the Christianity of the ancient churches of countries like Syria, Ethiopia and South India; Eastern Orthodoxy, which grew out of Hellenistic culture; Latin or Roman Christianity; and the Protestantism of northern Europe. Within the remains of these older forms there perhaps exists in germ a sixth and new form of Christianity adapted to the global scientific culture which has been emerging in the last three centuries. Only Buddhism has found expression in a comparable variety of cultures.

But the image of Jesus is perplexingly vague and blurred. It is not surprising that theologians have wanted (rightly or wrongly) to clarify and stabilize it. They have had little success, and their close study of the New Testament has only made matters worse. For by now the critics distinguish several different accounts of Jesus which can be discerned within the New Testament itself. Here are some of them, in broad outline:

Jesus himself was – and saw himself as – an eschatological prophet who proclaimed the imminent coming of the Kingdom of God. He did not make 'claims' for himself: he did not claim divinity, he did not claim to be the Christ, and he did not even call *himself* the Son of Man. But he did regard his own work as helping to usher in the Kingdom of God, and, whatever was to happen to him, he hoped to be vindicated by the Son of Man at the end of time.

The second interpretation of Jesus is that of the earliest Palestinian Christianity. It began with the baptism of the man Jesus, and described his ministry as a prophet and servant of God. After his death he was, in his followers' eyes, vindicated by God. He now waits in heaven, and his followers gather a band who wait on earth, for the time when he shall return as *himself* the Christ, the glorious Son of Man. When he comes thus, the present historical 'world' or 'age' will end.

The third interpretation of Jesus developed among the Greek-speaking Jews of the diaspora. Jesus is thought of as sent by God to be, during his life on earth, Son of David, Lord and Christ. At his exaltation he begins a period of heavenly reign over his church below which will culminate in the *parousia*.

The fourth interpretation of Jesus was that which appeared in the Greek world. The Gentile world longed for deliverance from sin, suffering and death. It was told of a pre-existent one, God's Word or Son, who descended to earth, became incarnate, defeated the demonic powers in a titanic struggle which ended his earthly life, returned in glory to his proper home in heaven, and now heads a new order of humanity which will be consummated in him.

Here, then, set out in a rather schematic way, are four very different accounts of Jesus to be found in the New Testament, which itself arose from the interaction of different cultures. Since the New Testament itself exhibits the translation of Christianity from one culture to another it is surprising that so many Christians are sceptical about whether Christianity can be so translated in our own time. And the development did not stop there, but has continued ever since, as Jesus has been ever more elaborately mythicized, demythicized and remythicized. Though the Christian tradition has almost constantly affirmed the reality of Jesus' manhood, it has with equal regularity idealized away, recovered, and then idealized away again his human characteristics, rather as in eastern Europe icons are effaced by pious kisses, repainted, and effaced again.

As there has been a long line of books attempting to isolate and define 'the essence of Christianity', so a great deal of ink has been spilt in endeavouring to give Jesus a clearer and more determinate outline. Indeed the 'quest of the historical Jesus' was undertaken in the hope of finding in him the essence of Christianity. Jesus is an example of the ancient philosophical problem of identity and change: it is hoped to distinguish the substance of what he is from the accidental dress in which various ages have clothed him. Surely if Christianity is one religion, and not many religions, it ought to be possible to say something about the one Christ in whom all Christians have in their different ways believed? Tradition has counted for a great deal in Christianity, and Christians have generally wished to affirm that they believe in the same Christ as St Paul believed in, and believe in him in the same way.

But Christians have been exceedingly diverse. An immense variety of ideals of character have been ostensibly based upon the example of Jesus: an historical man who lived only one life has been made the exemplar of a great range of different forms of life. Jesus has been declared to be a model for hermits, peasants, gentlemen, revolutionaries, pacifists, feudal lords, soldiers and others. Even if we restricted attention to the religious life of men in the Latin West alone, the diversity is great among the ideals of Benedict, Francis, Bruno and Ignatius Loyola.

One solution has been to recognize this diversity and generalize the notion of Christ. That is to say, the term 'Christ' is understood to denote an abstract principle of moral perfection, or of harmony with the divine, of which Jesus is one concrete and perfect instance but which may become concrete in other lives in a variety of different ways. Thus there may be a rough 'family resemblance' among all the actual Christ-lives, which justifies us in predicating 'Christhood' of them all, but they need not all closely resemble the life of Jesus himself. The traditional doctrine was that there is and can be only one Christ, namely Jesus, *in the same way* that there is and can be only one divine being, namely, God. So just as 'God' is both a predicable term and the proper name of an individual, so Christ is both a predicable term and the proper name of an individual. The result is that there is only one concrete way of being Christ-like, namely Jesus' own way. But this traditional and very 'strong' doctrine of the unity of Christ fails to explain the extraordinary variety of the Christian tradition. The historian notices how differently Jesus has been seen at different times and places, and what a variety of life-styles have been ostensibly based on his example: and the theologian must ask himself how the individual characteristics of the historical Jesus can be reconciled with the host of life-styles which he has been called upon to validate and exemplify.

Thus there has been a strong inclination to detach Christ from Jesus, or at any rate to change the logical knots by which Jesus and Christ have hitherto been tied together to make the complex entity 'Jesus Christ'.

A striking example can be quoted from Florence Nightingale. In her book *The Cause* (1929), Ray Strachey printed an extract from an unpublished confessional work by Miss Nightingale on 'the Woman Question'. She writes about the theological problem created for her by the extraordinary disabilities of women in the 1850s, and she sees herself as 'Cassandra', the prophetess of 'a female Christ, who will resume in her own soul the sufferings of her race'. Florence Nightingale was a Christian, but the position of women in her time was such that the full humanity of women was denied by society with, it seemed, the approval of the church. Jesus was a man and in Florence Nightingale's day hardly a man alive could understand what women were aggrieved about. The intellectual stress she suffered separated 'Jesus' from 'Christ' in her mind, and she became one of the first Christians to formulate the remarkably original idea of a female Christ.

Another way in which Christ could be detached from Jesus was through reflection on the limitations of our historical knowledge of Jesus. For Kant the idea of Christ was *a priori*: the term 'Christ' denotes the idea of moral perfection realized in a human being. We may find reason to judge that Jesus instantiated this concept historically; but such an historical judgment can never be more than probable, whereas we know with certainty what is really important to us, that moral perfection can be and must be realized in our lives. Thus for Kant the moral force of the Christ-idea is independent of any claim that it has been embodied historically in Jesus. When the possibility that Jesus had never lived was put to Tolstoy he said the same.[1]

For Hegel the term 'Christ' signifies the ideal union of human and divine spirits – a goal to which the entire historical process moves. The connection between Jesus and Christ is contingent, and certainly not exclusive.

So it would seem to be possible for people to experience a *religious* longing for a Christ, and the moral power of the Christ-idea, apart from any specific and exclusive claim that any actual man, such as Jesus, is the one and only Christ. One of the best examples is the Sufi doctrine of the Perfect Man. The Perfect Man somewhat resembles the idealized Adam of the rabbis, or the Heavenly Man of some ancient gnostics. He was the self-revelation of God, his visible image: he could be called the final cause of the universe, and the expression of God's will to be known. He could be seen as embodied in the Prophet, or the saints of Islam: he could also be seen in woman. R. A. Nicholson states that 'Ibnu'l-'Arabī went so far as to say that the most perfect vision of God is enjoyed by those who contemplate him in woman'; and Rūmī speaks in a similar vein.[2] The Perfect Man is in fact a schema – the notion of a human being perfectly responsive to God and so a revelation of him – a schema which different believers may apply and use in different ways. Its religious value and efficacy is not thought to depend on the claim that it has been embodied once for all in one particular person.

Our argument so far suggests a reason for the vagueness of Jesus. In the Christian phenomenon as a whole, 'Christ' has meant so many different things, and being Christ-like has meant so many very different ways of life, that talk of Christ must either break away from any exclusive association with Jesus of Nazareth or be severely pruned back. The first alternative was chosen by the

---

[1] Aylmer Maude, *The Life of Tolstoy: Later Years*, World's Classics edition (1930), p. 51. For Kant, see *Religion within the Limits of Reason Alone*, Harper Torchbook edition (1960), pp. 54–60.
[2] R. A. Nicholson, *Rūmī* (1950), p. 44. 'Ibnu'l-'Arabī (1165–1240) was an Andalusian, and the principal systematic thinker of Sufism. Jalalu'l-Dīn Rūmī (1207–73) was a Persian, and founder of the Mevlevi Order.

idealists, who made of Christ the general principle or pattern of relationship between the human spirit and the divine: a pattern which maybe was exemplified in Jesus but which may equally be exemplified in any number of other men. The second alternative was to try to fix the historical Jesus and use him to cut back the luxuriant growth of ecclesiastical Christianity. Christianity would be reconstructed on the basis of the Jesus of history, and in the process drastically simplified and clarified. The range of possible ways of being Christ-like and talking of Christ would be narrowed sufficiently for Jesus to be able to hold them together.

A liberal Christian who is told that the quest for the Jesus of history has failed finds himself wondering where he shall find his starting point. What is Christianity for him? Critics of Christianity sometimes try to play fair by defining at the outset what it is they propose to attack. And they discover that whatever they say Christianity is, someone will dispute the definition. The liberal Christian is in the same difficulty if he tries to say who Jesus Christ is, and what he means by the unity of Christ and by the finality of Christ.

We do not escape the difficulty if we turn to consider, not the historical Jesus himself, but the doctrinal propositions about him which have long been thought to constitute the *differentia* of Christianity. Four of these might be that Jesus was born of a virgin, that he was and is both divine and human (or that he is the Son of God), that by his death the forgiveness of men's sins has been procured, and that he rose from the dead. Each of these propositions seems at first sight tolerably clear and definite (whether it be thought true or false): but as soon as we begin the study of the history of Christian theology it becomes apparent that none of them is anything of the kind. There is no such thing as an orthodox christology, even though for purposes of church government it has often been claimed that there is. There is not even any such thing as a New Testament doctrine about Christ. As soon as you try to state it you are at once obliged to admit that your statement is interpreted rather differently by different New Testament writers. I doubt if you could write down *any* statement about Christ to which St Mark, St Paul, St John and the writer to the Hebrews would demonstrably have assented in precisely the same sense.

For example, the early Christians certainly held that Jesus was risen, but exactly what they meant by this is a matter of considerable and even acrimonious controversy. Did they mean that his corpse had revived in the grave, walked out of it again, and thereafter been physically seen by his disciples? Did they mean that at their meetings to break bread they had enjoyed visions of him while in a state of ecstasy? Did they mean that they had pored over the Old Testament and were now announcing, in the prophetic manner, that the God of Israel had approved the work and exalted the person of his servant Jesus? Did they mean that a divine man had descended from heaven, sojourned awhile on earth, and was now returned to his proper home? I have elsewhere argued for one of these opinions,[1] but I am bound to admit that some early Christians may have held one, and some another. I cannot assume that they all held the same opinion, when they manifestly speak about the resurrection in different ways.

Thus the diversity of Christianity is such that it is hard to see how a clear agreed picture of Jesus himself, or an agreed list of basic christological assertions, could be settled upon. One is bound to ask, how strong *is* Christian interest in the unity of Christ?

In the West people are used to the idea of visibly distinct religious communities. Christians sing 'One Church, one Faith, one Lord', and Judaism and Islam too have historically been hard-edged communities. A man was in no doubt to which he belonged. Westerners find Hinduism hard to understand precisely because it lacks such clear frontiers. To understand Hinduism one might invoke the famous disagreement between Socrates and Wittgenstein about universal concepts. Socrates thought that the prerequisite for rational enquiry in such fields as ethics was to establish clear and distinct universal concepts from which 'syllogizing' could begin. Wittgenstein, on the other hand, considered that the meanings of many important universal terms

[1] *Christ and the Hiddenness of God* (1971), pp. 138–67. For an authoritative recent discussion of the resurrection, see C. F. Evans, *Resurrection and the New Testament* (1970).

were not clear and distinct, and used the metaphor of a family resemblance among a class of individuals.

Similarly, our Western idea of the unity of a religion has in the past been Socratic, and the search for the essence of Christianity has been rather like Socrates' quest for exact definitions. But in Hinduism such a thing is plainly out of the question. What we find is rather a family resemblance among a large body of religious doctrines, cults, and movements.

Are we all moving in the direction of Hinduism? The religions used to be geographically distinguished in old atlases, but nowadays there are at least some adherents of most major religions in most countries. For centuries the influence of Jesus has by no means been confined to Christianity. For example, Tolstoy discerned in the gospels a repudiation of any exercise of coercive force. Gandhi picked it up from Tolstoy, and Martin Luther King picked it up from Gandhi. A religious idea twice moved across traditional religious frontiers within fifty years.

We may now tentatively suggest a few lines for further reflection. In the first place, as an historic organization Christianity, with its hierarchy and its discipline, had an almost military idea of its own unity. The slogan 'One Chuch, one Faith, one Lord' well epitomizes this, and in the ecumenical movement one can discern a nostalgia for that past ideal. Nevertheless it is in irreversible decline. Christianity is rather a family of monotheistic faiths which in various ways find in Jesus a key to the relation of man with God. It has and will continue to have almost as much internal diversity as Hinduism.

Both the unity and the diversity are important. It is important that the various forms of Christianity should maintain relations with the gospels, and that in each the Christ who is believed and preached today should interact with the Jesus who dimly emerges from the study of the New Testament. This common endeavour consolidates family ties.

But the study of the gospels has itself shown that Jesus' mission was not to draw attention to himself, or to promulgate doctrines about himself. He was a signpost, not a destination. He pointed men to God and told them about the claims of God and the nearness of God. His own career exhibited what it is to believe in God. To be a Christian is in one's own way to be stimulated by him to become engaged with the reality of God. It was always a mistake to make Jesus himself the direct object of worship. A good many forms of Christianity appear at first glance to fall into this error, and Jews and Moslems have rightly protested against it, as being incompatible with monotheism. But on closer examination one notices, for example, that in the historic Christian liturgies prayer was and is addressed *to* God *through* Christ. Official forms of prayer directly addressed to Christ or to the Holy Spirit are always uncommon, and for the most part late. Christianity has for the most part been a form of monotheism guided by Jesus seen as Christ, and if this were more generally understood relations between Christians and members of so-called 'other faiths' would be easier.

So I suggest that the problem of the one and the many in the Christian tradition – and particularly in the figure of Christ – is becoming a little easier. Modern study of the gospels tells against the opinion that the purpose of Jesus was to create a highly-unified cultus of himself as the divine Christ, a cultus definable in dogmatic formulae, and maintained by a sharply-defined church community. Jesus' legacy to mankind is rather an urgent appeal to each of us to acknowledge above all else the reality of God. I call him Christ insofar as I respond to this summons and find in the gospels the pattern or shape of what it is to obey it. But the way he is Christ for me may be very different from the way he is Christ for some other person, and (if I may speak crudely) he himself is not troubled by being many Christs, or Christ in many ways. Nor is he in the least concerned about the disintegration of the 'One Church, one Faith, one Lord' ideal. It was not followers in the Way who themselves invented the term 'Christian', and it is arguable that it is *almost* as serious a misnomer as 'Mohammedan' or 'Wesleyan'.

So I agree with the liberals that, in a rather loose way, allegiance to the historical Jesus holds together the various forms of Christianity. But we do not know enough of him to use him to prune back the variety of styles of faith and life which have stemmed from him. So I agree with the modernists in valuing that variety. Jesus' mission was not to create a cultus of himself as divine Christ, but to point away from himself to God. Hence his elusiveness, symbolized by St Mark in the so-called 'messianic secret'. God can be believed in and served in as many ways as there are people. In the Christian tradition Jesus is the paradigm of faith, but that paradigm may be re-enacted in a great variety of ways, and we need not labour to reduce their number.

PART III

CHRISTOLOGY AND HISTORIOGRAPHY

9

IS JESUS NECESSARY FOR CHRISTOLOGY?: AN ANTINOMY IN TILLICH'S THEOLOGICAL METHOD

JOHN POWELL CLAYTON

The requirement to do justice both to the concrete, historical foundation of Christianity and to the universal, trans-historical significance of that foundation inheres in any attempt to do christology. The problem of the relation which obtains between christology and historical enquiry is one point at which the tension between 'particularity' and 'universality' occasioned by this dual requirement has been keenly felt in modern theology. Paul Tillich, whom C. E. Raven once called 'that austere trans-cendentalist', was among the generation of theologians who inherited the unsolved problem of the relation of christology and historical research from the nineteenth century and who searched for a viable solution along lines radically different from the dis-credited *Leben-Jesu-Forschung*. I shall argue in this essay that Tillich's proposed solution rests on certain confusions which render it logically incoherent, but that it is nonetheless an instructive failure.

I

There is at least a *prima facie* case for arguing that an antinomy seriously undermines Tillich's proposed solution inasmuch as it seems to require that both the following be held simultaneously:

(i) A relationship of entailment exists between the confession 'Jesus is the Christ' and certain propositions about Jesus of Nazareth such that in order for the confession to be true, certain propositions about Jesus of Nazareth must also be true.

(ii) No relationship of entailment exists between the confession 'Jesus is the Christ' and any proposition about Jesus of Nazareth such that no propositions about Jesus of Nazareth need be true in order for the confession 'Jesus is the Christ' to be true. Clearly it cannot, at the same time and in the same sense, both be and not be the case that the basic christological confession entails statements about Jesus of Nazareth.

On the one hand, Tillich insists vigorously that the foundation of Christian faith ('Jesus as the Christ') is both an historical fact and 'the believing reception of Jesus *as* the Christ'. The whole theological enterprise is said to be undercut unless both these elements are preserved in the symbol 'Jesus as the Christ' [*ST*, II, 98–9 (113–14)].[1] For the basic Christian assertion is that 'essential God-Manhood has appeared within existence and subjected itself to the conditions of existence without being conquered by them'. In order to conquer existential estrangement, the power of 'new being' must be manifest in an actual person: otherwise the New Being would remain a quest and an expectation and would not be a reality in space and time. 'Only if the existence is conquered in *one* point – a personal life, representing existence as a whole – is it conquered in principle.' Elsewhere Tillich states emphatically that the foundation of Christianity would be denied if the factual element in it were denied [*ST*, II, 107 (123)]. He frequently emphasises that Jesus of Nazareth, the bearer of the power of new being, was in fact an individual, historical person existing in space and time and in comparison with whom all mythological divine figures are abstract expressions of the hope of new being, but not its bringer. It is precisely the concreteness of the biblical picture of a man, Jesus of Nazareth, as bringer of this power which gives the symbol 'Jesus as the Christ' its universal significance [*ST*, II, 151(175)]. This side of Tillich's christology cannot be adequately expressed by the phrase 'new being' alone, but must be expanded to 'the new being in Jesus as the Christ' inasmuch as 'new being' apart from 'Jesus of Nazareth is abstract and a-historical and, therefore, not a sufficient summary of 'the biblical picture of Jesus as the Christ' [*ST*, I, 49f. (55f.)]. Here there is

---

[1] References to the three-volume *Systematic Theology* (1951–63) appear in square brackets in the text. Corresponding page numbers in the English edition are cited in round brackets immediately after the page numbers in the American edition.

clearly a relationship of entailment between the christological confession 'Jesus is the Christ' and at least some statements about Jesus of Nazareth. According to the logic of this side of Tillich's position, Jesus is clearly necessary for christology.

On the other hand, Tillich insists equally vigorously that historical research can neither give nor take away the foundation of the Christian faith [*ST*, II, 113 (130)]. That is to say, no statement or combination of statements about the past *arrived at by historical enquiry* is allowed to count decisively for or against the truth of the 'foundation' of Christian faith. Tillich consistently argued throughout his career that Christian faith demands a foundation which is certain in the sense of being incorrigible and that historical enquiry is incapable of providing such a foundation since historical knowledge can never attain to more than a high degree of probability. For this reason, 'the historical Jesus' cannot be the foundation of faith; rather, 'the biblical picture of Jesus as the Christ' provides faith's foundation.

In 'Die christliche Gewißheit und der historische Jesus' ('Christian Certainty and the Historical Jesus'), an unpublished paper which was written in 1911 in the wake of the collapse of 'the quest of the historical Jesus' and the short-lived ascendency of the 'Christ-myth' movement,[1] Tillich considered the consequences for Christian theology if historians were to conclude that Jesus of Nazareth had never existed. Having distinguished between the confession 'Jesus is the Christ' and the contingent proposition 'Jesus, the Christ, existed', Tillich there argued that faith in the Christ of the biblical picture is authenticated by the presence of the transforming power of the Spirit and does not depend, either as a matter of empirical fact or as a matter of logical necessity, upon the incertitude of historical enquiry into the existence of Jesus of Nazareth. Indeed, such dependence is regarded as a form of heteronomy and, therefore, contrary to the protestant doctrine of

[1] The first edition of A. Schweitzer's *Geschichte der Leben-Jesu-Forschung* (*The Quest of the Historical Jesus*) was published in 1906 and A. Drews' *Die Christusmythe* (*The Christ-Myth*) appeared in 1909. Kierkegaard's *Philosophical Fragments* appeared in German translation only in 1910, although it had been published in Danish in 1844. E. Troeltsch published *Die Bedeutung der Geschichtlichkeit Jesu für den Glauben* (*The Importance of the Historicity of Jesus for Faith*) in 1911, the same year in which Tillich prepared his paper on the historical Jesus.

justification *sola gratia*. Nor is this radical bifurcation between confession of the Christ and statements about Jesus restricted to Tillich's earliest writings. Shortly before his death, Tillich commented that even if 'the biblical picture' were a fabrication of Mark the evangelist, it would still be a valid expression of the power of new being, for Mark would then have been 'the bearer of the Spirit through whom God has created the church and transformed…many in all generations, somehow including myself'.[1] It would clearly seem to follow from such remarks as these that there can be no relationship of entailment between the confession 'Jesus is the Christ' and any statement about Jesus, including statements pertaining to his ever having existed.

One possible solution to this apparent antinomy would be to postulate more than one way of acquiring knowledge of the past such that there could be both a 'scientific' way (namely, historical research) and a way of faith. If it were further granted that each of these ways is independent of the other, then it might be possible for faith to claim to be certain on its own grounds as to the truth of a given statement about the past (such as 'Jesus of Nazareth existed') without submitting itself to the alleged uncertainties of historical research. Tillich ostensibly rejects this alternative as untenable: faith is not able to bestow certainty upon statements about the past which historical research is incapable of giving them. Despite his adamant refusal to adopt such a view, it is less than clear whether he successfully avoided the procedure in practice. For Tillich does insist that faith can guarantee 'its own foundation' and that its foundation is in some sense historical or that it at least entails an historical proposition. Although faith is said not to be able to guarantee that Jesus of Nazareth ever lived, it is said to be able to guarantee 'the fact to which "Jesus of Nazareth" refers', namely that the power of new being became actual in an individual, historical person. Although admittedly less specific than the statement that the power of new being became actual in Jesus of Nazareth, even the more modest claim that this

---

[1] 'Rejoinder', *Journal of Religion*, XLVI (1966), 192. Tillich's remarks are in response to Professor D. Moody Smith's essay in the same number entitled 'The Historical Jesus in Paul Tillich's Theology', pp. 131–48.

power became actual in 'a personal life' remains or entails a contingent proposition about the past. Despite his protestation to the contrary, Tillich is thereby committed to the view that faith is capable of guaranteeing on its own grounds at least one statement about the past.

That an historical person corresponds to the biblical picture of Jesus as the Christ is said to be guaranteed by what Tillich earlier termed an 'imaginative intuition' (*fantasiemäßige Anschauung*) and later an *analogia imaginis* 'between the picture and the actual personal life from which it has risen' [*ST*, II, 115 (132)]. Tillich's argument would appear to run as follows: the power of new being cannot have become actualised except in and through an individual person; this power *is* actual in the biblical picture of Jesus as the Christ; there must therefore have been an individual person who corresponds to the symbol 'Jesus as the Christ', whether or not his name was Jesus.

Martin Kähler, Tillich's professor at Halle, actually adumbrated the *analogia imaginis* in his still-influential pamphlet published in 1896 entitled *Der sogenannte historische Jesus und der geschichtliche, biblische Christus* (*The So-called Historical Jesus and the Historic, Biblical Christ*). Having argued previously that the biblical picture of Jesus could not be merely an idealised composite portrait of the highest hopes of man or merely 'the loftiest poem of mankind',[1] Kähler asserted, 'We encounter precisely the historic [*geschichtliche*] Christ, not as an ideal to be realized in the remote future by scientific investigation nor as the fluctuating result of the biographers' disputations, but, rather, within a tradition which possesses the inherent power to convince us of its divine authenticity.'[2] This inherent power is said by Kähler to make Jesus the Christ 'directly accessible' and to make it impossible to differentiate the historic (*geschichtliche*) Christ from the biblical picture of Jesus as the Christ. Likewise, for Tillich, it is the inherent power of the biblical picture which is said to guarantee that an actual person corresponds to that portrait.

---

[1] M. Kähler, *The So-called Historical Jesus and the Historic, Biblical Christ* (1964), pp. 53, 78–9.

[2] *Ibid.* pp. 121–2.

F

Reference to a central aspect of Tillich's early thought further illuminates his understanding of the biblical picture and its component elements. In his programmatic essay 'Über die Idee einer Theologie der Kultur' ('On the Notion of a Theology of Culture'), Tillich indicated the mutual relatedness of 'form', 'content' and *Gehalt*[1] – a conceptual triad which, although not unprepared for in romanticist aesthetic theory,[2] was formulated by Tillich under the immediate impact of the expressionistic style of art initially as a foundation for his theological analysis of culture. In that essay, Tillich emphatically distinguished *Gehalt* and 'content' or *Inhalt*, the latter being defined as something objectively factual, and the former as the spiritual power which gives significance to form.[3]

Although all three elements – 'form', 'content', *Gehalt* – are said to be present in some measure in any given work of art, one or another element tends to predominate according to the style in which, for example, a portrait is painted. There are some styles in which both objective factuality (*Inhalt*) and expressive elements (*Gehalt*) are subordinated to such formal properties as line, shape and colour. The work of such non-representational artists as Josef Albers could be said to be dominated by form. Portraits in the cubist style, such as Picasso's *Fernande* or Leger's figures, might also be included here. There are other, more 'realistic' styles in which the object of art is regarded as the near-exact mirroring of the objectively factual. Most of the portraiture of the Renaissance could be said to be in such styles. Then there are expressionistic styles in which the object of art is to bring out the sometimes hidden meaning and significance of the subject matter, rather than to reproduce in exact detail its

1 The sense of *Gehalt* in Tillich's early works is difficult to convey in a single English word. Some, notably James Luther Adams and his students, have translated this key term as 'import'. After his emigration, Tillich himself came to employ several different English words (including 'power', 'dynamics', 'substance' and even 'content') in contexts where one might earlier have expected to find *Gehalt*. None of these alternatives, however, does justice to the richness of Tillich's use of *Gehalt*, a term perhaps better left untranslated.
2 See, for example, G. W. F. Hegel, *Vorlesungen über Ästhetik* (*Lectures on Aesthetics*) (2nd ed., 1842).
3 *Gesammelte Werke*, volume IX: *Die religiöse Substanz der Kultur: Schriften zur Theologie der Kultur* (1968), p. 20.

surface features. The break-up of traditional forms and the mini-malisation of the 'objective' in the late nineteenth century were not exploited by the expressionists merely for technical experi-mentation (as was the tendency in impressionism), important as that may have been for the development of expressionistic art, but were taken rather as an opportunity to bring expressiveness to a new intensity. Whereas the impressionists were primarily interested in the momentary effect of a situation (such as the play of light flittering through the trees in Renoir's technically superb *Le Moulin de la Galette*), the expressionists were more interested in the 'existential' significance or the 'inner meaning' of the subject matter. In Tillich's terms, this difference of focus in impressionism and expressionism is the difference between 'structure' and 'depth'. Although he became increasingly open to the religious dimensions of those styles in which form or content tend to predominate, Tillich generally regarded those styles in which the expressive element dominates as theologically the most important: for it is not the content or subject matter which is said to make a work of art 'religious' or 'secular', but the *Gehalt* which it brings to ex-pression. Thus, Tillich could on occasion claim there is more religious meaning in a still life by Cézanne or a tree by van Gogh than there is in a portrait of Jesus by the German romanticist Uhde![1] As examples of expressionistic portraiture, one might mention the self-portraits of Kokoschka or Modersohn-Becker and the frequently reproduced wood-cut of a *Prophet's Head* by Nolde.

It should come as little surprise that Tillich explicitly identifies the biblical picture of Jesus as the Christ as an expressionistic portrait [*ST*, II, 115–16 (132–3)]. I would like to suggest that Tillich's interpretation of the biblical picture, as well as the moves which he makes by means of the *analogia imaginis*, become more intelligible when seen in relation to Tillich's aesthetic model. The component elements of the biblical picture would appear to correspond in the following way to the components of artistic creations: 'a personal life' may be regarded as the form of the biblical picture; 'Jesus of Nazareth' and specific information about

[1] *The Religious Situation* (1932), pp. 88–9.

his life and teachings, that is, biographical material, supply its content; and 'the power of the New Being' must be understood as the portrait's *Gehalt*. Those who have been grasped by this power in and through the biblical picture can certify the experience of the power-full *Gehalt* of new being, although they cannot certify the objective factuality of the specific content of that picture: 'The concrete biblical material [in the biblical picture] is not guaranteed by faith in respect to external factuality; but it is guaranteed as an adequate expression of the transforming power of the New Being in Jesus as the Christ' [*ST*, II, 115 (132)]. Just as it is not content or subject matter which makes a piece of art a medium of religious meaning, it is not the specific content which makes the biblical picture of Jesus as the Christ a medium of the power of new being. This then is the significance of the aesthetic model employed by Tillich in his *analogia imaginis*: it is intended as a means of holding together the claim that the foundation of Christian faith is historical and the claim that that foundation is in principle unfalsifiable. For falsification of any aspect of the specific, factual content (*Inhalt*) of the biblical picture would not entail the falsification of the picture itself, as long as 'power' continued to be mediated through it.

II

Tillich's proposed solution to the problem of the relation of christology and historical research as it affects the single question of the christological necessity of the existence of Jesus of Nazareth must, in my opinion, be regarded a failure for four closely related reasons: certainty that something is the case does not entail that it is the case; 'intuitive' knowledge of the past is not incorrigible; knowledge of the past is not defective in comparison with other kinds of knowledge; and, although 'belief in' cannot be reduced without remainder to 'belief that', 'belief in' does nonetheless entail 'belief that'.

Discussions about the problem of certainty sometimes tend to conflate two basically different, though not unrelated, senses of 'certainty'. Since this conflation has at times given rise to confusion, it is important to distinguish between what might be termed subjective certainty and objective certainty. A statement such as 'I am certain that *p*' may be a true statement whether or not *p* is true. Not infrequently we are forced by circumstances to say such things as, 'I was certain that such-and-such is the case, but I was wrong.' But it would not follow from this admission that we were not *really* certain when we originally said, 'I am certain that such-and-such is the case.' For example, 'I am certain that the moon is a flat disc' could be a true statement, whether or not the moon is in fact a flat disc. This is what is meant by *subjective certainty*. On the other hand, there are other kinds of statements in which we use the term 'certain' in which it is decisive for the truth of falsity of the statement whether *p* is true. Neither 'it is certain that *p*' nor '*p* is true for certain' would be true statements if *p* were not in fact the case. 'It is certain that the moon is a flat disc' would be true only if the moon were in fact a flat disc. This is what is meant by *objective certainty*. I shall be using both senses of 'certainty' in what follows. My first two objections to Tillich's proposal have to do primarily with subjective certainty, whereas my third and fourth objections are more properly concerned with objective certainty. I shall assume that by 'faith can guarantee that *p*', Tillich means 'the subjective certainty of the believer can certify the objective certainty of *p*'.

The claim that historical research can neither give nor take away the foundation of Christian faith is, of course, a particular instance of Tillich's general attempt to make the truth-claims of theology immune from any form of empirical verification or falsification: no historical discovery must be allowed to count for or against the Christian's claim that 'the New Being appeared in Jesus as the Christ'. The following dilemma must be resolved if sense is to be made of such a proposal: *either* theology must relinquish its claim for the factuality of the foundation of its christology in order to secure immunity from historical enquiry into such claims *or* theology must relinquish immunity from historical enquiry into the alleged factuality of its christological foundation in order to secure the benefits of such claims to historical factuality. Now, Tillich proposed to evade this dilemma altogether by means of his *analogia imaginis*, which apparently came to replace his earlier notion of 'imaginative intuition'. The evasion is illusory, however, for the *analogia imaginis* can certify neither the existence of Jesus of Nazareth nor 'the fact to which "Jesus of Nazareth" refers', that is, 'the personal life' in which the power of new being is said to have become actual. For it does not follow that something is the case from the fact that someone is convinced that it is the case, except in very limited cases.

There are two classes of statements the truth of which may be said to be self-verifying. First, there are statements the very utterance of which entails their truth: for example, 'This sentence has five words'; 'I am now making a statement'; and perhaps 'I think, therefore, I am.' But Tillich's claim that faith can certify that an actual person, who was the bearer of the power of new being, is portrayed in the biblical picture clearly does not resemble any of these.

There is, however, a second class of statements, the truth of which is partially determined by whether one is convinced they are true. Here we may be closer to what is required for the *analogia imaginis* to be made intelligible. To illustrate this class of statements, I should like to allude to the 1970 British general election, although the 1948 U.S. presidential election could serve my purposes equally well:

(A) Mr Wilson was certain Labour would win the election.
(B) Mr Heath was certain the Conservatives would win the election.
(C) I, who was not eligible to vote, was certain the Labour government would be returned to office.
(D) Jones, who has been attempting to row round the world in a twelve-foot dinghy since two days before the election and who has not yet heard the results, is certain that Mr Wilson is still Prime Minister.

That certainty alone cannot 'guarantee' something to be true is clear from such statements as A, C and D. That certainty may in some cases contribute to the truth of that about which one is certain is allowed, but not entailed, by B. For it is not at all unlikely that in some situations a politician's certainty that he will be elected to office inspires similar confidence in his chances on the part of some undecided voters who then vote for him. This serves to illustrate two important limitations of those cases in which being certain that p contributes to the truth of p: certainty is never a sufficient condition for the truth of p, and certainty that p may contribute to the occurrence of p in the future, but not to its occurrence in the past. Assuming that Mr Wilson and Mr Heath were equally certain of victory, it is clear from A and B that certainty is not a sufficient condition since one of the parties lost, despite its leader's certainty of victory. Jones' certainty in D, no matter how strong, cannot change the fact that Mr Wilson was no longer Prime Minister after the 1970 general election.

Nor does it follow *solely* from the fact that someone discovers creative power in 'the biblical picture' that an actual person is portrayed there. For a fictional character in literature may be powerful without being a portrayal of an actual person. Indeed, a fictional creation is often more *power*-full precisely because it is a composite of characteristics of several individuals or because it epitomises common human experiences. Even though a character may expand one's self-awareness, challenge one's life-style, or make whole new dimensions of existential possibilities available to one, that would not 'guarantee' the existence of an actual, individual person who corresponds to the fictional creation of the author's imagination. This does not, of course, preclude the possibility that the character in question was in fact a 'portrait' of an actual individual. But this could be determined only by the marshalling of convincing evidence in support of the claim. For certainty that p is not a sufficient condition for the truth of p. Certainty is, rather, the 'tone of voice' in which one declares how things are but from which one does not infer that the declaration is justified[1]. And we have been taught by Locke and his heirs that the 'tone' appropriate in any given instance is directly proportional to the strength of the supporting evidence.

Tillich's proposal further rests upon distorted views as to the incorrigibility of 'intuitive' knowledge and the inherent defective-

[1] L. Wittgenstein, *On Certainty* (1969), §30.

ness of knowledge of the past acquired through historical enquiry. It is questionable whether intuition, which Tillich sometimes calls 'participation', is sufficient to verify any statement about the past, even one so general as 'an actual person corresponds to the biblical picture'. It is also questionable whether statements about the past are in principle significantly less certain than other kinds of contingent propositions, such as statements about the external world or about other minds.

The appeal to 'intuition' is the means whereby Tillich sought to neutralise the effects of his scepticism about the possibility of one's knowing for certain something which occurred in the past. Tillich's proposal falls within the tradition of what he terms the Augustinian–Cartesian refutation of radical scepticism through the immediacy of self-consciousness which authenticates itself by 'participation in being'. 'Participation, not historical argument guarantees the reality of the event upon which Christianity is based.' Furthermore, adds Tillich, 'No historical criticism can question the immediate awareness of those who find themselves transformed into the state of faith' [*ST*, II, 114 (131)]. Historical knowledge is corrigible and, therefore, an inadequate ground for knowledge of 'the event upon which Christianity is based'; intuitive knowledge or 'participation' is incorrigible and, there-fore, the only adequate ground for such knowledge. But, since even intuitive knowledge of the past must be knowledge of *the past*, Tillich is thereby committed to saying – despite his explicit denials – that intuition is another and even a more certain way to know at least some things about the past (such as 'the event upon which Christianity is based' and that 'an actual person is portrayed in the biblical picture') than is afforded by historical enquiry.

Let us assume for the moment that knowledge of the past could at least in certain instances be attained through some kind of intuition. Even if this were the case, the fact would remain that *no* statement about the past, whether based on intuition or historical enquiry, is incorrigible since no class of descriptive statements is incorrigible. Indeed, corrigibility is one of the essential features of descriptive statements: since they say something about what is or is not the case, there is at least the theoretical possibility of falsification of any descriptive statement, however it is arrived at. Whatever *is* may *not be*; whatever *was* might *not have been*. Consequently, even 'intuitive' knowledge of the past would be corrigible.

It does not follow from this, however, that descriptive statements or contingent propositions can be 'no more than probable', that descriptive statements or contingent propositions are somehow defective in comparison with analytic statements or necessary propositions. It only follows from this that the kind (but not necessarily the degree) of certainty which may be appropriate to a contingent proposition is not identical to that which may be appropriate to a necessary proposition. Even Moore, that most confident of philosophers, distinguished the sort of certainty appropriate to necessary and contingent propositions.[1] Yet, he insists that it is not always inappropriate to claim to be certain – even *absolutely* certain – of some contingent propositions. The degree of certainty which may be legitimately bestowed upon any contingent proposition – whether the statement be about the external world, other minds or the past – is relative to the decisiveness of the supporting evidence. Now, although statements about the past present some peculiar problems (some of which are considered by Dr Carnley in his essay in this present volume), it does not follow merely from their being about the past that they cannot be reasonably regarded as certain. I would suggest the following as statements about the past which may be regarded as certain: 'The battle of Waterloo took place on 18 June 1815'; 'In 1492 Columbus sailed the ocean blue'; 'Plato was a student of Socrates'; and, 'George Washington did not assassinate Julius Caesar'.[2]

Any one of the propositions expressed by these statements could be false in the sense that the contrary of none of the four is self-contradictory. That is to say, it is not self-contradictory to say, for

[1] G. E. Moore, *Philosophical Papers* (1959), p. 237.

[2] Examples have been limited to statements about the distant past, that is to statements appertaining to events which we do not 'remember' in the sense that we might remember events to which we were eye-witnesses (such as a friend's wedding) or even events to which we were not eye-witnesses but which occurred 'within memory' (such as the assassination of President Kennedy).

example, 'George Washington assassinated Julius Caesar', although it would be self-contradictory to say of any circle that that circle is a triangle. It does not follow from this alone, however, that we have not the right to be certain of all four of these statements about the distant past.

Statements about the external world and about other minds, as well as statements about the past, all express contingent propositions. So far as I know, Tillich never entertained the view that knowledge of the external world or of other minds can be 'no more than probable'. Nor does consistency require him to have been sceptical about all forms of empirical knowledge in order to have been sceptical about historical knowledge. Yet it is nonetheless the case that sceptical arguments could be constructed to cover our knowledge of the external world and of other minds, as well as of the past, and that the structure of such arguments is in each case similar: only the sort of knowledge in doubt is different.

For example, since our knowledge of other minds is at least partially contingent upon the adequacy of our opportunities of observing other individuals' behaviour (including speech) and since we often are mistaken in our observation even when we have had adequate opportunity for observation, one might be tempted to infer that our knowledge of other minds is seriously defective and that there is no sufficient warrant for claiming to know other minds. Yet, we *do* have knowledge of other minds. Likewise, sceptical arguments could be constructed in regard to our knowledge of the external world since we are frequently deceived by our senses. Yet, we *do* have knowledge of the external world. And, we *do* have knowledge of the past as well.

Whether the historical propositions (however many or however few that may be) entailed by the confession 'Jesus is the Christ' can be said to be true for certain cannot be determined *a priori*: for, since certainty is proportional to evidence, the supporting evidence for each such proposition must be weighed before a judgment is given. Nor, as has been argued above, can the certainty appropriate in each case be decided intuitively or by 'participation'. Whatever role intuition (of the sort required by

Tillich's *analogia imaginis*) may play in our coming to know something in the distant past, it cannot be regarded as sufficient to warrant our claiming to know for certain something in the distant past. One must not confuse the way one comes to know that *p* and the grounds on which *p* may be said to be true. For example, the role of intuition in scientific discovery is sometimes emphasised. It may of course be true that many, if not all, of the most important scientific discoveries originated as intuitive insights. But it is also important to remember that many, if not most, of any given scientist's 'intuitive insights' fail to be confirmed when subjected to appropriate experimental testing. That is to say, the intuition that *p* must be confirmed by evidence for *p*. But it is precisely this which Tillich refuses to allow, for the certainty of faith must remain independent of 'the way things go'. But can faith stand aloof from the way things go and yet claim the dividends which accumulate from claiming to have a foundation which is historical?

A confusion implicit in the *Systematic Theology* is more explicit in the account of the relation of 'the truth of faith and historical truth' in *Dynamics of Faith*, in which Tillich apparently equates the following: faith is not identical with or reducible to historical knowledge; faith is not 'based upon' historical knowledge; and, the truth of faith does not in any sense entail historical factuality.[1] But these three statements clearly do not express the same proposition. Although Tillich is surely correct in arguing that Christian faith cannot be reduced without remainder to historical knowledge, and that faith cannot supply historical certainty (even if he is inclined to ignore this in practice), he is surely mistaken in his argument that the truth of the symbol 'Jesus as the Christ' is not in any sense dependent upon the results of historical research: for, although the existence of a man Jesus of Nazareth is not a sufficient condition for the truth of the symbol 'Jesus as the Christ', it nevertheless remains a necessary condition. Although some beliefs – of which belief in Jesus as the Christ may be an example – cannot be reduced without remainder to 'beliefs that', *all* 'beliefs in' entail 'beliefs that' inasmuch as one cannot legitimately

[1] *Dynamics of Faith* (1957), pp. 85–9.

believe *in p* without also at the same time believing *that p*.[1] That is to say, whereas 'Jesus is the Christ' is not in its theologica application strictly speaking an empirical statement, it does nevertheless entail at least one empirical statement, namely, 'There was a man Jesus who has been called "the Christ".' Thus, there is a sense in which theology is 'at the mercy' of historical research inasmuch as descriptive statements are subject to empirical verification or falsification. Tillich is certainly correct in emphasising that the risk of faith is not *merely* a historical risk, but he is mistaken in his inference that historical risk is in no sense entailed by the risk of faith [*ST*, II, 116–17 (134)].[2] For, to cite Professor MacKinnon slightly out of context, in christology 'finality belongs somehow to that which is particular and contingent, to that which has definite date and places, to that which is described by statements that are not . . . "necessary propositions" '.[3]

Tillich's inability to incorporate the contingent into his christology without its ceasing to be contingent contributed to the marked lack of specificity in his interpretation of the biblical picture. Whether or not it was in a man named Jesus of Nazareth, the power of new being became actualised in 'a personal life': but, if one cannot specify with some certainty the *particular* person in whom existential estrangement is alleged to have been conquered, what warrant is there for the claim that it has been conquered in *a* person? This problem of specification in Tillich's christology is both illustrated and made more acute by his comment cited above that even if 'the biblical picture' were a fabrication of Mark, the picture would still be a valid expression of the power of new being, for Mark would then have been its bringer. This telling remark suggests the extent to which Tillich had been misled by the aesthetic model he had employed as a means of interpreting the component elements of 'the biblical picture'. Indeed, Tillich would have done well to have heeded his

---

[1] See H. H. Price's recently published Gifford Lectures on *Belief* (1969), pp. 426–54.
[2] This passage in the *Systematic Theology* is apparently directed against C. H. Dodd, who – according to Tillich – once suggested to him that historical risk could be an aspect of the risk of faith. See Tillich's 'Rejoinder', *op. cit.*, pp. 193–4.
[3] D. M. MacKinnon, *Borderlands of Theology* (1968), p. 58.

own warning of the tendency of art dominated by the expressive element to degenerate into meaningless subjectivity unless the expressive is held in check by other elements, including the empirical or what he earlier termed *Inhalt*.[1] The inherent weakness of expressionism is its inability to produce a criterion by which its product can be checked against that which it allegedly brings to expression. Therein lies one of the limitations of Tillich's aesthetic model which is duplicated in his *analogia imaginis*.

At the outset of this essay, it was claimed that, although a failure, Tillich's proposed solution to the problem of the relation of christology and historical research is nonetheless an instructive failure. The proposal is instructive to the extent that it shows clearly the futility of any attempt to resolve the problem on the one hand by claiming that the foundation of Christianity is historical and on the other hand by exempting it from the possibility of falsification through historical investigation. For there is no logically coherent way of making these two claims simultaneously without equivocating in the use of the term 'history': the two claims are and must remain antinomously related.

Whether Jesus of Nazareth may be said to have lived for certain, as well as whether the biblical picture may be regarded as 'a good likeness', are issues which lie beyond the scope of the very limited concerns of this essay. They are christologically crucial problems, however, and they must be faced squarely: for the confession 'Jesus is the Christ' cannot be more certain than is warranted by the evidence for the empirical propositions entailed by that claim.

---

[1] *Systematische Theologie* (1966), III, 90–1. Unfortunately, this paragraph on the ambiguity of the expressive element in cultural creations does not appear in the English-language editions of the *Systematic Theology*. It was added to the German edition at Tillich's request.

10

THE POVERTY OF HISTORICAL
SCEPTICISM

PETER CARNLEY

One of the recurring characteristics of much twentieth-century theology is its historical scepticism. It is my thesis that this scepticism is based on poor and inadequate philosophical reasoning, that it is therefore an unjustified scepticism, and that theologies which have been conditioned by it are in need of revision.

I

Roots of the kind of scepticism with which we are concerned can be found in the work of German theologians early in this century. As the tide began to turn against the nineteenth-century preoccupation with 'the Jesus of history', Martin Kähler and Wilhelm Herrmann argued that it was a fatal error to attempt to establish the basis of faith by means of historical investigation because faith, as a complete and final commitment and not a mere tentative acceptance, must necessarily be based on something fixed and secure. Historical research was disqualified because it was 'constantly constructing afresh' and modifying the results obtained from the records. More explicit reasons for the permanent insecurity of historical conclusions were advanced by Ernst Troeltsch, who pointed out (a) that the everpresent possibility of a future discovery of new evidence prevents us from achieving certainty in the present, and (b) that relativity in historiography is unavoidable since the historian's judgments are always conditioned by his world view.

The same scepticism holds an important place in the work of Bultmann who goes beyond the affirmation that historical results have 'only relative validity' to declare that in historiography 'the conception of truth is dissolved'. Tillich, as was seen in the previous essay, holds a similar sceptical position and rejoiced in the fact that the consequent emancipation of faith from historical research constituted the 'greatest contribution of historical research to systematic theology'. Meanwhile, even the protagonists of the so-called 'new quest of the historical Jesus' often affirm that faith cannot and should not be dependent on the change and uncertainty of historical research, new quests notwithstanding.[1]

But this position is not confined to the Lutheran/Reformed tradition in twentieth-century theology. John Knox, the contemporary North American Anglican theologian, presents one of the clearest statements of the kind of scepticism which I wish to challenge when he writes:

> Since even the best attested fact of the history of the past can possess no more than a very high degree of probability and since, by definition, Christian and indeed all religious faith must from the believer's point of view be absolutely certain and secure, can faith ever be said to depend upon a historical fact, no matter how well established? Faith must *know* its object in a way we cannot know a historical fact.[2]

Clearly, Professor Knox believes that one cannot have historicity without risk and that faith cannot be made to rest on anything as uncertain, vulnerable and insecure. Thus, besides the difficulties of conclusively verifying many *particular* historical judgments, occasioned by the ambiguous and meagre nature of the gospel evidence, Knox has come to recognise the permanent uncertainty of *all* historical judgments. There is always a theoretical possibility, he asserts, that a 'chance discovery of an ancient document or a new conclusion of historians' could cause us to reconsider even our 'best attested' judgments about the past. If faith is based on so tenuous a foundation there is *always* the possibility that we could be robbed of it.

---

[1] On all this see: W. Herrmann, *The Communion of the Christian with God* (1906), esp. p. 77; M. Kähler, *The So-called Historical Jesus and the Historic, Biblical Christ*, tr. Carl Braaten (1964), and compare Paul Tillich's Foreword, p. xii; E. Troeltsch, 'Historiography', *Hastings' Encyclopaedia of Religion and Ethics*, VI (1913), 716–23; R. Bultmann, 'The Quest for Meaning in History', *The Listener* (1 Sept. 1955), p. 329, *Faith and Understanding* (1969), p. 30 and *Essays Philosophical and Theological* (1955), p. 18; Paul Tillich, *Systematic Theology*, II (1957), 108ff. (Amer. ed.), 125ff. (Eng. ed.) and Mr Clayton's essay in this volume; G. Ebeling, *Word and Faith* (1963), pp. 56–7 and E. Fuchs, *Studies of the Historical Jesus* (1964), p. 213.

[2] *The Church and the Reality of Christ* (CRC) (1963), p. 16. F. Gerald Downing's *The Church and Jesus* (1968), pp. 185, 187 contains similar examples of the same sceptical trend.

It is in the face of this scepticism that Professor Knox has been led to place more and more confidence in his concept of the church's continuing 'corporate memory' of Jesus as the basis of the judgment of faith. He has come to espouse the conviction that faith must be essentially related to historical fact concerning Jesus, for how would a living presence be recognised as the 'presence of *Jesus*' if we did not have *some* information about his nature from the past? And yet, he has been obliged to admit that historical research is inherently incapable of establishing this essential information. Knox does not subscribe to the view that the judgment of faith must necessarily be independent of all rational support, yet he is convinced that in the moment of faith the believer knows that he is not venturing anything important on the results of the researches and deliberations of historians. Faith, he says, 'is not, it simply cannot be, as tentatively, as precariously poised, as our historical knowledge must be' (*CRC* p. 16). Thus, he calls on the church's continuing 'corporate memory' with its alleged certainty and security, to provide a basis for the judgment of faith. Consequently, though Knox has never repudiated his belief in the worth of historical investigation for the Christian religion and has never abandoned the quest of the historical Jesus, he has moved away from historical research at least to the extent of seeking to raise his concept of the 'church's corporate memory of Jesus' to the status of a kind of *sturmfreies Gebiet* for faith.

Many of Knox's readers, however, find difficulty in his concept of the church's continuing 'corporate memory' of Jesus and cannot see how, if it provides the Christian with a knowledge of Jesus, it can be completely independent of the researches of the critical historian. One would perhaps expect that the scientific historian could at least be called upon to verify the church's ostensible 'memory of Jesus'. But, for Knox, the Christian cannot rely on the historian for this kind of support, for, be believes, all historical conclusions are themselves uncertain and less than fully verified.

Consequently, we are able to say that historical scepticism is both a widely held and important element in twentieth-century theology. For the historian's alleged inability to achieve any

assured results has led theologians to seek a basis for faith in some
other sphere – the preaching of the kerygma, the idea of the new
being, the memory of the church, for example. Or else, it has led
to the conviction that, in so far as faith includes historical assertions,
it must always be a commitment marked by risk or lack of
complete assurance, for a complete assurance is something that
historical research is incapable of providing.

We must now look at some of the arguments which are brought
forward from time to time in support of this scepticism, with a
view to ascertaining whether it is in fact a justified scepticism.

II

In this theological opinion concerning the uncertainty of all
historical judgments there are two closely related, though slightly
different, arguments. The first is that we are unable to achieve
certainty in our judgments about the past because we can never
be sure that a chance discovery of a new document will not cause
us to reconsider our present judgments; the second is that we
can never be sure that a future historian will not reassess the evidence *now* possessed from a different point of view and come to a
different conclusion. We must first say something about this latter
kind of argument.

The first thing to say about it is that, as it has just been stated, it
involves a *non sequitur*. The fact that different historians see the
past from different points of view, or write different histories of
the same historical events, and that a future historian may write
a different account of the past from the one we now possess, does
not entail that any one of them is necessarily invalid and untenable,
or that we cannot entertain *all* of them with certainty. The mere
fact of difference does not entail that we must begin to doubt.
Relativism, in other words, does not necessarily involve us in
scepticism.

Introductory books on logic are quick to point out that the
logic of descriptions allows us to admit many different but equally
true descriptions of the same object. A ball may be described as
red, large, soft, not very bouncy and a bad buy. None of these

descriptions is in logical competition with any of the others. We do not strike trouble if somebody describes the ball as red and another describes it as large, but only if one person were to describe the ball as red and another as yellow. This is trivial, but the corresponding case concerning descriptions of past persons and events, in the reflections of theologians about the theory and method of history seems to be constantly overlooked. Bultmann seems to overlook it, for example, when he says: 'How widely the pictures of Jesus presented by liberal theologians differ from one another! How uncertain is all knowledge of "the historical Jesus"!'[1] It may be an injustice to Bultmann to assume that he believes that the first of these statements entails the second. Yet, this entailment is suggested also by his contention that relativism (i.e. different histories because of different points of view) involves the dissolution of truth.

It might be admitted that many of the lives of Jesus of the nineteenth century are unsatisfactory because the statements which constitute them are supported by evidence that, at best, warrants them with a degree of probability only, and that other statements are ill-founded, totally unsupported by evidence, partake of the nature of romantic speculation and are, therefore, patently false. But the ability to pronounce a statement about the past false seems to have been surrendered by Bultmann; if the conception of truth is dissolved the conception of falsity dissolves with it. Thus, Bultmann is unable to say that it is certainly true that many of the statements in the nineteenth-century lives of Jesus were false! He is obliged to say that the lives of Jesus *differ* and implies that, *on these grounds*, none of them can be *certain*. However, the fact that theologians differ does not necessarily entail that *all* historical knowledge is uncertain. We may admit that different historians may give different descriptions of the same event or person of the past without necessarily being obliged to conclude that any one of them or that all of them must be accounted untrue and uncertain. Historical relativism does not in itself entail that 'the conception of truth is dissolved.'

Often this issue is confused by the use of the word 'objective'.

1 *Faith and Understanding*, p. 30.

Because every different description of an event or person of the past is a description of an aspect or a description formed from a 'point of view' it is said not to be objective, and because all history is written from a point of view of some kind, it is alleged that *no* history is 'objective'. Aspects and points of view are the aspects and points of view of knowing subjects; they are therefore said to import a subjective element into historiography. The conclusion is then drawn from the fact of this minimal element of subjectivity that cannot be eliminated from any piece of historical writing, that historical research is viciously subjective; that is to say, that it is not objective in the sense that it never achieves certain and fixed results, that it actually *knows* no facts, does not report what is the case, and even that 'the historian cannot see the historical reality but only the images in his own mind'.[1]

But the words 'objective' and 'subjective' are very deceitful ones, their uses various and liable to mislead. For example, in *Christian Apologetics* (1947), Alan Richardson equates 'objectivity' with 'omniscience'. It follows that, by definition, an historian cannot be said to produce an objective account of the past simply because he is not God. Because God alone sees everything in one sweep of his eye, his knowledge is not limited by aspects and points of view; therefore God alone could produce a truly objective account of the past. A human historian looks at the past from *an* aspect and this is alleged to entail that what he says does not report what is the case. He never gets at 'what really happened'.

Maurice Mandelbaum seems to hold a secularised version of the view that 'objectivity' is synonymous with 'omniscience'. Objectivity for Mandelbaum is the complete account of what happened in the past, the resulting account of the past that is obtained when all aspects and points of view are taken together. Objectivity is a kind of encyclopaedism. Only when we know everything about a past event will we be approaching objectivity. But the number of different descriptions of a past event is infinite. This means that 'objectivity' can never really be obtained. Thus,

1 Alan Richardson, *History Sacred and Profane* (1964), p. 192. Cf. Carl Becker, 'Detachment and the Writing of History', *The Atlantic Monthly*, CVI (1910), 528: 'The reality of history has forever disappeared, and the "facts" of history, whatever they once were, are only mental images or pictures which the historian makes in order to comprehend it.'

Mandelbaum has to settle for a 'modified encyclopaedism'; we do not have to know exactly everything there is to know, so long as different histories taken together are regarded as the objective ideal.[1]

Both these thinkers, in different ways, equate 'objectivity' with what Morton White has called the 'whole truth'. However, one can describe a ball as red, and, if it is the case that the ball is red, this may be called a perfectly true and objective description of the ball, without also having to say that it is made of rubber, has a hole in it, and was not a good buy, or any other of an infinite number of things that could be said about it. To claim objectivity, and indeed, certainty in the accuracy of one's description of an object, does not mean that one must state everything that could be stated about it, but that one must have sufficient justification *for what one does assert.* In the case of the red ball one must look to see if the ball fulfils the requirements for what, under standard conditions of lighting, is conventionally called 'red'. Why should the description of a past event or person be intrinsically different? Provided one has the grounds for describing a past event or person in a particular way, it is not necessary to know *everything* that could be known, or to see as God sees. One must simply possess the grounds to justify *what one does assert.*

On the other hand, there are those who contend that objectivity is not achieved when *everything* that could be known is known, but when the ideal essence of the event is described. Instead of equating objectivity with 'omniscience' or 'the whole truth' it is equated with a particular, 'deeper' truth. In other words, it is intimated that, amongst various descriptions, there is one which is *the* objectively true history. E. H. Carr argues, for example, that *the* objectively true history is the most durable one, the one which will prove to be most interesting for ages to come. In *What is History?* he argues that the 'historian of the past can make an approach towards objectivity only as he approaches towards the understanding of the future'.[2] In order to write objective his-

---

[1] M. Mandelbaum, 'Objectivism in History' in Sidney Hook (ed.), *Philosophy and History* (1963), pp. 43–56.
[2] *What is History?* (1961), pp. 118–20.

tory the historian must be a prophet as well as an historian; he must choose the 'right facts' and judge them according to the 'right standard of significance' so that future ages will see in them a movement or development towards occurrences that are then coming to pass. This means that history can be judged to be objective only in retrospect. One cannot say that a present history is 'objective'.

In theological writing the assumption that there is only *one* objective history of the past is often made. For example, we are often told that the account of the past which the historian gives us is to be compared with a portrait rather than with a photograph. It is implied that a photograph gives an objective representation whereas a portrait is the product of the artist's intentions and interests or 'point of view'. On analogy, it is argued that, because of the distorting factor of the historian's point of view, the account of the past that he gives cannot represent what really happened. Once again, Alan Richardson provides us with a clear statement of this kind of argument. Quoting from Walther Hofer, he says: 'Naive historical realism, according to which something like recognition of an historical object "in itself" (*an sich*) is possible has long since been overcome.' This is a highly questionable contention. In any event, he goes on:

The picture which we form of the past must not be compared to a photograph but to a painting. And, just as we can see a landscape only from a given place, similarly all historical vision is determined by that place from which we view it. It means seeing in *perspective*. Broadly conceived, an historical problem, therefore, is always a question by the present to the past. Hence, in point of fact the questioner's interest and principle of selection and in the final analysis his value system and his ideology, are decisive factors in the definition of the question.[1]

However, even Benedetto Croce, the doyen of idealist philosophers of history, saw the weakness in this kind of argument. In *Aesthetic* he drew attention to the fact that a photograph is the product of a photographer who arranges his camera, sets the lens and shutter speed, and composes the picture to capture just such-

[1] Alan Richardson, *History Sacred and Profane*, p. 183, quoting Walther Hofer, 'Towards a Revision of the German Concept of History', in Hans Kohn (ed.) *German History: Some New German Views* (1954), p. 188.

and-such an effect. Indeed, even the most fumbling amateur points his camera at an object from a 'point of view'. And how often do we hear that a photograph is 'nothing like' the person photographed! Even a camera can distort and misrepresent. On the other hand, is it not a fact that we sometimes say that a portrait really and truly represents a particular aspect of a person's character with an accuracy that is astonishing? The difference between a photograph and a portrait is perhaps better made by saying, not that one is objective and the other subjective, but that the photograph represents what is the case from the point of view of a 1/250th of a second glimpse, whereas the portrait embodies the product of continued observation and social intercourse and can capture the character of the person whose portrait it is in ways that the photograph cannot. Both, however, may truly and objectively represent different aspects of a person.

A similar view is found in the writings of John Knox. Professor Knox does not often use the term 'objective' and when he does he does not use it consistently. However, he does seem to think that only *one kind* of description can be called 'objective' and has something analogous to the photograph/portrait distinction in mind in bringing out his meaning. He says that the church's image of Jesus is one which tries to express the concrete and particular quality of the love that was remembered to have been in Jesus and something of the concrete meaning he had for those who knew the impact of his love. This is the church's particular impression of Jesus and Knox says that it is not an 'objective' picture. In order to suggest what would be a purely 'objective' picture he draws a distinction, not between a photograph and a portrait, but between a portrait and a thumbnail sketch.[1] A thumbnail sketch is apparently to be understood as embodying a few 'bare facts' about Jesus; it is said to be 'objective' but, apparently, 'abstract', just as a map or a diagram are 'abstractions' from the full concrete richness of the realities they represent. The full concrete quality of Jesus' love is captured in 'a full length portrait in colour'. This does not just consist of a few 'objective'

---

[1] *Christ the Lord* (1945), p. 5. He also contrasts a picture and a map, a living body and a diagram.

facts, but is a picture formed from the point of view of the church.

However, despite the fact that Knox intimates that the portrait is not 'objective' he claims that it is nevertheless true. It is clear that he believes that the church's image of Jesus is that of an actual person, and that the figurative or mythological language that is used to fill out the bare historical facts does express a truth about the quality of love that was remembered to have been exhibited in his life. On the other hand, he implies that the 'objective' and 'abstract' thumbnail sketch is not true! It is said to be too cold and dispassionate to represent, fully and truly, what is the case. It is a very curious and idiosyncratic use of the words 'true' and 'objective' which places them in logical tension. More recently, however, in *Myth and Truth*, in comparing a map of Venice and a Turner painting of Venice, Knox resolves this tension and claims that they are both, in their own way, true *and* objective; both may represent Venice from different aspects truthfully and thus be 'objectively true', though clearly different.

Consequently, though his thought is blurred by a strange use of the word 'objective' in relation to the concept of 'truth', it is clear that what is constant in Knox's thought is that a portrait, whether he says it is objective or not objective, is, in its way, and given what it sets out to represent, true. Indeed, in *Myth and Truth* Knox asserts that there may be several very different, but equally true, portraits of the same person. The intimation is that each portrait may truly represent a different aspect of a person's character.

This, in effect, concedes the point I wish to make. It is a mistake to think that there is only *one* objective or true account of any event or person of the past. It follows that though there is a possibility that a future historian will write a *different* account of the same historical event or person from one held to be true at present, this, in itself, does not necessarily entail that the one at present entertained is not true, not objective, not validated by appeal to evidence, or that the certainty with which it is asserted is not justified. In order for it to be possible for a future account of the past to call a presently held account into question it will not only have to be different; it will have logically to contradict what is at present being asserted. It will have to be not only an alternative description but also a description that is in logical competition with a presently held description. Moreover, it will have to show that the grounds on which it is asserted are more reliable than those on which our present assessment is based or that the arguments which support our presently held convictions are erroneous. Thus, much more than a '*new* conclusion of historians' will be necessary before a presently held description will be called in question.

However, this does not dispose of the scepticism which was outlined in the first pages of this essay. If it is conceded that there may be many different true descriptions of a past event or person, the argument could be recast in the following way: it could be argued that it is impossible to achieve certainty in the present because of an ever-present possibility that, in the future, an historian may write, not only a *different* or *new* account of the past but an account which will in fact be in logical competition with one we at present entertain. Indeed, if he were pressed on this issue, Bultmann would undoubtedly argue that historical judgments are always uncertain on the grounds that the liberal lives of Jesus were not only *different* but *incompatible*. This, in fact, seems to be a widely accepted outcome of Schweitzer's *The Quest of the Historical Jesus*. But even the fact that the liberal lives of Jesus were all different and incompatible is not sufficient to demonstrate that *all* knowledge of the historical Jesus is uncertain. To say that all the nineteenth-century biographies of Jesus were different and incompatible may help to convince us that it is not possible to write a biography. But, even if we cannot write a biography of Jesus, it does not necessarily follow that we can know *no* historical facts concerning Jesus whatsoever. It does not mean, in other words, that we must necessarily deny *every statement* in every life of Jesus or that *all* historical results 'have only relative validity'.

In any event, perhaps we can strengthen the argument for historical scepticism at this point. It could be argued that there is always the possibility that circumstances will arise which will call any individual statement concerning Jesus in question. Indeed, the

argument outlined in the opening section of this essay is that, not
only statements about Jesus, but any historical statement whatever,
including, as Knox says, statements asserting our 'best attested
facts of the history of the past', are always subject to future
revision and correction. The contention remains, therefore, that
it is impossible to achieve a complete verification of any particular
historical statement, and therefore impossible to achieve really
assured and certain knowledge, because we must always take
cognizance of the fact that there is a permanent theoretical possibility that in the future, for one reason or another, it may be
necessary to amend 'even the best attested fact of the history of
the past'.

III

In affirming that we can never achieve absolute certainty with
regard to any statement about the past, the theologians involved
have adopted a position not unlike that of some philosophers,
notably C. I. Lewis and Rudolf Carnap, who have insisted that no
empirical assertion whatever can be absolutely certain. This has
sometimes been called 'fallibilism'.[1]

The contention of fallibilism is that every empirical statement,
and this, of course, includes statements about the past, is 'less than
absolutely certain'. This means that no empirical statement can be
completely verified, or established beyond all doubt, or conclusively proved to be true, or known for certain. In other words, no
empirical statement can, without some possibility of doubt, be
regarded as factual. And this is so, it is argued, because for any
empirical statement there is an infinite number of tests that we
could perform in order to verify it. Because there is an infinite
number of means of verification, and since, theoretically, it is
possible that any one of these could prove the statement to be
false, and because not all of the tests can be performed, their

---

[1] Cf. Arthur Pap, *Elements of Analytic Philosophy* (1949), pp. 150ff. This position is stated
by C. I. Lewis, *An Analysis of Knowledge and Valuation* (1946), p. 180; also, *Mind and the
World-Order* (1929), pp. 279–82; Rudolf Carnap, 'Testability and Meaning', *Philosophy
of Science*, III (1936), IV (1937). See also *Philosophy and Logical Syntax* (1935), pp. 11–13,
The Logical Syntax of Language (1937), p. 246.

number being infinite, it is not possible to verify any empirical statement conclusively. There is always a residual element of doubt, a theoretical possibility of mistake, for the possibility that a further test, if made, would yield a negative result, cannot be precluded.

Now, it has been noted that statements about the past are empirical statements. This means, if the argument just stated is right, that no statement about the past can be conclusively verified, because if it is asserted that a certain event occurred, there will be an infinite number of tests which must be applied before we can be *completely* certain of its factuality. The result is that we have to admit that we can never be absolutely certain of any statement about the past.

There is, therefore, a clear point of contact between the argument of Lewis and Carnap and that of the theological opinion with which we are concerned. Irrespective of whether we are talking about all empirical statements or only statements about the past, there is the commonly held view that absolute certainty is out of our reach because of the impossibility of achieving a complete verification. In the argument of Lewis and Carnap this impossibility is said to be due to the fact that for any statement there is an infinite set of tests, any one of which could yield a negative result. If the statement is 'there is a piece of white paper on the table', there is an infinite number of tests of the statement, all of which must be shown to be true if the truth of the statement is to be completely verified. And because the number of tests that could be carried out, and that must be carried out before complete or absolute certainty can be guaranteed, is infinite, there is always a permanent possibility of correction. The residual element of doubt cannot be eliminated. As C. I. Lewis says:

No matter how fully I may have investigated this objective fact, there will remain some theoretical possibility of mistake; there will be further consequences which must be thus and so if the judgment is true, and not all of these will have been determined. The possibility that such further tests, if made, might have a negative result, cannot be altogether precluded; and this possibility marks the judgment as, at the time in question, not fully verified and less than absolutely certain.[1]

[1] *An Analysis of Knowledge and Valuation*, p. 180.

Rudolf Carnap, expounding his form of this argument, admits that in normal, practical circumstances, after a few tests, the degree of confirmation will be 'so high that we practically cannot help accepting the sentence' as true. But even in this case, he says, we must admit that there is still a 'theoretical possibility' of denying the truth of the sentence.[1]

The similarity of this argument to that of the theologians whose work has been mentioned will be obvious, though Lewis and Carnap present an argument that has an apparent tightness that is lacking from the arguments of the theologians. Once again, there is a permanent possibility that the statements, in this case statements about the past, could be subjected to further tests, perhaps prompted by the discovery of a new document, which could yield a negative result. The possibility of this happening is said to be a permanent one, for one thing, because we can never know when a new document might be discovered, and for every discovery there is a theoretical possibility of another discovery to modify it. No matter how well established an historical statement may be, the possibility of future modification or correction allegedly hangs over us like a dark cloud. Indeed, John Knox says that even the 'best attested facts' of the past are subject to this defect. Complete verification can never be achieved, and consequently, absolute certainty is beyond us; there is always an element of risk.

The arguments of Lewis and Carnap and those of the theologians are different in the sense that the theologians are thinking only of statements about the past, the judgments of historians in particular, whilst Lewis and Carnap argue that all empirical statements are subject to the same limitations. At least one theologian, T. A. Roberts, however, does seem to endorse the conclusion that no empirical statement whatever can be verified with complete certainty. Clearly, Roberts' belief in the impossibility of achieving absolute certainty is not confined to statements about the past; it is a defect of the judgments of the empirical sciences generally. Indeed, he affirms that 'absolute certainty belongs only to the conclusions of *a priori* deductive systems such as mathematics or logic'.[2]

---

[1] 'Testability and Meaning', *Philosophy of Science*, III (1936), 426.
[2] *History and Christian Apologetic* (1960), p. 37.

With regard to the contention that all historical judgments are probability judgments of one degree or another, Roberts is writing under the acknowledged influence of Marc Bloch. However, I suspect that on the particular issue of the uncertainty of all empirical judgments he is uncritically accepting a notion of A. J. Ayer, whose work he draws upon elsewhere in his book, and who, like Lewis and Carnap, urges that it is impossible completely to verify any empirical statement: 'no proposition, other than a tautology', says Ayer, 'can possibly be anything more than a probable hypothesis'.[1]

It is true that, as far as I am aware, no theologian has actually said that the possibility of further modification or revision of historical conclusions is 'infinite'. But clearly, the possibility of further correction must be, if not infinite, then unlimited, or indefinite if the argument is going to carry the weight that is put on it. For if the possibility of further correction is finite, limited or definite then, certainly in theory and possibly in practice, it would be possible to carry out all relevant tests and thus arrive at a complete verification and hence absolute certainty. In order to justify the argument for historical scepticism the possibility that our judgments about the past may have to be revised must be an unlimited possibility, in the sense that there is always the possibility of correction. We can never know when *all* possible discoveries of new documents have been exhausted, nor do we know, apparently, when all possible conflicting interpretations will have been put on the evidence already at hand. Consequently, while the number of possible new discoveries may not be infinite, it is certainly indefinite, and this means that no matter how thorough an historian may have been in verifying statements about the past there is always the theoretical possibility of correction.

Moreover, when we realise that it is not only the possibility of further discoveries that allegedly makes it impossible to achieve absolute certainty, but also the possibility that further testing of the old evidence will produce a new result, 'the fresh sifting of facts by criticism' that could produce a new conclusion, as Troeltsch puts it, then the argument of the theologians becomes exactly

1 *Language, Truth and Logic* (1936), pp. 24 and 132; see also *The Foundations of Empirical Knowledge* (1940), pp. 42–5.

parallel to that of Lewis and Carnap. For the number of tests that could be employed to verify a statement about the past is infinite, and in theory, any one of them could produce a negative result.

IV

The argument of the theologians has been brought into deliberate association with that of Lewis and Carnap for a specific purpose. In the last generation the kind of fallibilism represented by Lewis and Carnap has been subjected to a sustained onslaught by G. E. Moore, J. L. Austin, Ludwig Wittgenstein, Norman Malcolm and other philosophers who have been influenced by them. Indeed, twenty years ago Professor Malcolm published a long and thorough critique of the argument of Lewis and Carnap.[1] Nobody, as far as I am aware, has drawn out the parallels between the arguments of Lewis and Carnap and that of post-Troeltschian theology, nor has the relevance of Professor Malcolm's refutation of Lewis and Carnap to the argument for historical scepticism been noted by contemporary theologians.

Before any attempt is made to bring Malcolm's refutation to bear on the theologian's argument it is necessary to make some points which are not, in fact, made by Malcolm. The first is that it is important to distinguish between *knowing* and *claiming to know*, between the *validation* of a claim itself, and the *justification* for making it, and between *knowing* and *being certain*. The fact that somebody discovers evidence to show that a person of the past cannot have known that an event occurred because the claim that the event occurred is not validated by the evidence at present possessed, does not mean that the past person was in fact not *certain* that the event occurred. Nor does it mean that he was not *justified* in *claiming to know* (with certainty) that the event occurred. For example, we now know that the world is not flat. We are able to say that the claim that it is flat is not validated, and that nobody in the past can have *known* that it was flat. We may nevertheless admit that twelfth-century people were *certain* that it

---

[1] See 'The Verification Argument' in *Philosophical Analysis*, ed. by Max Black (1950), republished in N. Malcolm, *Knowledge and Certainty* (1965), pp. 1–57.

was flat, and, indeed, we may admit that they were *justified* in thinking or claiming to know that it was flat. That is to say, we may admit that they possessed what they regarded as good reasons for thinking that the world was flat. It is for this reason that we do not censure them. They had *justification* for making this claim, and sincerely and confidently asserted it, even though we do not now admit that the claim itself is *true*, and though we now deny that they actually *knew* that the world was flat.

Similarly, we may say that a person of the past did not *know* that an event occurred if we find that the claim itself is not validated; but, at the same time, we may admit that the person concerned was *justified* in making the claim, and justified in his certainty and confidence.

Consequently, it is possible that the Christian may have *justification* for making certain *claims to know* particular facts about Jesus. If at a future time it is discovered that the claims are untrue (not validated) this would then entail that the Christian of the past cannot have *known* these facts. But it would not mean that he was not *justified* in *claiming to know* them, nor that he was not *certain* about them. Thus, it is possible to be certain, and to make *claims to know* facts of the past which turn out to be wrong in the final analysis.

However, whilst 'being certain' and 'knowing' are not synonymous, a necessary condition of *claiming to know* is that one is sure or certain. And the argument that one can never reach assured results about the past entails that one is *never* really justified in *claiming to know* a fact of the past, and that all historical statements are really 'hypotheses', 'mere interpretations of the evidence', or probability judgments. That is, they are statements that must be tentatively asserted. In this view we may claim to *believe* particular statements about the past, but we can never be sure enough about them really to claim to *know* them. Thus, the argument for historical scepticism is that we can never really make claims to know facts of the past, thereby expressing certainty, or claim to *be* certain about the facts of the past, in the face of the permanent possibility of correction.

It is at this point that Professor Malcolm's article is of enormous help. Consequently, in the following pages the crux of Professor Malcolm's argument will be adapted to show that the contention that one can never achieve complete assurance with respect to historical judgments or claim to know an historical fact with certainty *because* of the permanent theoretical possibility of future correction is erroneous.

Let us suppose that an historian living at time t_1 possesses evidence from which he infers that a certain event, E, occurred. Furthermore, the evidence he possesses is of such a nature that he believes he is justified in asserting that he knows that it occurred. The argument for historical scepticism put forward by the theologians, if I understand it rightly, is that, given this state of affairs, it is theoretically possible that at any future time, t_n, a piece of evidence could come to light which would provide good grounds for believing that the event, E, did not occur, or else that it is theoretically possible that at a future time, t_n, a further sifting of the evidence at present possessed might provide good grounds for thinking that E did not occur. This is a permanent theoretical possibility, and it is argued, in the light of this, that at no time can it be completely certain that E did occur, and that, therefore, one cannot claim to know this historical fact with certainty without falling into a self-contradiction.

Let us suppose that this theoretical possibility is actualised, that at time t_2 a piece of evidence does come to light which provides grounds for believing that the event, E, did not occur. In other words, at time t_2 it is alleged that there is a reasonable doubt, based on the evidence of a newly discovered document, whether an assertion at time t_1 that E occurred is really true. The proponents of the argument for historical scepticism would say that if at time t_2 there is a reasonable doubt that E occurred, then it cannot have been the case at time t_1 that it was known with certainty that E occurred. But Malcolm has shown that this is not true.

The argument for historical scepticism is that the discovery at t_2 of grounds for doubting that E occurred *entails* that at no previous time can it have been known with certainty that E did in fact occur, and therefore, to assert the conjunction of these two propositions, that is, that at t_2 there are grounds for doubting that E

occurred *and* that at t_1 it was known with certainty that E occurred involves a self-contradiction.

However, the first proposition, that at t_2 there are grounds for doubting that E occurred, does not entail the second proposition, that at no previous time can an historian have known with certainty that E did in fact occur, and to assert the conjunction of both propositions is *not* to fall into self-contradiction. For clearly, the fact that somebody at time t_2 has *grounds for doubting* that E occurred does not entail that E in fact did not occur, and therefore, it is still possible that E did occur. If we admit that it is still possible that E did occur, then we may admit that an historian at t_1 could have made absolutely certain that E did occur, and could have known with certainty that it did occur.

Let us take an example. Eadmer, St Anselm's biographer, may have claimed to know with complete certainty at t_1 that Anselm promulgated a certain theological argument for the existence of God. An historian at t_2 may discover grounds to doubt that Anselm was the author of this argument, or indeed, grounds to doubt that Anselm ever uttered the argument. Let us suppose, for example, that he finds grounds which suggest that the *Proslogion* was a later composition. But the fact that the historian at time t_2 has reasons which suggest that Anselm might not have uttered the argument, does not entail either (1) that Anselm *certainly* did not utter the argument, or (2) that Eadmer cannot have made absolutely certain that Anselm did utter it. Clearly, it is possible that an historian knew with complete certainty at t_1 that E occurred, and now at t_2 another historian has grounds for believing that E might not have occurred. To assert both these things does not involve a self-contradiction.

Therefore, from a statement of the fact that there are at t_2 some grounds for believing that E did not occur, it does not follow at all that a person in the past cannot have known with certainty that E did occur. The fault of the argument is that the proposition that at t_2 there are *grounds for doubting* that E occurred does not necessarily entail that E did not occur.

Professor Malcom suggests a way in which the argument may be strengthened at this point, to which we will turn in a moment.

G

For the present we note that if it is not entailed that E did not occur, then it is logically possible that E did occur and therefore we must admit that it could have been known with absolute certainty at t_1 that E did occur. Despite the fact that there are reasons for doubting at t_2, if it is still possible that E did occur, then it is possible that somebody could have made absolutely certain that E did occur. Clearly, it just does not follow from the fact that because somebody discovers evidence to suggest that E might not have occurred, that no person at a previous time can have known with absolute certainty that E did occur.

However, the argument can now be strengthened to avoid this defect. It is possible that at t_2 the newly discovered evidence will be of such a nature that, from a statement of it, it will be entailed that the event E certainly did not occur, and in this event, it follows that nobody in the past can have made absolutely certain that E did occur. This entailment will be possible if the evidence discovered at t_2 is of such a nature as to constitute *absolutely conclusive grounds* for inferring that E did not occur, and not just *evidence to suggest* that E might not have occurred. For it seems perfectly true that if at time t_2 there is absolutely conclusive evidence that E did not occur, then it is impossible that an historian at t_1 can have known with certainty that E did occur. This is impossible in the sense that it would be self-contradictory to assert: 'There are at t_2 absolutely conclusive grounds that E did not occur and an historian knew with absolute certainty at t_1 that E did occur.' That this is self-contradictory can be shown from the fact that the assertion that at t_2 there is absolutely conclusive evidence that E did not occur implies that E did not occur, and the assertion that at t_1 an historian knew with absolute certainty that E did occur implies that E did occur. Therefore, to assert both propositions is to imply 'E certainly did not occur and E certainly did occur.' This is plainly contradictory.

Clearly, if it is known with absolute certainty at t_2 that E did not occur, then a previous claim that it was known for certain that E did occur must have been mistaken. In other words, it does follow from the fact that at t_2 there is absolutely conclusive evidence that E did not occur, that at no previous time (t_1 or any other time) could anyone have *known* with absolute certainty that E did occur.

However, Malcolm points out that this does not mean we have proved the argument. The discovery of new evidence providing absolutely conclusive grounds that the particular event E, of which we have been talking, did not occur does constitute a proof in this particular case, that nobody can have known at any previous time that E occurred. But the argument for historical scepticism is a thoroughly *general* argument. Even if the discovery of absolutely conclusive evidence at t_2 that E did not occur could be used to show that no previous historian at time t_1 could really have *known* for certain that E did occur, it cannot be used to prove the general argument that *no* statement about the past can be known with absolute certainty, because a fundamental premise of the argument asserts precisely what needs to be proved! In order to assert that nobody in the past can have known with absolute certainty that E occurred we need to know for certain that E did not occur. But those who use the argument for historical scepticism assert that we can never know *any* statement about the past for certain. In other words, in order to show that it is impossible that anybody knew with absolute certainty at t_1 that a particular statement was true, we have to be able to show that, at t_2, it is absolutely certain that the statement is false. But this is exactly what the argument for historical scepticism denies. Therefore we cannot assume this. If one premise of the argument assumes that the falsity of an historical statement can be conclusively established, it cannot be employed to prove the general argument that *no* statement about the past can be conclusively established. Consequently, by strengthening the argument, it has become completely circular. And the dilemma is that, unless it is strengthened in this way, it is logically incorrect. For if we do not have conclusive evidence at t_2, but only grounds for believing that E might not have occurred, then the proposition that E did not occur is not entailed, and we are able to assert without self-contradiction that at t_1 somebody can have known for certain that E did occur.

It seems, therefore, that the argument which Tillich declares is 'the greatest contribution of historical research to systematic theology' and which many contemporary theologians accept and, indeed, which has led twentieth-century theology to seek a *sturmfreies Gebiet* for faith in complete independence of the alleged permanent insecurity of historical results, is a faulty one.

V

Moreover, John Knox says that we must admit that even 'the best attested facts of the history of the past' are subject to future correction and that we cannot claim to know them with certainty. Indeed, it is once again important to stress at this point that the argument for historical scepticism is a perfectly general one. It is not argued that there is a particular piece of evidence that shows that a particular statement about the past is untrue or uncertain, and that this statement cannot be asserted in the face of the available evidence. Rather, it is argued that, with respect to *no* statement about the past can we be hopeful of ever achieving complete certainty with respect to its truth, because of a permanent *theoretical* possibility of future developments that could prove us wrong. It is not the point that a particular statement about the past is false. It is not that some reason is known to exist which renders our conviction, for example, that there was a Jesus, and that he died on the cross, untenable. 'It is inadequate', says Tillich, 'to point out that historical research has not yet given any evidence to support such scepticism. Certainly, it has not yet! But the anxious question remains whether it could do so sometime in the future!' [*ST*, II, 113 (130–1)]. Or, as Knox says, the problem is that 'historians could *conceivably* rob us' of our faith (*CRC*, p. 17), not that they have actually done so. Indeed, even those facts of the past for which we have sufficient evidence to justify calling them 'the best attested facts of the history of the past' are said to be subject to this conceivable possibility. Consequently, Knox's position is, not that there *are* grounds which conclusively prove that Jesus never existed, nor that he did not die on the cross, nor, presumably, that he did not exhibit a particular kind of love, but that it is possible to *conceive* of grounds which could possibly or conceivably be shown to exist in the future, and that the possibility of being able to conceive of these grounds makes it impossible, in the sense of self-contradictory or not logically possible, to claim to know with certainty that the events concerned did occur. The implied argument is that we cannot assert that any event occurred with absolute certainty whilst entertaining the possibility that there *could* be evidence which *could* count against the assertion.

However, to be able to *think* that evidence which would demonstrate that an event did not occur could exist and could be discovered, does not entail that such evidence does exist, nor that there is not conclusive evidence in existence which proves that the event did occur. Logical possibility of error does not entail actual possibility of error, and to be able to *think* of possible evidence that would demonstrate that the event did not occur does not mean that an historian cannot be perfectly justified in asserting with absolute certainty that he *actually possesses* evidence which proves with certainty that the event occurred.

Indeed, the point about 'the best attested facts of the history of the past' is that they are precisely those facts for which we *already possess* the evidence which allows us to discount this future or theoretical possibility. If we have consulted the relevant evidence, and find that we are justified in claiming to know a fact of the past with certainty, we mean to indicate precisely that the evidential support is of such a calibre that it concludes the issue. That is to say, it is what historians call 'conclusive evidence'. 'The *best* attested facts of the history of the past' are thus those facts for which the evidential support is so conclusive that the theoretical possibility of future revision of these facts, or future discoveries which would cause us to revise these facts, can be discounted. Indeed, that we can *think* of evidence which would count against the evidence we now possess is irrelevant. The fact that I can think that King's College Chapel does not exist is irrelevant with respect to the fact that I actually possess the best of reasons for claiming to know with certainty that King's College Chapel does exist. Similarly, though the evidence on which historical asser-tions are based is obviously different from that on which I may base my claim that King's College Chapel exists, it is nevertheless true that, if I possess conclusive evidence, I may justifiably claim to know historical facts with certainty. The ghostly possibility that future discoveries may be made which would count against an historical assertion can, with conclusive evidence, be laid to rest.

There is a certain impropriety about claiming to know a fact of the past if one is not in the position to know it. If one claims to know a fact one signals not only that one is sure or certain, but that one has evidence sufficient to warrant such a claim, otherwise one normally uses a more guarded expression, such as, 'I *think* that so and so', or, 'I *believe* that so and so'. Such statements are compatible with error. One may say 'I *think* that *p*, but I could be wrong'. But to say 'I *know* that *p*, but I could be wrong' would be absurd. In other words, a claim to know signals that one is prepared to defend oneself by exhibiting the grounds which warrant the claim, and if one claims to know, it is entailed that the grounds one possesses are of such a kind that further investigation has lost its point.[1]

Consequently, the point about 'the best attested facts of the history of the past' is that the evidence on which they are based is not just good, but as good as one could wish. If I claim to *know* the date of the outbreak of World War I, I express certainty; I signal that I am not guessing or making a stab at it, but that I have consulted evidence relevant to this claim, have no reason to believe that I am dreaming or seeing illusory documents, and that therefore, I am perfectly justified in asserting that I know this fact with complete certainty. To say that it is an 'hypothesis' or 'mere interpretation of certain pieces of evidence' or that I do not *know* this fact but only *believe* that it is (probably) true, would be quite absurd.

Moreover, I intimate, when I claim to know a fact of the past with certainty, that I propose to disregard any additional documents which could be consulted further to verify the claim; I imply that I cannot see that any further information or further

[1] See Douglas Arner, 'On Knowing', *Philosophical Review*, LXVIII (1959), 84–92 for a very convincing treatment of this point. For example, p. 89: ' "Know" is used to assure others in a special way. It indicates that the evidence is not merely good but is as good as can be, that further investigation has lost its point. "Know" closes questions, stops debates.' See also Jaakko Hintikka, *Knowledge and Belief* (1962), pp. 19–20.

testing of the evidence I have consulted would lead to a conclusion that would be in logical competition with the one at which I have already arrived.

It is true that the New Testament material presents particular problems of its own, that the evidence concerning the person of Jesus is meagre, that once we move beyond certain fundamental assertions, such as that he was a man, lived in Palestine, died on a cross, expressed a distinctive and compelling love, we must, as historians, be prepared to accept statements as being less than completely certain. The important thing is that it is not legitimate to argue that faith cannot be based on *any* historical judgments or must be *totally* independent of historical research and autonomous, because *no* historical judgment is *ever* justifiably claimed with certainty. Thus, to search for a *sturmfreies Gebiet*, as something that is altogether independent of historical research, and to drive a firm wedge between faith and historical research is, at least on the grounds here discussed, an unnecessary and mistaken move.

THE GOSPEL TRADITIONS AND EARLY CHRISTOLOGICAL REFLECTION

G. N. STANTON

It is not surprising that motifs such as 'Jesus as the Man for others', and, indeed, the humanity of Jesus in general, should be so prominent in the recent work of systematic theologians, whether or not one agrees that the most adequate modern christology will start 'from below'. Much more surprising is the width of the gap between this current interest in the life and character of Jesus of Nazareth and the conclusions of many New Testament scholars. For many New Testament specialists are becoming more and more vociferous in their insistence that there was no close relationship between early christological reflection and the life and character of Jesus; the most primitive christologies did not arise from the church's interest in or memory of the type of person Jesus showed himself to be in his teaching, actions, and relationships with others, but from expectations of an imminent *parousia* which were deeply influenced by apocalyptic.

If the primitive church was not interested in the 'past' of Jesus, why, then, did the church produce gospels which, at a cursory glance at least, look so much like lives of Jesus? A wide variety of answers has been given, all of which argue that only at a relatively late stage in the long development from the earliest preaching of the gospel to the church's acceptance of four gospels did the church understand its traditions about Jesus as historical or biographical reminiscence of any sort. Some point to the important step taken by Mark when he first linked gospel traditions together to make a 'story' about Jesus; many others insist that Luke is the innovator, for he has carefully placed his biography of Jesus within the framework of his overall understanding of the Christian message; others point to the effect of the so-called delay of the *parousia*, to the needs of the Hellenistic churches or to a reaction which set in against primitive Christian *Enthusiasmus* which had partly overlooked the earthly Jesus. When the gospel traditions did eventually come to play a more central role in the life and faith of the church, they were understood in the light of firmly established christological convictions; convictions which, it is often argued, deeply influenced or even largely created the church's traditions about Jesus.

The systematic theologian is placed in something of a quandary by expositions of the development of the christology of the early church which proceed along these lines. If the humanity of Jesus is to be central in christological thinking and if the christology of the New Testament is to be taken at all seriously, the earliest stages of christological reflection must be by-passed deliberately and attention paid to later developments. Just conceivably, the systematic theologian may be tempted to throw his hands in the air and conclude that since New Testament scholars cannot provide a consensus of opinion and since the various christologies in the New Testament arose at different stages and clash so strongly with one another, he is forced to work out his christology in isolation from historical uncertainties.

I should want to argue that various lines of evidence, taken cumulatively, indicate that Luke and Mark have done little more than use their literary and theological talents to refine a pattern which is very much earlier: in its proclamation of Jesus, especially in its initial missionary proclamation, the primitive church included reference to the past of Jesus of Nazareth, to his life and character, and often used gospel pericopae for this very purpose. Opponents will immediately retort that this is a naïve view which can be defended, firstly, only by reading the gospels and the traditions they enshrine as biographical documents, thus totally misunderstanding their perspective, and, secondly, only by assuming that the primitive church was interested in the 'past' of Jesus, for which there is in fact no *Sitz im Leben*.

I make no apology for advancing an unfashionable point of view by re-examining these two widely cherished convictions. New Testament scholarship has moved so quickly in recent decades that reconsideration of generally accepted conclusions is very much the order of the day. New theories may or may not emerge, but an intensive resifting of the evidence will, by indicating which conclusions are well grounded and which not, provide firmer foundations for further research.

I

The often-repeated dictum 'the gospels are not biographies' needs careful reappraisal. I certainly do not want to argue that the clock must now be turned back many decades and the gospels read as biographies. The gospels are unique. There is little point in considering which ancient biography is closest in form to the gospels. But a comparison of the gospels with roughly contemporary biographical writing is by no means irrelevant, for it underlines some important characteristics of the gospels which have often been overlooked in recent discussion.

The fundamental difference between the gospels and all biographical writing, whether ancient or modern, has often been used as a quick way of confirming that the gospel traditions were not originally understood as 'historical reminiscence' or 'biographical' portrait of Jesus.

The gospel form [writes Norman Perrin] was created to serve the purpose of the early Church, but historical reminiscence was not one of those purposes. So, for example, when we read an account of Jesus giving instruction to his disciples, we are not hearing the voice of the earthly Jesus addressing Galilean disciples in a Palestinian situation but that of the risen Lord addressing Christian missionaries in a Hellenistic world.[1]

Standard New Testament textbooks usually point out that the gospels are not at all comparable with Hellenistic biographies, for they make no attempt to set out a detailed chronological record of the events in the life of Jesus, nor do they depict the main stages in the psychological development of Jesus, nor do they contain either a sketch of the character of Jesus or a description of his appearance, nor do they set Jesus against the wider historical background of his time; Luke, it is admitted, is a partial exception.

---

[1] N. Perrin. *Rediscovering the Teaching of Jesus* (1967), pp. 15f.

The gospels and the gospel traditions which circulated in the church before and after Mark wrote are not related to any biographical interest on the part of the early church. They are proclamation, not report. Such conclusions are usually taken, if not as an axiom, then at least as an assured result of the form critical revolution; the word 'biographical' has become to a form critic like a red rag to a bull. But this general understanding of the perspective of the gospels is bound up with a quite surprisingly inaccurate assessment of ancient biographical writing.

Greek and Roman biographical writing reached its zenith shortly after the gospels were written, in the work of Tacitus, Plutarch and Suetonius; but all three writers drew, in different ways, on traditional techniques. When some of the literary conventions used in depicting the life of a significant person in the Graeco-Roman world of the first and early second centuries are examined, the profound difference which emerges is not so much between ancient biographical writing and the gospels, as between all forms of ancient biographical writing and its modern counterpart.

The gospels do show comparatively little interest in chronological order when compared with modern biographical writing, but the loose structure of the gospels is by no means unique. It was once customary for classical scholars to divide ancient biographical writing into two streams: chronological order was a feature of the Peripatetic biographers by whom Plutarch was deeply influenced; the Alexandrian biographers, and later Suetonius, dealt with a life *per species*, grouping together material on topics such as conduct, business, family, attitude towards society, friends. However, since the discovery of fragments of Satyrus' *Life of Euripides*, the only first-hand Peripatetic biography extant, this division is seen to have been an oversimplification. Although Satyrus was one of the last Peripatetic biographers, writing in the second half of the third century B.C., the extant sections of his work reveal a clear tendency towards an orderly grouping of material, but only one section which can in any way be called chronological. There is now little doubt that the Peripatetics, who so strongly influenced both Greek and Roman biographical writing of the first century A.D. and later, ordered their material by topics, not chronologically.

Nor does Plutarch make any attempt to adopt a precise chronology; the chronological expressions he does use are nearly all vague, phrases such as 'about this time', 'some time after this', being common. Campaigns are presented chronologically, but Plutarch's basic method is *per species*. Later writers, such as Arrian, Philostratus and Diogenes Laertius present a similar picture. Concern for chronological order was not a characteristic of ancient biographical writing; Tacitus and Cornelius Nepos are partial exceptions who prove the rule. As a stylistic technique, presentation of material *per species* is much more common than a precise chronological order or framework.

Since chronological order was not common, it is not surprising to find that to trace development of character was not a *sine qua non* of ancient biographical writing. Early encomiasts, such as Isocrates and Xenophon, were not interested in development of character, for they attempted to delineate their subjects in terms of their own notions of exemplary character traits. Nor did Peripatetic biographers, and those who later inherited their techniques, trace development of character or personality, though the phenomenon of human alteration was not unknown. Instead of tracing character development, ancient biographical writing from Plato onwards generally started and finished with the mature character of the person concerned. The idea that a person can be understood only by tracing the development of his personality is modern and is hardly found in the ancient world.

Nor is the brief character sketch a common convention in ancient biographical writing. Plutarch, for example, sometimes does include a character summary, but he makes no attempt to analyse internal development of personality. Plutarch aimed to 'paint personality', but he did not always do this in his own words.

Much more prominent as a method of character portrayal is the recognition that a person's actions and words sum up his character more adequately than the comments of an observer. This is a deeply rooted tradition in ancient biographical writing. In his

Agesilaus Xenophon states that the deeds of a man best disclose the stamp of his nature. Direct analysis of the subject's character was almost certainly rare in Peripatetic biography; the actions and words of a person were allowed to speak for themselves. At the beginning of his life of Alexander Plutarch expounded the principles on which he worked: 'In the most illustrious deed there is not always a manifestation of virtues and avarice, nay, a slight thing like a phrase or a jest often makes a greater revelation of character than battles where thousands fall, or the greatest armaments or sieges of cities.' This method of indirect characterisation, in which the personality of the author himself remained in the background, was a widely practised technique in ancient biography generally.

The gospels also show little interest in character development, portraying Jesus from the beginning to the end of his ministry in essentially the same way and allowing his actions and words to show the sort of person he was. While it is impossible to find clear traces of ancient biographical conventions in the gospel traditions, the gospels' presentation of the life of Jesus is much less distinctive than has been claimed.

Attention has often been drawn to the fact that, unlike ancient biographical writing, the gospels fail to set Jesus against the wider historical background of his time. But this feature of modern biographical writing was not known among the Greeks, for consciousness of different historical epochs was lacking in antiquity. Biography and history were carefully held apart.

There is a little more justification for drawing attention to the absence of personal descriptions of Jesus from the gospels, but even this was not a universal feature of ancient biographical writing. Xenophon only rarely mentions traits of physical appearance. Both Plutarch and Diogenes Laertius have descriptions in some but not all of their biographies. Tacitus gives only a very brief account of the appearance of Agricola, while Nepos omits such a description of Atticus.

It is not difficult to draw attention to the wide gulf between the gospels and ancient biographical writing; the gospels have nothing comparable to the many personal anecdotes, some of which were widely used 'stock' situations which Plutarch and Suetonius included simply to satisfy the curiosity of their readers. The travellers' tales cast in biographical form perform a similar function in Philostratus' *Life of Apollonius of Tyana*.

The gospels must be read against the backdrop, not of modern biographical writing, but of their own times. When this is done, the gospels do not emerge as biographies of Jesus, but their presentations of the life of Jesus are seen to be much less distinctive than is usually believed. Recognition of the fact that, unlike Plutarch, Suetonius and other ancient biographers, they do not draw on a long literary tradition, supports this conclusion. For if the modern preoccupation with chronological precision, historical background, personal appearance and character development are all largely missing in ancient biographical writing with its *literary* tradition, their absence is even less surprising in the gospels, which can scarcely be described as literary productions. 'Sophisticated' ancient biographical writing very often used the simple technique of portraying character by allowing the actions and words of a person to speak for themselves; hence there is no reason to agree that 'unsophisticated' gospel traditions can appear to portray the character of Jesus by reporting his words and actions only if their intention is misunderstood.

However Hellenistic the gospels may be, they are firmly anchored in the Jewish world. But Jewish accounts of the life and character of a person comparable in any way with the gospels are almost non-existent. The Qumran literature, for example, reminds us that it was by no means the usual practice in the ancient world to compile an account of the life of a founder of a community such as Qumran, nor even of many other types of significant figures. In spite of the influence and importance of Qumran's Teacher, the community seems to have survived on a minimum of tradition *about* him. The nature and extent of material relating to the life and character of the Teacher show clearly that by comparison the gospels are rich in material about Jesus, however the historian may evaluate it. Similarly, the variety and richness of the gospels' materials about *one* person stand out when they are placed alongside the rabbinic literature. We know exceedingly little about the life of Yohanan Ben Zakkai, one of the most important and influential rabbinic teachers. Rabbinic traditions refer to almost as many different rabbis as there are pericopae.

That the uniqueness of the gospels lies primarily in the impact of the resurrection on the primitive church is not in doubt. But the uniqueness of the gospels also lies not so much in the ways they differ from Greek and Roman biographical writing, as many have insisted, but in the fact that in Jewish writings, from the Old Testament right through to the rabbinic corpus, there is nothing comparable to the gospels' concentration on the words, actions and relationships of one person.

The dictum 'the gospels are not biographies' is still as firmly established as the standard solution to the synoptic problem, but this dictum cannot be used to deny that the gospels and the gospel traditions were intended to portray the life and character of Jesus. If, as one of his main purposes, Mark had wished to set out an account of significant aspects of the life of Jesus and to indicate the sort of person Jesus was, would the end result have been strikingly different from the gospel we now have?

Once this understanding of the perspective of the gospels is acknowledged as plausible, it is by no means difficult to accept that there is a good deal of material in the four gospels which portrays the character of Jesus. Many traits emerge from the gospel accounts of the actions and teaching of Jesus, and of his relationships with others. To this extent the gospel traditions may be described as 'biographical'. However, this expression has so many modern connotations (especially concerning personality) which are foreign to the ancient world that (if it is not to be misleading) it can be used of the gospel traditions only with careful definition.

But it is certainly true that no tradition about Jesus was retained by the church *solely* out of historical interest or biographical curiosity, for the traditions are kerygmatic and were used in the service of the preaching of the primitive church. There is no reason either to quarrel with this general conclusion or to rehearse the reason which lie behind its widespread acceptance since the rise of form critical study of the gospels. But the very commonly suggested corollary, that since the gospel traditions are kerygmatic they are neither 'historical' nor 'biographical' in their perspective, is untenable: the kerygmatic role of the gospel traditions has not smothered interest in the life and character of Jesus. The dual perspective of the gospel traditions is inescapable: they intend to proclaim Jesus, they are also concerned with his life and character. To by-pass or minimise either aspect is to miss the finely-held balance of the traditions themselves: they are neither purely 'biographical' nor 'historical', nor are they kerygmatic to the exclusion of concern with more than the mere *fact* of the historical existence of Jesus.

The earliest preaching of the Christian message must surely have taken pains to sketch out briefly the kind of person Jesus was, in the context of its call to commitment to the one raised by God from the dead. Since the gospel traditions 'report' the life of Jesus and 'portray' his character, they were particularly appropriate for use in the initial missionary preaching of the church. This is not to deny that gospel traditions were used in ethical instruction, in apologetic, in instruction of believers, in worship, and in a variety of other ways in the life of the church.

II

In the preceding paragraphs we have been using the dual perspective of the gospel traditions to establish their *Sitz im Leben* in the primitive church. This procedure looks dangerously like a circular argument: the interest of the primitive church in the past of Jesus is established from the *form* of the traditions, but the very form of the traditions is interpreted in the light of their use in the primitive church. At this point we must also take up briefly the objection that since the primitive church was at first uninterested in the life of Jesus, the gospel traditions cannot have been understood and used in the way we have described. However, there are other lines of evidence which minimize the risk of a circular argument and also suggest that the early church, especially in its missionary preaching, was interested in the past of Jesus and that traditions about Jesus were understood and used, as far back as we can trace them, as both proclamation and report about Jesus.

The only explicit accounts of initial missionary preaching in the New Testament period are to be found in Acts.[1] While it is impossible to date the traditions lying behind the speeches in Acts with any precision, these speeches (especially Acts x.36–43 and Acts xiii.16–41) are certainly pre-Lucan and seem to stem from a very early period. Luke indicates that as soon as the gospel was preached to audiences unfamiliar with the story of Jesus, the first evangelists included in their preaching a sketch of the life and character of Jesus. Peter's speeches in Acts make it quite clear that the primitive church did not proclaim the risen Christ and over-look the pre-resurrection events and the character of Jesus of Nazareth.

As Paul refers to the content of his initial missionary preaching only rarely in his epistles, he may well have used gospel traditions in his preaching – but there is, of course, no explicit evidence for this in the epistles. Paul's knowledge and use of gospel traditions must be left as a partially open question. But even if Paul did not refer to the life of Jesus precisely in the *form* of the gospel traditions which have come down to us, there are good grounds for main-taining that Paul was neither ignorant of, nor uninterested in the life and character of Jesus and that his preaching included some reference to the sort of person Jesus was.

The proclamation of Jesus was used in the primitive church to proclaim him. Jesus' message is already, *in nuce*, a message about himself; his actions and words are inseparable. Jesus' message is very much bound up with his conduct and character, his 'obscure' background and the unpromising outward circumstances of his ministry. The nature of Jesus' proclamation encouraged the primi-tive church to sketch out his life and character – including the 'scandal' of his background – as part of its proclamation of him.

The very fact that Jesus could not be fitted into any of the categories of the day meant that the primitive church could not

---

[1] The arguments which are advanced briefly in the following paragraphs have been ex-plained and defended in much greater detail in my forthcoming book, *The Primitive Preaching and Jesus of Nazareth.*

simply make a theological pronouncement about him, and assume that no further explanation either of what sort of a person he was or of what sort of a life he had lived was necessary. For Jesus broke all Jewish preconceptions about the promised one; Hellenistic categories were no more adequate.

III

If then, the primitive church included a sketch of the character of Jesus in its preaching, it had a stake in transmitting and using traditions which it understood as referring to the past of Jesus; it was also much more aware of the distinction between the 'past' and the 'present' of Jesus than many scholars have recently argued, and it was therefore less likely to confuse its own understanding and experience of the risen Christ with its account of who Jesus of Nazareth was. And if the earliest christological proclamation and traditions about Jesus were not at first separate entities which were only later linked together, there are still further implications for our understanding of primitive christology.

What were the factors which influenced the earliest christological reflections of the church? The church's experience of the risen Christ, its apocalyptic expectations of an imminent *parousia* and its interpretation of the Old Testament are all seen as influential at particular points. But the christological terminology employed by the primitive church in its confession and proclamation of Jesus Christ was partly developed in the light of its traditions of the teaching, actions and character of Jesus.

Take, for example, the confession 'Jesus is Messiah', one of the earliest, if not the earliest, ways in which Jesus was proclaimed. Why was Jesus called Messiah? Whether Jesus avoided the title completely (either because it was politically dangerous or because he did not consider himself to be Messiah), or whether he was simply extremely reticent about using it, there is a gulf between the explicit teaching of Jesus and the preaching of the primitive church. One currently popular answer argues that the Palestinian church used Messiah of Jesus in the specific context of his *parousia*, as an equivalent for the apocalyptic title, Son of Man; hence there was no danger of confusing the title with the political type of Messiah.[1] This view places a great deal of weight on Acts iii.20 which is understood to mean that at the *parousia* Jesus will return as 'the Christ appointed for you'. But this is not the most natural interpretation; the immediate context confirms that Jesus is already Messiah, not merely at his *parousia*. And in addition there are serious objections to be raised against the view that Son of Man was an apocalyptic title first used by the church in connection with its *parousia* expectations, then of the passion and resurrection of Jesus, and finally applied to the ministry of Jesus. The hypothesis that the primitive church's christological reflection (especially its use of Messiah–Christ, Son of Man, and even its interpretation of Old Testament passages) moved 'backwards' from the *parousia* to the life of Jesus is surely an oversimplification of the evidence.

Nor can one answer the question 'Why was Jesus called Messiah?' merely in terms of the resurrection. What was there about the resurrection which led the earliest believers to make a link between Jesus and Messiahship? One may legitimately insist that the resurrection confirmed, declared or even revealed the Messiahship of Jesus, but the resurrection alone did not *make* Jesus Messiah.

Peter's speech to Cornelius points us in a rather different direction: 'God anointed Jesus of Nazareth with the Holy Spirit and with power (made him Messiah–Christ, *echrisen*). He went about doing good and healing all who were oppressed by the devil, for the active presence of the Holy Spirit of God was with him' (Acts x.38).[2] The primitive church announced the Messiahship of the one raised by God from the dead because of its conviction, now confirmed by the resurrection, that this Jesus had been anointed by God's Spirit, for his life and ministry were not merely consistent with this claim, but provided evidence that God had begun to act in a new and decisive way in Jesus of Nazareth. The proclamation of Jesus as Messiah was no doubt filled out and

[1] R. H. Fuller, *The Foundations of New Testament Christology* (1965), p. 159.
[2] See W. C. van Unnik, 'Jesus the Christ', *New Testament Studies*, VIII (1961–2), 101ff., and ' "Dominus Vobiscum": the Background of a Liturgical Formula' in A. J. B. Higgins (ed.), *New Testament Essays in Memory of T. W. Manson* (1959), pp. 270ff.

supported by traditions about the life of Jesus – for example, by traditions which showed that his relationships with others, which were so revolutionary as to prompt constant critical questioning, were grounded in his unique relationship to God, and by traditions which claimed that Jesus' actions were not those of a madman but were done by the finger or Spirit of God. The kind of person Jesus showed himself to be by his actions and relationships with others, and not merely such explicit teaching as he gave about his own person, may very well have influenced the kind of christological confessions the church made about Jesus.

But there remains the possibility that this understanding of Messiahship in terms of the anointing of Jesus with God's Spirit is Luke's theological achievement, for it is certainly an important theme in Luke–Acts. At the opening of Luke's account of Jesus' ministry, Jesus announces in the synagogue at Nazareth: 'The Spirit of the Lord is upon me, because he has anointed (*echrisen*) me, he has sent me to announce good news to the poor' (Luke iv.18f.). Isaiah lxi.1f. lies at the heart of both Acts x.38 and Luke iv.18f. But in both passages Isaiah lxi.1f. is tightly woven together with other Old Testament passages in a way which is typical of early Christian exegesis of Old Testament texts, but not typical of Luke himself. In addition, both passages contain a number of features which are not characteristic of Luke, but point to pre-Lucan tradition.[1]

And it would be rash to argue that the portrait of Jesus has been created by the church, for many aspects of the gospels' portrait of Jesus are represented so widely in various sources, strata and forms of the gospel traditions that their substantial reliability is established on the basis of the criteria of multiple attestation, coherence and consistency.

Perhaps we shall never know *precisely* the influences at work in

---

[1] Luke vii.22 (Q) also weaves together Isaiah lxi.1f. with other Old Testament passages. Isaiah lxi.1f. is alluded to in another Q passage, Luke vi.20f. H. Schürmann has recently suggested that Luke iv.16–30 contains some material, including the citation of Isaiah lxi.1f., which is characteristic of the Q material, but not of Luke or his L material. ('Zur Traditionsgeschichte der Nazareth-Perikope Lk 4,16–30', in *Mélanges Bibliques en hommage au R. P. Béda Rigaux*, eds. A. Descamps and A. de Halleux (1970), pp.187ff.) If this is so (and Schürmann's case is strong), Isaiah lxi.1f. must have deeply influenced the theology of the Q material.

the earliest christological reflections of the church. To claim that the christological beliefs of the primitive church have not left their mark upon the gospel traditions would be to fly in the face of clear evidence to the contrary. But we may be sure that traditions about the life and character of Jesus played an important part not only in the preaching of the primitive church, but also in its christological reflection: both began with Jesus of Nazareth.

12

ON THE RESURRECTION AS AN HISTORICAL QUESTION

J. C. O'NEILL

That the resurrection is an historical problem is not the truism it seems. I find it necessary to argue the case both against those who assert that the idea of the resurrection is philosophically untenable, and against those who assert that to insist that the resurrection is an historical problem is injurious to faith.

I propose to begin by examining the arguments that purport to prove that the idea of the resurrection is philosophically untenable. Then I attempt to carry the historical quest further by meeting the best historical argument against the resurrection that I know. Finally, I draw out some of the theological conclusions that follow from the assertion that the resurrection is an historical question.

The meaning of the resurrection of Jesus Christ in the New Testament documents is scarcely in doubt, although we shall later have to examine the case for saying that some of the early witnesses to the resurrection implied something different. The resurrection of Jesus Christ in most, if not all, parts of the New Testament meant that whereas the bodies of men like the patriarch David crumbled away in their tombs, the flesh of Jesus did not 'see corruption', and Jesus was raised from the dead by God the Father (Acts ii.24–36). The earthly body was transformed into a spiritual body (I Cor. xv.44).

On the surface it would appear obvious that the truth of the assertion that Jesus was raised from the dead could be tested historically or not at all. Either an historian would find evidence to prove that the assertion was false, or evidence to prove that the assertion was true, or evidence which left the issue open. However, the matter is not so simple, for it is argued that the very idea of such a resurrection, the resurrection of Jesus or the alleged resurrection of any other man, is incoherent.

There are two versions of this entirely general argument which I wish to examine. The first version asserts that the idea of resurrection is meaningless. The argument may be put in the following form. Even if it be granted that we can talk in terms that do not necessarily involve space and time (as when we talk about numbers or values), we cannot talk about an object which one moment continuously inhabits time and space and the next moment does not continuously inhabit time and space. Our criteria for talking about objects are destroyed; therefore we cannot talk about the risen Jesus.

In reply, I agree that the idea of the resurrection is different from the idea of waking from sleep. If it were not, it would not be resurrection. I cannot see that the difficulties involved in describing this idea can be allowed to count against the possibility. A square circle is by accepted definition impossible. I do not see how to get every man who uses words sensibly to agree that resurrection is by definition impossible. The existence of the word 'resurrection' is a standing challenge to the imagination, which refusal to accept the challenge will not make go away. A man may decide not to believe that the resurrection happened, but the decision is a decision about facts, not a decision that the word is meaningless before he has examined the evidence.

The second version of the entirely general argument that the idea of the resurrection is impossible is this. The physical laws of the universe preclude resurrection. Since the time when the idea of resurrection was coined, we have discovered laws (about the conservation of energy, for instance) which rule out in advance the conception that a corpse could escape destruction and be transformed into a body which does not seem to be simply part of the universe.

In reply I appeal to David Hume. He argued that no series of observed regularity can establish absolute laws of nature. It may be objected that in practice we assume that the regularities do represent laws, and that this practice has led to such success in prediction about the physical universe that we are justified in assuming that there are these laws, and that these laws are immutable.

If the argument is made pragmatic in this way, I am justified in bringing a pragmatic defence, which is as follows. The assertion of the resurrection of Jesus Christ need in no way weaken the ability of a man to operate efficiently and creatively as a scientist. In asserting a breach of the natural laws in a very special set of circumstances, he is in fact asserting that the natural laws normally hold. (He may perhaps be pardoned for adding: 'God sees to that', without claiming that belief in God is necessary in order to work the 'laws'.)

At this point David Hume brings another argument to bear. He says that we are bound to subtract the experience which lies behind the human testimony to a miracle from the experience which assures us of the laws of nature, and embrace an opinion, either on one side or the other, with that assurance which arises from the remainder. This argument does not necessarily hold. The acceptance of a miracle may, in fact, strengthen the assurance with which we assert that the laws of nature obtain. It depends on the miracle.

David Hume may even be called to witness in favour of my proposition that the resurrection is an historical problem. In his famous argument on the absurdity of believing, on the best of testimony, that Queen Elizabeth died on the first of January 1600, was interred for a month while her successor was proclaimed, and then appeared, to resume her throne and govern for three years, Hume stated a principle. His principle was that we have to compare the instances of the violations of truth in the testimony of men with those of the violation of the laws of nature by miracles, in order to judge which of them is most likely and probable.

I grant the general probability that violations of truth in the testimony of men are more likely than violations of the regularity observed by men in the countless circumstances in which no interest is involved, but I deduce the corollary that the only court of appeal is the testimony of men. Hume decided that 'men of sense' had sufficient grounds for rejecting the alleged fact of the resurrection of Queen Elizabeth, and even for rejecting it without further examination, but this is a statement of his reading of the probabilities. I should even agree, in the case of Queen Elizabeth.

If he is forced to argue further, however, under pressure of an intrinsically plausible case, he must then ask whether or not in this case the human testimony is to be taken seriously. He has argued that the resurrection is improbable, and I accept that argument. He has not argued that the resurrection is impossible, and he has implied that the only test would have to be historical.

There is no room in this essay to examine all the historical debates about the resurrection. My present purpose will be served if I can show that the historical argument against the resurrection that I consider the most telling will not withstand examination. The argument may be stated in this form. The earliest testimony to the resurrection is found in I Cor. xv. Even if those witnesses believed that they were testifying to the resurrection of Jesus Christ, their testimony is sufficient only to lead us to conclude that they were convinced Jesus appeared to them. The further stories of the empty tomb which are told in the gospels were made up in order to provide 'evidence' to support the assumption that the appearances of Jesus implied his resurrection from the dead.

Although it is not necessary for their case, the supporters of this argument usually try to strengthen their position by supposing that the first witnesses did not themselves assume that the 'resurrection' they were talking about included a transformed body and a tomb left empty. When I Cor. xv.4 says that Christ was buried or entombed, the words do not imply (so the argument goes) that the next assertion, 'he was raised', has anything to do with a transformation of the body.

This interpretation of the words is, however, highly unlikely. If the author had believed what he is supposed to have believed, he would more naturally have omitted the words 'he was raised' and have written, 'he was buried and on the third day appeared to Cephas'.

A further argument is drawn from the statement in I Cor. xv.50, 'flesh and blood cannot inherit the kingdom of God, nor does the perishable inherit the imperishable'. It is held that this rule precludes the resurrection of the body. I think the rule precludes the resuscitation of the body in the case under discussion, but do not see how it precludes the transformation of the body, about which the surrounding argument in this chapter is concerned.

The words in I Cor. xv seem to imply resurrection in the normal meaning of the word in the New Testament.

Nevertheless, the evidence brought forward in I Cor. xv is not in itself sufficient to support the resurrection, being evidence only of appearances. The conclusion seems to follow that a great deal of weight must be ascribed to the testimony to the empty tomb in the gospels. The gospels are generally agreed to have been written many years later than I Corinthians, and are therefore less likely to be reliable.

I admit that the general considerations mentioned do have to be taken into account by an historian, but an historian also knows that the later date of an account is not necessarily an argument against its truth. Each historical account has to be put to the test, and made to yield up its secrets; we cannot tell in advance precisely what those secrets will be.

We have already found reason to doubt that the gospel accounts of the tomb can be disposed of too quickly. If the first witnesses to the appearances of Jesus believed that he had been raised from the dead, their assertion could have been refuted by producing the body. We have no evidence, apart from late Jewish stories, that any attempt was made to produce the body of Jesus. All traditions, whether Christian or non-Christian, agree that Jesus' tomb was empty. They disagree about whether the body was raised or hidden elsewhere.

There is little reason to doubt that Jesus' body was put in a tomb, and that the man responsible was a Jew of some standing (Mark xv.42-6; Luke xxiii.50-4; Matt. xxvii.57-60; John xix.38-42; Acts xiii.29). The closest disciples certainly did not bury Jesus, and we may doubt whether Matthew's and John's statements that Joseph of Arimathea was a disciple of Jesus are quite accurate.

The gospels contain four separate accounts of the discovery that the tomb in which Jesus' body had been placed was empty. The first is that certain women made the discovery (Mark xv. 47 – xvi.8; Luke xxiii.55 – xxiv.11; Matt. xxvii.61 – xxviii.1-3,

5–8). The second is that Jewish guards on the tomb awoke to find the tomb empty (Matt. xxvii.62–6; xxviii.4,11–15). The third is that one woman made the discovery (John xx.1). The fourth is that Peter and 'the other disciple whom Jesus loved' were told by that one woman about the empty tomb, and went to see for themselves (John xx.2–10).

Three of these accounts go on to tell that witnesses of the empty tomb also saw the risen Lord. But this seems to be a mere appendix to the central narrative of the empty tomb. The disjunction between the two types of resurrection narratives, narratives of an empty tomb and narratives of appearances, has encouraged the idea that the latter once existed without the former, and that the former are legends designed to prove the latter. This is the best argument I know against the resurrection, and a discussion of this argument lies at the heart of the historical problem concerning the resurrection.

I doubt very much whether this simple account does justice to the evidence. I propose to examine the hypothesis that the accounts of the empty tomb are Christian fabrications, and I shall confine myself to the account in Mark xv.47 – xvi.8.

Before we examine the evidence for the hypothesis that the Marcan account is a Christian fabrication, we must examine the other hypothesis, that it is a true story misunderstood. Kirsopp Lake suggested that the women were really told by a man at the tomb that Jesus' body was not there but (pointing) elsewhere. The women were so terrified that they immediately ran away, and believed they had seen an angel who had announced the resurrection. They accurately reported the words they had heard, except for the addition of one word, *ēgerthē* (he is risen).

This hypothesis is very unlikely to be true. It is possible that the women mistook the tomb, but very unlikely that anyone would be present to tell them their mistake. If a gardener were present, it is unlikely that he would startle women who had come to anoint a body. If he did startle them, it is unlikely that he would allow them to run off without reassuring them.

The words themselves point in an entirely different direction. The first thing the young man says is not the statement (or question) of someone trying to help bewildered women to find a tomb. It is rather a dramatic device, put into the angel's mouth, to prepare for the great affirmation which is to follow. These words belong to the storyteller's art, not to a verbal recollection of what was actually said.

If this account is not simply a misunderstanding of an ordinary incident, but a dramatic proclamation of the resurrection, we have to ask the historical question of whether or not the whole is a fabrication. Sometimes form critics assume that any story told by the religious community of the church in order to affirm faith must *ipso facto* be made up. The conclusion does not follow, although it remains one of the possibilities to be considered. A story told to encourage the faithful may or may not be based on fact, and only a close examination of the evidence can decide.

We must first establish the original wording of Mark's account. The first difficulty is to decide how many women are said to come to the tomb. Most manuscripts list three: Mary Magdalene, James' Mary, and Salome. The Codex Bezae omits from xvi.1 the reference to the passing of the sabbath and the names of the three women. This manuscript states rather that the two women who noted where the grave was situated (xv.47) were the same who brought the spices to anoint him. The two women named in xv.47 are Mary Magdalene and Joses' Mary. The group of three has been mentioned before, in xv.40, as witnesses of the crucifixion. There they are named as Mary Magdalene, Mary the mother of James the less and Joses, and Salome.

The shorter text given in Codex Bezae is more likely to be original than the longer text; it is easier to understand how an editor would surmise that all three women mentioned as witnesses of the crucifixion would have become witnesses of the resurrection and add this detail, than it is to understand how an editor would omit information so precious as this.

If the threefold list was added to xvi.1, the editor who added it must have had the list in xv.40, the source of his addition, in a slightly different form from us. He probably read that the second Mary was *hē tou Iakōbou* (James' woman). Our text of xv.40, which says *Maria hē Iakōbou tou mikrou kai Iōsētos mētēr* (Mary the mother of James the less and of Joses), looks like a later attempt to identify the second Mary in xv.47 with the second Mary in xvi.1. This was only possible on the assumption that the genitive of relationship designated the child of the woman rather than the father of the woman. That assumption is not likely, unless the context forces such a conclusion. My argument is that the wording of xv.47 or xvi.1 taken by itself does nothing to suggest anything else than that one Mary was the daughter of Joses and the other the daughter of James – either that, or the wife of Joses and the wife of James.

I conclude, following Wellhausen, that Mark had two separate traditions. The first, reproduced at xv.40, was that Mary Magdalene, Mary the daughter of James the less, and Salome witnessed the crucifixion. This tradition was reproduced as an addition to xvi.1, and later expanded in xv.40 to take account of the conjunction of xv.1 with the other list in xv.47. The other list in xv.47 belonged to Mark's source, and speaks of Mary Magdalene and Mary the daughter of Joses. These were the women who visited the tomb to anoint the body.

Even this conclusion, which reduces the amount of information about the women, may be too optimistic. Mark's sources may originally have been still less explicit. Luke, who may have been using a purer version of Mark than we possess, does not give any names at all, either in his account of the women who observed the crucifixion (Luke xxiii.49), or in his account of the women who watched the entombment (Luke xxiii.55), or in his account of the early morning visit to the tomb (Luke xxiv.1). Names are not given until the end of the last-named pericope, and the names are Mary Magdalene, Joanna, James' Mary and others (Luke xxiv.10). Perhaps we should conclude that all names were later additions to originally anonymous accounts.

Who were these women? Mark assumes, perhaps on the strength of the name of the Galilaean town Magdalene, that they were Galilaean women who followed Jesus there and came to Jerusalem with him (xv.41). I think that this is merely Mark's guess, for the pericope we are discussing gives a different impression. We must turn to the words of the angel.

The first problem has to do with Mark xvi.7. The problem does not lie in the supposed contradiction between a command to tell the disciples something and the flat statement in the next verse that the women said nothing to anyone. Verse 8 cannot be taken literally. The real problem in verse 7 concerns the words, *hoti proagei humas eis tēn Galilaian; ekei auton opsesthe* (that he goes before you into Galilee; there you will see him). There is no trace of them in the Lucan parallel, except perhaps in the words, *en te(i) Galilaia(i)* (in Galilee) (Luke xxiv.6). But even this reference to Galilee is a coincidence, being due to Luke's assumption that the women came from Galilee (Luke xxiv.10). I used to assume that Luke had simply altered a verse which would have thrown out his scheme for setting all the resurrection appearances of the Lord in Jerusalem, but I now find it more and more unlikely that Luke altered his sources as drastically as that.

We must consider the possibility that the reference to Jesus' proceeding his disciples to Galilee was added to Mark's text later.

The first argument in support of this hypothesis is that the previous prophecy to which this saying refers is very likely also a later addition. The words, *alla meta to egerthēnai me proaxō humas eis tēn Galilaian* (but after I am risen I shall go before you into Galilee), in xiv.28 are absent from the citation of something very similar to Mark xiv.27–30 in the Fajjum Fragment. In any case they have nothing directly to do with the context, which is about how the disciples will be 'scandalised' when the shepherd is smitten. The parallel account in Matthew contains the words, but they are absent from Luke xxii.31–4, the nearest parallel in that gospel.

The second argument for doubting whether the angel's words originally included a reference to going to Galilee is based on the words themselves. Codex Bezae reads: *alla hupagetai [sic for hupagete] kai eipate tois mathētais autou kai tō(i) Petrō(i) hoti idou proagō humas eis tēn Galilaian; ekei me opsesthai [sic for opsesthe] kathōs eirēka humin* (but go and say to his disciples and to Peter, Behold I am going before you into Galilee; there you will see me as I told you). Strictly speaking this could be read as a message from Jesus which the angel was passing on verbatim, but the awkwardness of this reading must very soon have produced the third person version we find in most manuscripts. But there can be little doubt that Codex Bezae offers the better text, since we cannot imagine any scribe's producing this text from the text to which we are accustomed.

Matthew preserves one isolated part of the first person text. In Matt. xxviii.7 the angel ends the message with *idou eipon humin* (Behold, I have told you), and perhaps here we have a clue to the true history of Mark's text. Let us suppose that Mark's original text was this: *alla hupagete eipate tois mathētais autou; idou eipon humin* (but go speak to his disciples. Behold I have told you). Luke had this version in front of him. He took the last words as a quotation of the words of Jesus, and used this as an occasion for introducing a reminder of the Galilaean predictions of the passion and resurrection. Mark's text then was glossed by a glossator who possessed a separate account of a resurrection appearance in which the Lord said, *idou proagō humas eis tēn Galilaian; ekei me opsesthe* (Behold, I go before you into Galilee; there you will see me). This gloss was incorporated into Mark's text, where it was later assimilated in various ways. Matthew reproduces one way of assimilation, which retained the original form of the ending; the usual text of Mark reproduces another way; and the Bezan text of Mark yet another.

Striking confirmation of the hypothesis that the words about preceding the disciples to Galilee are drawn from an independent resurrection appearance is provided by Matt. xxviii.9,10. Jesus appears to the women and says, 'Do not fear. Go, tell my brothers to go to Galilee, and there they shall see me.' This pericope uses the term 'brothers' for the disciples, and seems therefore to be quite independent of Mark xvi.7.

I conclude that Mark's gospel originally contained no more than the angel's command to the women to announce the news of the resurrection to the disciples.

What, then, is the meaning of the last sentence, about the fear of the women and their failure to tell anyone (xvi.8)? It has been suggested by Wilhelm Brandt[1] that this notice was designed

1 *Die evangelische Geschichte und der Ursprung des Christenthums* (1893). Brandt was followed

to explain why the account of the empty tomb came into the apostolic tradition very much later than the accounts of resurrection appearances. This hypothesis is very unlikely, because no Christian at the time would ever have drawn the conclusion from reading verse 8 which, according to this hypothesis, he was meant to draw. He would simply have understood that the women said nothing to anybody until they had obeyed the angel and spoken to the disciples. Their fear could not be quelled until they knew the whole context of what had happened, and this they could only learn from the disciples.

Slowly the true interpretation and history of this pericope is beginning to emerge. The final piece falls into place when we observe one further peculiarity in the angel's words to the women. He says, *mē ekthambeisthe; Iēsoun zēteite ton Nazarēnon ton estaurōmenon* (Do not be afraid; you are looking for Jesus the Nazarene, the crucified) (xvi.6). Two manuscripts, codices Sinaiticus and Bezae, omit *ton Nazarēnon*, and Codex Bezae puts an article before *Iēsoun;* but these are attempts, like that found also in Matthew, to remove the description of the Lord as *ho Nazarēnos*. There is no need to discuss whether or not this form or the stranger form *Nazōraios* is the original term applied to Jesus. The only point of importance for us is that in Mark this designation of Jesus is otherwise only employed by outsiders, and never by disciples (Mark i.24; x.47; xiv.67). If Mark is consistent, the angel, in describing Jesus to the women as 'the crucified Nazarene', is implying that they knew him only from outside. The women who came to anoint Jesus' body after his crucifixion are, by implication, pious women who have observed Jesus' ministry from outside, and have come to do what they could to honour him as a good man.

Everything that we have observed about the original form and wording of the pericope lends support to this conclusion.

The names of the women who came to the tomb are uncertain, and we cannot trust the assumption that they were close followers of Jesus. The angel addresses them as outsiders to the circle of

by von Soden, *Theologische Literaturzeitung* (1895), p. 5; H. J. Holtzmann; J. Weiss; A. Loisy.

disciples and directs them to go and speak to the disciples. They
are so astonished at what they have seen that they do not confide
in anyone else until they see the disciples.

I have assumed that every detail in the original pericope is told
with great art in order to build up the body of believers. It is
worth adding that the pericope thus understood forms a magnifi-
cent end to Mark's gospel. He ends with independent testimony
to the resurrection, and implies that all who are struck with fear
at what they read should, like the women, go to the disciples
to learn the import of the resurrection. The meaning of the
resurrection can only be gathered from a reading of the whole
gospel, in which the passion is constantly proclaimed as the
necessary prelude for understanding the risen glory of Jesus
Christ.

What does this reading of the pericope contribute to our understanding of the historical problem of the resurrection? The story
is told with art and with evangelical point, but that fact does not
decide one way or the other the truth of the account.

The main thing to note is that the event spoken of is not
intrinsically unlikely. We possess another similar account concerning Stephen's martyrdom.[1] After Stephen's friends were
scattered far and wide from Jerusalem, we are told that 'pious
men buried Stephen and made a loud dirge over him' (Acts viii.
2). Jesus too was buried by other than his close followers, and it is
not unlikely that pious women would also wish to take part in
the mourning.

We cannot eliminate the possibility that the church made up
the incident, but we have other evidence to show that the community, left to itself to make up incidents, would probably have
produced something rather different. The tendency in all the other
accounts is for the witnesses of the empty tomb also to see the risen
Lord. Matthew adds the independent tradition immediately after
his parallel to the Marcan account (Matt. xxviii.9,10); John puts Mary
Magdalene's encounter with the man she takes for the gardener immediately after her words to the angels in the tomb (John xx.14–18);
the later ending to Mark states that Jesus appeared first to Mary Mag-

[1] J. C. O'Neill, *The Theology of Acts in its Historical Setting* (2nd ed., 1970), pp. 88ff.

dalene (Mark xvi.9); and even Luke implies that the women are present with the disciples when the Lord appears to them all (Luke xxiv.33–6). Mark's account alone restricts the witness of the women to a witness of the empty tomb.

Of course one could still believe that Mark's tradition was the result of the wish of the early church to have independent testimony to what they believed, but against that possibility must be set the fact that the anti-Christian Jewish accounts all agree that the tomb in which Jesus' body was placed was found empty. All these accounts start from that point, and then go on to suggest other explanations for the fact.

I conclude that Mark xv.47 – xvi.8 provides reliable evidence that some pious women who wished to honour Jesus' body discovered that his tomb was empty. There is no space to discuss the other accounts of the empty tomb. I merely suggest that the other accounts, the account of the guards in Matthew, the story of the one woman in John, and the account of the two men, also in John, may have originally been stories about how outsiders discovered that the tomb of Jesus was empty.

It will immediately be clear that in asserting that the resurrection is an historical question I have not been asserting that an historian as historian can establish that Jesus rose from the dead. The historian in this case can only show whether or not the evidence makes it at all plausible to assert that Jesus rose from the dead. I have been examining the specific argument which asserts, first, that the earliest accounts do not wish to say that Jesus rose from the dead in the way this was later understood, and, secondly, that the stories about the tomb's being empty are later fabrications designed to support a later view of the resurrection. I have tried to show, first, that there is no evidence for the alleged early view of the resurrection, and, secondly, that the stories about the discovery of the empty tomb probably stem from independent witnesses.

Even if my case is granted, there are many other possible explanations for the evidence. The women may have mistaken the tomb. The body of Jesus may have been stolen. Both these hypotheses are unlikely, but both are also possible. A decision depends on judging the whole nexus in which the resurrection is embedded.

What theological consequences follow?

If it be granted that the resurrection is an historical problem, one could then decide that the resurrection, as usually understood, did not happen. There would open up the familiar choice between a reinterpretation of New Testament language about the resurrection in terms that are 'significant' but which do not require belief in the event, and an excision of this part of the New Testament message in order to hold whatever remains. These possibilities have been explored often enough. If I had to choose, I should prefer the second, the 'liberal' interpretation, to the first, the 'existentialist' interpretation.

I am more interested in the implications that flow from deciding, on all the evidence, that God did raise Jesus of Nazareth from the dead. The evidence for this decision would have to include a judgment on the evidence from the women. However, it would also have to include a judgment on the evidence from the apostles, a judgment about the evidence concerning Jesus' ministry, and a judgment about the meaning of the Old Testament. It would be quite possible to believe that God raised Jesus from the dead, and not to believe that he was Messiah.

The faith of those who believe that Jesus was raised from the dead and who call themselves Christians is consequently a judgment about events in history, that they are events in which God has directly intervened, and upon which he has bestowed meaning for all men.

To the charge that such belief is injurious to true faith, because it assumes that God's ways are open to our observation, the answer would have to be, How do you know that God does not wish his ways to be open to observation? The charge in fact springs from a particular conception of God. Once that assumption is challenged, the Christian faith, as set out in the Bible, has a chance of being understood for what it is.

To allow that the resurrection is an historical question is already to allow the possibility that the God of the Jewish Christian tradition is living and trustworthy. That allowed, how should the historical enquiry be pursued? There is a place for the ruthless single-minded search of a detached investigator, in the manner of a detective, provided the detective does not delude himself that this one problem, when solved, will clinch the case. The detective need never slacken his vigilance, but he must turn into another man. He must become like a stranger who suddenly sees someone who may turn out to be a friend, who watches every gesture with the most patient attention. Or he becomes like a geologist who has pored over the seismic maps, examined thousands of samples, and walked over the whole country, who looks for the last sign to show that the precious mineral is indeed where he suspected. The resurrection is that sign, faint but unmistakeable, to him who knows the country.

The search may have to be solitary; the finding is not.

PART IV

THE LOGICAL GRAMMAR OF CHRISTOLOGY

13

WHAT IS A 'CHRISTOCENTRIC' THEOLOGY?

J. K. RICHES

I

From time to time words gain currency in theology which, though apparently terms of some technical exactitude, turn out on closer examination to be patient of a baffling variety of uses. 'Kerygma' was, or perhaps still is, one; 'existentialist', 'dialectical', 'paradox', 'dynamic' and 'static' others. A glance at the dictionary articles[1] is enough to convince one that 'christocentric' is a worthy addition to the list. The article in *The Oxford Dictionary of the Christian Church* refers to 'systems of theology which maintain that God has never revealed himself to man except in the Incarnate Christ', which on the basis of a literal interpretation of Matt. xi.27 'preclude the possibility of natural theology altogether'. By contrast with this largely negative definition, the Roman Catholic dictionaries give a more positive, and unmistakeably more enthusiastic account of the term. According to the *Lexicon für Theologie und Kirche* a theology is to be adjudged 'christocentric' insofar as 'all its tractates are moulded in the light of Christ'. The term is also used frequently of Barth's theology by his commentators,[2] but, surprisingly, receives cautious treatment from Barth himself. If anything emerges from this initial glance, it is firstly that, for some, christocentric theology is taken

[1] See the relevant articles in *The Oxford Dictionary of the Christian Church* (1957), ed. F. L. Cross; *Lexikon für Theologie und Kirche* (1958), eds. J. Höfer and K. Rahner; *New Catholic Encyclopaedia* (1967). *The Oxford Dictionary of the Christian Church* lists as modern advocates A. Ritschl, W. Hermann and K. Barth.

[2] Cf. above all H. U. von Balthasar, *Karl Barth, Darstellung und Deutung seiner Theologie* (2nd ed., 1962), pp. 335–72 for an exposition of the Catholic view; K. Küng in *Lexikon für Theologie und Kirche, s.v.*; H. G. Pöhlmann, *Analogia entis oder analogia fidei* (1965), who argues that Barth's position is to be characterised as a 'christomonistic actualism'. Pöhlmann's study is of the greatest relevance to the question of the relation of natural and revealed theology. See too D. M. MacKinnon, 'Masters in Israel: III. Hans Urs von Balthasar' in *The Clergy Review* (November 1969), pp. 859ff.

to be inimical to natural theology and hence to put itself beyond the reach of human reason; secondly, that the term is closely associated with the theology of Karl Barth; and thirdly, that there is a great deal more confidence in the benefits of christocentricism for theology in Roman Catholic than in Protestant circles. If one reflects that natural theology has traditionally been looked upon more favourably in Roman Catholic theology than in Protestant theology, the state of affairs appears decidely odd.

Part of the reason for this multiplicity of use undoubtedly lies in the looseness of the term itself. It seems reasonable to assume that 'christocentric theology' means 'a theology which is centred on, which has as its centre, views the surrounding territory from the stand-point of Christ'. But such a definition leaves much which is undefined. How wide are we going to draw the boundaries of such a theology? Is Christ the centre of the closed circle of revelation or would we want to include not only the study of the Bible and, possibly, church history and doctrine but also secular history, philosophy, comparative religion? Again, if Christ is the centre of theology, in what sense is it implied that he is normative for theology? It would certainly be possible to envisage a theology which gave a central position to Christ's person and teaching and yet still submitted his person and teaching to a critical assessment. On the other hand some theologians clearly see Christ both as the most fruitful, if not only, source of our knowledge of God and also as the ultimate standard by which all theologies are to be judged. Thus the same term can be applied to theologies which differ very considerably both in the way they define theology's proper sphere of enquiry and in the way they spell out the relationship between natural and revealed theology.

This initial impression of the ambiguity of the term hardens into conviction when we turn to its history. It is, I suppose, most often applied to the theology of Karl Barth. Yet if we say that for Barth theology must steer its course between the anthropocentrism of Schleiermacher's theology of experience and the theocentrism of the Catholic *analogia entis*, we are brought up sharply by Barth's own use of the term. For the fact is that within Protestant theology the term has often been used of Schleiermacher himself!¹ There is a most interesting section of the *Church Dogmatics* where Barth introduces the term in the course of a discussion of the doctrine of election.² The theologian, so Barth argues, cannot choose Christ; if he is not himself already chosen, if his theology is not *von Haus aus* christocentric, then no amount of systematic skill and effort will make it so. We cannot simply draw on the reserves of Christian experience, morality, world-order and make these the central subject of our study. God can be known to us only insofar as he freely chooses to reveal himself to us in the Son. The theologian is one who has been called, who must be obedient to his call, a servant of the Word which he has freely received.

Thus we are confronted with the important question of the relation of the theologian to his subject. What is it, if anything, that distinguishes a Christian theologian, *qua* theologian, from, say, a student of comparative religions studying Christianity?³ They may both see Christ as the 'focal point' of Christianity, but in what way will their view be affected by their own relationship to Christ? It is of course possible to argue that for some purposes it makes no difference whether one believes in the existence of the focal point or no. It is argued that a phenomenology of religion can be given without reference to the question whether the 'focal point' of religion actually exists. I can see no reason why this should not be so, why it should not be possible thus to produce a careful analysis of rites, observances and practices in the Christian religion and of their relationships to beliefs held in the various Christian bodies and to follow this with a comparison of such beliefs and practices with those of other religions. But would this

¹ Indeed there is good reason for this. Schleiermacher, in *Der christliche Glaube* (1960), ed. M. Redeker, pp. 74ff., sees the distinctive element of Christianity as lying in the fact that 'everything in the same is referred to the redemption wrought in Jesus of Nazareth', and in the same section, in a marginal note, refers to the 'centrality' of this state in the Christian religion and its 'realisation in Christ'. See also E. Schaeder, *Theozentrische Theologie* (1909), for a discussion of the inadequacies of the christocentrism of Schleiermacher and Ritschl.

² *Church Dogmatics* I/2 (1956), 350ff.

³ See Prof. Ninian Smart's forthcoming book on the phenomenology of religion. Also G. van der Leeuw, *Religion in essence and manifestation, a study in phenomenology* (1938); J. Hermelink, *Verstehen und Bezeugen. Der theologische Ertrag der 'Phänomenologie der Religion' von G. v. d. Leeuw* (1960); H. U. von Balthasar, *Herrlichkeit*, I (1961), 477ff.

be *von Haus aus* christocentric, or would such study reduce Christianity to a set of 'ideal types' which failed to portray its distinctive character? Equally we may put the question the other way round and ask of the believing theologian what it is that he knows and portrays which is missed by the phenomenologist and why it is that his belief in Christ thus puts him in a privileged position.

This question leads us on to a second one about the general intelligibility of such a christocentric theology. For even if we admit that the theologian may know and talk about something which is not caught in the net of a phenomenological analysis of Christianity, we may still ask how far such knowledge of God is communicable, indeed in what sense it is entitled to be called 'knowledge' at all. If such knowledge is the exclusive possession of the believer, then how can it be expressed in terms which are intelligible to others? Does the christocentric theologian when he talks about 'God' mean by it something *totally* different from what others intend? And if so, does his use of the term have any meaning at all, even to himself? If such a theologian claims to speak about God, then must he not in some way know what he means by 'God' before he receives the revelation in Christ – or would he else be able to receive it as a revelation of *God*? What we are doing here is to press the theologian to say whether his knowledge of God is derived solely from Christ or whether he must take into account other means of coming to know God as necessary conditions of the intelligibility of the revelation of God in Christ. Now I think it possible to give answers on both these points, but only if we have a rather more precise idea of what a theology which is *von Haus aus* christocentric might be. So before returning to these questions I will attempt to give what can be no more than the briefest sketch of a possible christocentric theology.[1]

II

The subject of theology is the revelation of the glory of the divine love

[1] The following section owes a great deal to the work of H. U. von Balthasar. Cf. especially *Love Alone: the Way of Revelation* (1968) and his great work *Herrlichkeit: eine theologische Ästhetik* (1961—)

in Jesus Christ. To speak of the subject of theology as the revelation of the glory of the divine love in Jesus Christ is to suggest a way of conceiving it which emphasises the transcendence of the subject of our study without putting it entirely beyond our grasp. The subject of theology is love. What it shares in common with human love is its givenness and its irreducibility. We cannot choose to be loved; though we might wish it, we cannot force someone to love us. Love is a *free* gift of the self, full of grace. Thus we cannot explain the love of a man for a woman exhaustively in terms of environment, circumstance, psychology, biology. True we may be able to trace similar patterns of behaviour in the animal world, similar psychological features, but to accept such explanations as exhaustive would be to deny the uniqueness of this love, to fail to grasp it as the free, spontaneous act of the lover, as a breaking of the bonds of heredity and environment. Such love is a gift, not merely in the sense that it is undeserved, unforced, but in the sense that it is a gift of the *self*, an offering by the lover of himself in complete openness, so that the other may know him as he is. In this sense every love is different, distinct, this love and no other; but what all human loves share in common (though in varying degrees) is the giving of the self *to be known*, as he truly is, without deception or withholding.

Yet to speak thus is to be reminded of the forces which endanger human love, to be reminded of its frailty and subjection to the very forces from which it would set men free. The subject of theology is the divine–human love in Christ, which, though subject to the forces of fear and death, triumphs over them in the supreme act of suffering love on the cross. In the cross Christ is glorified and glorifies the Father. In it the divine–human love shines in majesty and glory. This is to speak in deliberately aesthetic terms, to stress the analogy with the great works of the human creative imagination. The glory of the last quartets of Beethoven lies in their rightness, in the perfectness of their form, in the matching of thematic material and its development with rhythm, harmony and tone-colour to give something uniquely beautiful, something which is as it is and could not be otherwise unless Beethoven had chosen to make it so. Again as in the analogy with human love there is an element of the sheerly given, of irreducibility. But what I want to stress here is the *form* of the revelation, its rightness and truth 'full of grace and truth'. Only so, now we have beheld its glory, is the divine love conceivable. In the relation of Christ's mission and existence, of his sending from the Father and his obedience unto death on the cross as he bears our sins, in his sending of the Comforter ('it is expedient for you that I go away'), the movement of the Old Testament, its hopes and despair, its message of promise and judgment, is brought to fulfilment: in Christ men's hopes and longings find their goal, not albeit as they had thought or can conceive ('how can a man enter a second time into his mother's womb?') but in a manner which outstrips and yet fulfils their fondest imagination.

Theology is possible only on the basis of a loving response to the revelation in Christ, which response is in turn only made possible by the divine love itself. Just as in our human loving we come to know the love of another for what it is only when we return that love, so too it is with the divine love: we can know it for what it is, only when we respond to it in love. Let us start by taking the first half of the analogy. What is it to say that we come to know the love of another for what it is only when we return that love? It is not, of course, to deny that a man may well be aware of another's love without returning that love. But such knowledge, though it may be of different kinds, is not the knowledge which would be enjoyed by the man who returns that love. At the lowest level a man may register such love merely as a part of his own history, more or less pleasant, more or less threatening, but still essentially to be considered as part of what is happening to him. At another level those who have loved and have known what it is to love may, by analogy, be able to grasp something of what that love must mean to the other. But what is the other way of knowing, which is peculiar to the lover? What is it but seeing, knowing the other *as other*, as over against one, as free, yet giving themselves, ready to embark upon the 'great adventure',[1] the going out to meet each other in a way that is radically new. It is in loving that

---

[1] Cf. St John of the Cross, 'On a darksome night', and von Balthasar's study of his work in *Herrlichkeit* II.

we know what it is to be loved, that the way is opened to the deepening and growth of mutual knowledge, that the mutual knowledge is born.

But here we encounter a paradox: for while on the one hand we want to say that it is only in loving that we know the other, that we can understand the other's love as the gift of themselves, there is also a sense in which it is only the love of the other which makes possible our own loving, whether we will or no. So Goethe:

> Fesselt dich die Jugendblüte,
> Diese liebliche Gestalt,
> Dieser Blick voll Treu und Güte
> Mit unendlicher Gewalt?[1]

Nor is the paradox removed, but only heightened, if we think of love which is given, as it were, simultaneously. For the paradox rests on conceiving the evoking of the response after the manner of cause and effect in a temporal sequence of events, whereas in fact both the initiative of love and the returning of that love are free acts, which cannot be exhaustively described in terms of their concrete manifestations. True, the lover's tale can be told, the moments marked, but the giving and receiving are events which, though they have their biography, cannot be equated with words or actions or meetings, but are free, 'timeless', 'eternal'. (To speak thus is to come close to the language of idealism. But in one sense at least what I am arguing is substantially different. For although it is necessary to distinguish between the transcendental act of loving and its concrete manifestations, it would be wrong to draw too hard a line between the two, or to attempt to reduce human loving to a single essence. For the loving is the gift of this particular self, is unique, and this very uniqueness is reflected in its particular history. The point which is to be stressed here is the transcendence of the loving over and above its concrete manifestations. It is by means of this analogy that we may break out of the anthropocentricism of a theology of experience. I will attempt

---

[1] From 'Neue Liebe, Neues Leben'. 'Are you ensnared by the bloom of youth, by that lovely figure, those eyes so faithful and kind – ensnared with irresistible force?' Translation in: *Goethe. Selected verse* (1964), trs. D. Luke.

to develop this point more fully under the third head of this section.)

To point out this paradox is fruitful in more than this one respect. It emphasises the transcendence, the freedom of love, but it also brings out the constraints which are placed on human love. For however timeless or eternal our loving, it finds its expression in the concrete, contingent stuff of human living. Love may be sworn eternally but such pledges will have to stand the test of time and change, and ultimately to be confronted by the reality of death. The gift may be cherished, the love may grow, but it may also grow cold, it may fall victim to the 'everydayness' of things. Indeed the very newness and excitement of loving may lead to a search for new loves; and in face of the short time we have to live, is not Don Juan's sheer appetite at least understandable, if in the end self-destructive? And more: our love is cloyed by guilt. The very possibility of growth, of maturity, brings with it the possibility of falling short, of failure. The demands which love makes may prove too great; the end is resignation, guilt.

What then of man confronted by the divine love? How can he return the infinite self-giving of God? How can he return what he has not, how can he receive the light, dare to become a Son of God when the effort of human loving stretches him to his limits and beyond? What is more true than George Herbert's lines:

> Love bade me welcome: yet my soul drew back,
> Guiltie of dust and sinne.

And so we are brought to the second half of our analogy. Just as we can know the love of another only when we return that love, so too we can know the love of God as it is revealed in Christ only when we are enabled to return that love. But how is such a loving response possible? Here I can offer only the briefest outline, but some such outline is necessary in order to carry the main line of the argument through. 'Unless a man be born again of water and the spirit he cannot enter into the kingdom of heaven.' But the answer to the question how this is possible, though hinted at in the reference to Moses lifting up the snake in the wilderness, is not given fully until we come to the farewell discourses, where Jesus, in the closed circle of his disciples, expounds the mystery of our incorporation in him, of our being taken up into the love-relationship between the Father and the Son in the Spirit. As Jesus shares in the Father's love, so too we may share in Jesus' love; moreover the love which he shows us in his works, in the pedilavium, in his death on the cross, is the Father's love, and in him we may return that love and bear fruit (cf. esp. John xv). Or to put the matter in epistemological terms: 'all things have been given to me by the Father and no one knows the Father except the Son and he to whom the Son chooses to reveal him' (Matt. xi.28, *pace Oxford Dictionary of the Christian Church*). It is Christ who reveals to us the true nature of God, who is the gift of God himself to us men. 'For God so loved the world that he gave...' But equally it is Christ who enables us to return that love, who himself provides the archetype of our faith in his loving obedience to the Father. It is only in him that we can know the Father's love as it is, that we can know the Father as he gives himself to us in the Son. Only on the basis of such knowledge can we begin to do theology.

Theology is not possible as an abstract, detached science; theology is possible only on the basis of a loving faith. The danger lies in imagining that the theologian is in some way in a privileged position where, by sheer intellectual effort he can plumb the mysteries of God without entering upon the venture of faith; or alternatively that some justification can be found for faith by standing back and attempting to reconstruct from rational principles what we already believe. Either approach is doomed to failure from the start, and can lead at best to some kind of 'liberal' reduction.

Theology is a meditation on the mystery of the divine love in its engagement with the world as revealed in Jesus Christ. In the previous paragraphs little reference has been made to the form of love, either human or divine. The importance of the concrete expressions of love may have been underestimated because of the emphasis laid on the 'timeless', free act of self-giving as the essence of love. But at least where men are concerned, love, though not reducible to its concrete manifestations, is intimately bound up with them. Moreover it is precisely through the form of love that it is apprehended. It is the '*liebliche Gestalt*' which holds us captive. In the form, the manner of the giving, we learn the value of the gift. It is in the form of the love that its beauty, its uniqueness is perceived, and its beauty, its gracefulness vouches the genuineness of the gift.

Perhaps I can put the matter as follows. The actions, events, words which make up the biography of a love cannot be equated *tout court* with that love. Love 'transcends' its concrete manifestations, and yet it is only through its manifestations that it can be apprehended. How else can we know the love that is given except through the words and actions and demeanour of the lover? These actions have a form, a shape, a pattern: where the love is genuine they have a rightness, a grace, a beauty which vouches their genuineness, which speaks of their truth. The notion of a 'trial of love' is misconceived, because it overlooks the proof that is already given and demands what will still remain ambiguous for those who have not eyes to see. Love is in this sense its own measure, that although we may have broad, general standards by which we measure the sincerity, integrity and goodness of human actions, these will not adequately measure the depth and quality of this particular love. Similarly we may have rules of thumb for assessing works of art, but still find them curiously inadequate when confronted by a Giotto, a Rubens, a Monet. This is not to say that there are no criteria, no means of judging the genuineness of love, nor indeed that these are entirely discontinuous with the rules we employ in assessing other forms of human behaviour, but to insist that the rules do not exhaust the reality and particularity of our loving and being loved.

If then the subject of theology is love, and if the form of the divine love is the sending of the Son to suffer and to die that all that believe in him might have life, we may now say something about the task of theology. Theology has in the first place the task of meditating on the form of the divine love. It is, or should be, concerned to spell out the form, to present it in such a manner that the pattern and shape of God's engagement with the world become clear, and in a way which shows the centrality in this of the form of Christ. In this respect its task can be likened to the task of the literary critic, which is not so much to paraphrase, to tell us the meaning of a work of art before we have read it, as to open our eyes to the work in such a manner that we read it with greater understanding, that we are able the more clearly to grasp its meaning. Thus, for example, a faithful theological interpretation of the Bible will not be so much concerned to wrest from it some metaphysic, some doctrine of man, some general *Schriftprinzip*, as to show how its various parts together mediate to us the form of Christ.

In this, theology will not be working as it were within the closed circle of revelation. To present the Bible or the doctrine of the church, in however sophisticated a manner, simply as a promulgation of divine mysteries, is to overlook the manner in which the Bible encompasses and perfects men's own searchings after God. Whatever else recent biblical scholarship, and in particular the work of the *religionsgeschichtliche Schule*, has shown us, it is that both the Old and New Testaments are firmly rooted in the religion and culture of their times. This only serves to point out to us the way God chooses to reveal himself to us: not by setting aside all human thought as worthless, but by taking it up, judging it and exalting it. Of course on the one hand the word of the cross is folly to the Greeks and a stumbling block to the Jews, but on the other hand it is precisely in the language of Judaism and Hellenism that St Paul spells out the meaning of the gospel. Thus the theologian will attempt not only to show the centrality of Christ within the biblical witness, but also to show the centrality of Christ among the religions and philosophies of the world.

III

I can now attempt to answer the questions I posed at the end of the first section. Under the three heads above I have attempted to outline a possible christocentric theology. Such a theology is christocentric in the first place because it takes as its subject matter the revelation of the divine love in Christ. It will attempt to set out the pattern of God's activity in creation, in salvation-history, in the life of the church, so that those who will may see in it the marks of the divine love which is perfectly and uniquely revealed in the divine condescension in Christ. But, I have suggested, there is another sense in which it is christocentric, 'von Haus aus' christocentric. For true knowledge of Christ is possible only when we are drawn into the circle of the divine love, when 'in Christ' we are enabled to return the divine love and to begin to know it as it is. Thus theology, however sophisticated, however far it proceeds with its reflection on the philosophical and historical conditions of the possibility of such a revelation, will always speak the language of faith. My position can be pin-pointed by saying that in a christocentric theology we should always be able to discover both the language of confession, such as is found in the earliest recorded Christian utterances, Jesus Christ is Lord, and also the language of meditation: 'we beheld his glory, the glory as of the only-begotten of the Father, full of grace and truth'.

It is possible now to tackle the question which is raised by a comparison between the type of theology we have been suggesting and a phenomenological study of religion. What is it that a christocentric theology catches in its net that a phenomenological approach does not? A full answer would require at least as full an account of what a phenomenology of religion might be as we have given here of a christocentric theology, but let us say at least this much. A phenomenology of religion (and here I shall use the term broadly in the sense employed by G. v. d. Leeuw) must in the first place be distinguished from a 'history of religions'. It does not set out to plot the development through history of different religious beliefs in terms of cause and effect, origin and development, still less to trace the many religions back to a primal religion, or to extrapolate from its study a general, universal religion. Its prime aim is to grasp religious phenomena as they show themselves to us, to name them, to describe them, to categorise them into 'ideal types'. Such a process of understanding requires on the one hand that we should enter into the beliefs and practices of other cultures and peoples with imagination and sensitivity, guided by our own experience, but ready to discover new possibilities of human experience, ready to have our understanding of such phenomena corrected and deepened. Only by such *methodologisches Miterleben* can we see the phenomena. But at the same time we are able to leave open the question of the reality of that of which such phenomena claim to speak. There is a 'bracketing' of the question of the existence and value of that which is said to appear in such phenomena.

Now there is little doubt that such an account can and indeed has been given of Christianity. Nor should we be surprised that Christianity can thus be categorised according to general religious types, for the simple reason that it is an historical religion. The Old Testament is embedded in the religious and cultural world of the Middle East; Jesus himself was a man of his times: his ministry has much in common with that of the prophets and other founders of religions; Christianity takes over the language of Judaism and Hellenism. What then distinguishes the two approaches to Christianity? On the basis of what we set out above it cannot simply be that theology takes over where phenomenology leaves off, providing arguments for the existence of God, attempting to evaluate the relative merits of what has been described. Nor can theology be based simply on a leap of faith (so G. v. d. Leeuw) after the phenomena have been described. What then does theology catch? The question looks fatal, for there is nothing else of a concrete, phenomenal kind to catch. Anything we could suggest would be suitable material for the phenomenologist.

But can we accept the phenomenologist's account of his procedure? Is it as neutral and objective as it claims to be? Do his own religious convictions have no bearing on the manner and results of his study? However much the phenomenologist may remain silent about the existence and value of the reality behind the phenomena, the very method by which he seeks to grasp the phenomena makes such a silence arbitrary and artificial. For he can only understand the phenomena in their structures by recourse to his own experience, by *die Einschaltung des Phänomens in das eigene Leben*. Such *Er-leben* is possible, so van der Leeuw maintains, on the basis of a common human essence. *Homo sum, humani nil a me alienum puto*. But this is to raise the question which in one form or another has provided the main theme of this essay. Is all human experience equally accessible to all of us, or are there some kinds of experience which are, in a sense, open only to the initiated? What I have been arguing is that there are certain types of experience, certain types of knowledge which, though properly human, are not open to us in the way that, say, the experience of going to a cricket match is open to us, or indeed that of 'going to church'. We can only know a person fully when we love them and are loved by them, for only then do we know them as other, as unique, do we know them as they give themselves to be known. And this sort of knowledge is not open to those who have never loved or been loved. I have also suggested that such knowledge of the other is mediated to us through the form of their actions, words, demeanour, i.e. of their appearances, in such a way that the beauty, the rightness of the form vouches the value, the truth of their love. I have further claimed that our knowledge of God is to be seen as analogous to this kind of knowledge. Now what this means in the present context is that if we are to 'read' religious phenomena aright, if we are to enter into them imaginatively, we can do so only if we have already enjoyed some such religious experience. Moreover it means that we cannot exclude the evaluation of such phenomena if we are to understand them fully. This is not to say that we cannot given some general religious typology, but what we will not grasp the (relative) uniqueness of the various types, we will not be able to see them as glimpses of the eternal, as *Lichtungen des Seins*, and we certainly will not be able to place them in relation to one another, if we exclude all consideration of their value. In short, what a christocentric theology grasps is the glory of the divine love in its concrete manifestations, a glory which vouches its uniqueness and truth.

But still we may ask in what sense this is intelligible. When all is said and done what is being claimed is that in Christ the nature of the world, of man and of God is revealed to us and unless we can attach some meaning to 'God' and indeed to the 'world' and 'man' it is hard to see how such a claim can be meaningful. To put the point more bluntly, unless we were thinking, rational beings, who could form ideas of God and being, then God could not, logically could not, reveal himself to us. Unless we had some

knowledge of what it was to love, we could not know God as
perfect love, we could not begin to understand what was meant
by saying that in Christ we may behold the glory of the divine
love. It might well appear that the sort of theology I have been
proposing attempted to dispense with any such knowledge of
God prior to the revelation in Christ and it would then indeed
have to face the serious charge of unintelligibility. To raise this
question is to help to clarify the implications of the theology
outlined above. For what I have been trying to argue is not that
Christ is the *only* source of our knowledge of God, but that he is
the central, most fruitful source of such knowledge and that it is
by knowledge thus gained that we must judge such knowledge as
we may derive from other sources. Just as we can only know the
true worth, the value, the beauty of another's love when we
return that love, so too we can only know the full meaning of
God's love, and hence know the true nature of God as he gives
himself to be known, when we are enabled to respond to that
love. God meets us as other, as other than our preconceived
notions of him, and we can only know him when we return his
love. But the fact that he reveals himself as other than our preconceived notions of 'God' does not necessarily mean that he is
therefore unrecognisable, that he ceases to be God. Just as we
shall be unlikely to say when we love someone that we were
entirely mistaken about them before we loved them, so too with
our prior notions of God. What are we committed to saying is
that there is *some* truth in such ideas. But for such ideas we would
indeed be unable to grasp the idea of revelation. But such ideas,
such a prior understanding of God, should not be confused with
a natural theology, if by the latter we mean something that can
provide a rational basis for our belief in God, which can act in
internal theological disputes as a court of appeal, which forms a
body of doctrines assured by reason and to which revealed theology must conform. For to say that there is some truth in our
prior ideas of God is not to say that such ideas can be erected into
a canon by which to judge revealed theology. On the contrary
we shall only discover what that truth is when we have seen God
fully revealed in Jesus Christ. Thus we may have some notion of a

creator God, and we may conceive such a God as a being of such infinite power that he can create the universe out of nothing, but the manner in which we conceive of that power and the way in which we regard the world which he creates will be radically altered when we see the supreme manifestation of God's power in the powerlessness of the cross, when we see Christ as the 'heart of the world'. For then we shall know what it is to say that God created the world 'out of his fatherly goodness', out of the same graciousness and love for the world which sends the Son that all may live, and which is supremely realised in the love between the Father and the Son; and we shall know that despite appearances the world is grounded in love, in the boundless love which suffers all in order that he may draw all men to him.

In conclusion a few very general remarks. It may seem that it is untimely to advocate such a very dogmatic theology. Ten years ago the authors of *Soundings* were unable to persuade themselves that the time was ripe for major works of theological construction or reconstruction. And this has been a cry which has been repeated often enough over the past decade. Nor can one point to any major change in the philosophical and general cultural situation which would suggest that the times were any more favourable. Nevertheless the time does seem ripe for a change in theological emphasis. The last ten years have been fruitful in the sense that they have exposed many of the confusions and uncertainties which lay behind much Christian assertiveness. But it seems to me that there could be a danger of settling into a style of theologising which would be liberal only in the sense that it eschewed making any claims for Christianity unless it was certain that it had an answer for every possible objection. I am not, that is, advocating a retreat from dialogue, putting up the shutters and turning up the sound to keep out the shouts from the street. Nor am I arguing for a return to a simply assertoric style of theologising, but I am suggesting that if the dialogue is to bear fruit we must be ready to advance our claims, to reflect deeply on the meaning of those claims, and to try and 'understand the world better than it understands itself'. It should be evident that if such an attempt at understanding is not to be vain in both senses of the word, it must listen seriously both to the world and to Christ.

14

THE LANGUAGE AND LOGIC OF 'MYSTERY' IN CHRISTOLOGY

STEVEN T. KATZ

The aim of this essay is to focus attention on some of the interesting and curious logical and linguistic problems raised by the use of the word 'mystery' in religious discourse. This paper does not attempt to construct any unified, positive theory of theological meaning or usage, but is intended to be therapeutic in character. It attempts to show that there are certain minimal conditions of logical and linguistic adequacy and propriety which even the mystery theologian cannot ignore with impunity.

No one historical account has been singled out for criticism. Instead, the focus is on the necessary and essential features of any theological system which gives 'mystery' a central place. The essential intention is to analyse a specific method and not to criticize any specific school or the work of any individual. To begin, let the following proposition serve as a tentative shorthand of the mystery technique which this essay proposes to examine and criticize: 'Let ø be any predicate and M any subject', then 'for any ø, M is not ø'. There are many theologians who intentionally advocate and follow this type of analysis with eyes wide open. Yet, there are an even greater number who, despite sincere intentions to the contrary and a conscious commitment to another sort of theological analysis, slide, in the working out of their positions, into this form of debate. My discussion is intended as a useful and corrective analysis of what is involved when any variety of the mystery position is adopted or appealed to in theological argument, regardless of whether this appeal is explicit and conscious or merely implied and the result of logical backsliding.

Insofar as the essential critical model is a composite of various positions it might be argued in criticism of this paper that it has constructed a straw man. In anticipation of this criticism let me say only this: the essay attempts to spread its net widely enough to snare anyone who employs any variation of the mystery method. If not every criticism applies to every theologian who broadly belongs to this school of thought, no matter. Take whatever criticisms are relevant to any specific approach and apply them. Look upon this paper as an A la Carte menu.

I

Theologians who exploit the category of 'mystery' argue that religion is concerned with realities that exceed our grasp in terms of any conceptual system we may employ. When we say that the objects of religious discourse are transcendent, we imply that no extension of the categories of human understanding can assimilate them. The 'states of affairs' to which religious language points do not belong to the empirical world, that is, the world revealed to us by sense perception. Although we may use such substantives as 'God' to refer to 'states of affairs', these abstractions, unlike substantives such as mountain, house, tiger, etc., do not indicate an individual entity that can be isolated from its environment whether in landscape, in town, or in jungle. By referring to such 'states of affairs' as objects of ultimate concern, we indicate that they have a character totally unlike those relative constants of our natural environments. The very indistinctness of our language emphasizes that such 'states of affairs' are not identifiable particulars that can be considered as substantial by virtue of their constancy, their internal coherence, and the possibility of our specifying change of a sort distinctive of their identifying structural character.

This opacity of the divine to human understanding is, we are often told, an expression of human finitude. Indeed, some theologians seem to explicate the alleged mysteriousness of the divine in terms of the latter's freedom from the inherently limited character of human experience. And this in various ways. Thus the divine autonomy is entrusted with all the obstacles set in the way of human fulfilment by circumstance, that which Heidegger referred to by use of the term *Geworfenheit*. Again, God's omnipresence is represented as the absence of all that flows for human experience from the fact that man can only be in one place at one time, that although technological advances may reduce the time taken to pass from Cambridge to New York, Trinity Street and Broadway can never be simultaneously directly perceived by the same individual.

Theocentrism, treated in the manner of the mystery theologian, is exceedingly problematic, and the difficulty is compounded by the necessary christocentricity (this is not a technical Barthian usage) of Christian theology. In christocentric accounts the negative stipulation of the mystery theologian requires the following sort of exegesis. God, who in his majesty is unknowable and whose self-revelation must always assume the form of mystery, now, through the incarnation, becomes human. The manner of the presence of the human and divine in one person is formulated ontologically as 'hypostatic union'. However, the use of this formula involves a proviso which severely limits the intelligible content we may assign to this conception. In fact, so powerful is the force of this circumscriptive proviso that it has become normative in Christian theology to treat the sense of the self-revelation of God in christological form as one of the ultimate mysteries of faith.

II

Before discussing the central issues a few facts must be made clear. The word 'mystery' is quite familiar to most people and they are able to use it correctly in ordinary speech. Precisely because we can use the word, and we know what 'mystery' means when it is used non-theologically, we also think we know what we are doing when we use it theologically. Our facility in employing the penumbra of ideas connected with non-theological mysteries lulls us into assimilating the non-theological and theological uses of the word, and into thinking that we can work with the latter as easily as with the former. In fact, however, the word 'mystery' as used in ordinary statements and the word 'mystery' as employed in theology are very different *words* and the two cannot and should not be conflated, nor should we think that because we understand the use of 'mystery', for example, with reference to historical mysteries like that surrounding the ship *Marie Celeste*, or the possible implication of Mary Queen of Scots in the murder of Robert Darnley, we also understand the use of the concept of 'mystery' when it appears in Tillich's *Systematic Theology* or I. T. Ramsey's *Models and Mystery*.

In addition two important aspects of the way the word 'mystery' is used in ordinary speech must be made explicit. In the first place, an important feature of the ordinary meaning of 'mystery' is the essential demand that the situation be, *in principle*, formulable in ordinary language or in the relatively technical language e.g. of mathematics. We must be able to give an intelligible account of the situation which demands a solution. Thus, when Sherlock Holmes is faced with the horror of a seemingly supernatural beast on the Devonshire moors he is able to communicate to even a Dr Watson what is unnatural and puzzling about the situation in which they find themselves. Or consider the example presented by the physical sciences in relation to quantum theory. Even though the secrets of quanta are still not exhausted, causing the working physicist tremendously complex difficulties, it is possible to explain, through language, the sorts of problematic behaviour which require the need for further and more exhaustive research into the character and activity of light and energy.

A second, and even more important, feature of non-theological mysteries is that, *in principle*, they are held to be soluble. Any non-theological mystery is assumed, *a priori*, to have an explanation and solution. Often there are many possible solutions, only one of which can be correct, but an abundance of possibilities is not a logically significant obstacle. It may, at any given time, be beyond the possibilities of either the criminal or scientific investigator to solve an especially difficult 'mystery', but this never precludes or alters the essential demand for solubility *assumed* by both. In a detective story, the investigator is faced with the fact that, for instance, a man has been found dead in a locked room to which no one could have possibly gained access, from a wound which could not have been self-inflicted. Again, some years ago empirical cosmologists were confronted with entities named quasars that at first they found hardly possible to identify or to relate to other familiar features of the cosmos. When one talks of 'mystery' in these instances, one talks about phenomena or occurrences which are perplexities, a different sort of perplexity in each example no doubt, but perplexities which can be solved.

If at this point some theologian would make the following interjection: 'But that is precisely how I, too, use the word "mystery"!' my retort would be as follows: 'Any theologian who uses the word "mystery" in theology in the same way as the scientific investigator or as Sherlock Holmes is represented as doing in his cases, stands outside the scope of this paper and its critical remarks.'

III

It has now been argued, and the examples should make it clear, that the first essential feature of the ordinary use of the concept of 'mystery' is that one is able to say what is puzzling in language which itself is not at all puzzling. What about theological language? Does the same condition obtain here too? Can a theologian sustain and explain the need for talking about the mysteriousness of M while rejecting all predicates in language which itself is not reducible in form to some instance of the circular and uninformative statement: 'M is a mystery because it is mysterious'?

It appears that the mystery theologian can make statements of the sort required which do not commit him to a vicious logical circularity. For have not many Christian theologians who have talked in terms of 'mystery' and the 'mysterious' carried on hoary debates about the essentials of Christian faith? Ironically, the fact that the debate over what constitutes heresy *vis-à-vis* the christological mystery has occupied such a large part of Christian theological history supports the view that theologians do indeed have some understanding of the realities of their discipline; how else could they label certain views orthodox and others heterodox and heretical?

An important interjection must here be made. It should not be thought that the demand that theological discourse, in order to be intelligible, need be reducible, without remainder, to empirical or observable phenomena. The notions of synonymy and equivalence are not being invoked here. That is, I am not making the strict demand that all theological propositions of type P *must* be translatable into non-theological propositions of type Y so that all P statements can be reformulated without remainder in Y statements. I am fully aware that the dangers of reductionism are nowhere greater than in theology. Too often in the past, and unfortunately it continues to be true today, we have been overly hasty in applauding and adopting non-theological schemata as suitable explanatory models of theological realities. Just as the psychologist must fight against falling prey to the all too easy behavioural explanations of human action, so, too, the theologian must staunchly resist the idea that the fleeting fashions of the day are truly descriptive accounts of ontological and metaphysical entities.

It is important that no one should treat the argument presented in this paper as reductionist, and fear it on that account. Theologians should be able to defend and account for the logical and theological need of their statements in non-theological language, and should be able to state why their investigations are necessary. If theologians can only explain the need for theological language and argument by using theological language and argument, they exhibit a circularity in their reasoning parallel to that exhibited by the man who, in trying to answer the question of the sceptic, 'How can we know anything about the past?', uses statements about the past to argue his case.

The actual effect of this requirement is the grounding, at least in the first instance, of the nature and cause of theology in the real world. It does not limit the possibility of acquiring sense-transcending knowledge, as some may think. What it does do is circumscribe the limits of the free play of the theological imagination. The products of the unconstrained imagination, whatever their charm and internal coherence, cannot illuminate the contents of our world, which are bounded and determinate. The justification for theology must emerge from the character of determinate human experience. This is all that is here being asked.

In christology this logical request takes the following sort of form. What is it about the historical Jesus that requires an elaborate christological systemization? What is it about the historical Jesus that logically requires the elaborate philosophical and theological architectonic of Christianity? What is it indeed about the historical Jesus that even requires the introduction of talk about 'mystery'? On the face of it this seems a minor problem, for all that needs to be said in order to generate the whole elaborate edifice is: 'Jesus is the Christ' or 'Jesus is One with the Father'. Granted this, it easily follows that what Christian theology is about is trying to clarify and explicate these identifications and what they entail for man and the created world. The problem seems easily solved.

Unfortunately it is not quite so simple, for there is a small but vital step in the move from: 'what is the ground of christology?' to the statement (1) 'Jesus is the Christ', or (2) 'Jesus is One with the Father God'. This step is the ability to identify in case (1) not only facts J about Jesus but also facts C about Christ; and in case (2), to identify facts J about Jesus and facts G about God. Then, in case (1) to be able to say, if $a, b, c, \ldots n \ldots$ is J then some $a, b, c, \ldots n \ldots$ is C; and in case (2) to be able to say, if $a, b, c, \ldots n \ldots$ is J then some $a, b, c, \ldots n \ldots$ is G. In other words, what is required to make an identification of A with B is a rule of identification not only for A or for B but for both A and B. It will not suffice to say, for example in case (1), that Jesus exhibited Christ-like attributes and exercised Christ-like prerogatives, unless I am able, if nothing else, to specify and individuate what those attributes and prerogatives are. Again, in case (2), we cannot say Jesus was God incarnate unless we have some minimal understanding of what the word 'incarnate' means and unless we can identify by some minimal set of marks what predicates are God-like and how we can identify their presence. (We must demand the ability to identify the presence of the specific attributes or we do not really have a rule of identification.)

A way of making this point clearer is to consider the following exercise. We ask the theologian to make two exhaustive inventories, on the one listing all the things which can be predicated of Jesus, and on the other, itemizing all predicates which are predicable of the Christ. Then we compare the two lists to see if there are at least a small and relevant set of attributes predicated of Jesus which are also predicated of the Christ and thus whether there are grounds for making the statement 'Jesus is the Christ'. We can see at once that if we are able to construct only one of the two required inventories (which one being immaterial for the purposes of this argument), but not a list for both Jesus and the Christ, it would be contradicting sound reason to conclude that 'Jesus is the Christ'.

The importance of these minimal conditions of linguistic (and conceptual) adequacy cannot be too strongly pressed. When the word 'God' is used it must have some bare features of intelligibility or Christians could not distinguish themselves from Buddhists or even atheists. If the difference between theists and atheists is to be maintained, the word 'God' must describe a 'state of affairs' over which they can disagree. To speak of the term 'God' as relating to a 'state of affairs' as has just been done requires one additional clarifying remark. Such language clearly rests on the assumption that 'God' is, at least in part, a 'disguised description' and not *only* a proper name as some have argued. It may not be *only* a 'disguised description', but it seems apparent that it must always have, as a necessary constitutive factor, a descriptive component. The term 'God' does not function like a proper name, and it is a mistake to treat it solely as such.

In the peculiarly Christian context the issue can be put with still more sharpness and point. It is the general view of western theology that Jews and Christians worship the same God. Yet Christians believe that God became incarnate and was present on earth in a unique way in the life and person of Jesus Christ and in his crucifixion and resurrection. Thus, for Christians, both trinitarian and incarnational notions are properly ascribed to God. On the other hand, Jews deny the possibility of 'God becoming man'. For Jews, the word 'God' does not include either trinitarian or incarnational notions, nor, they argue, could it ever do so. One could say that Jews regard the ascription to God of incarnational and trinitarian concepts as category mistakes. Now, either Jews, or Christians, or both, are using the word 'God' incorrectly, that is, they are giving erroneous descriptions. Finally, in the most intimately and specifically Christian and christological context, the issues being raised are central in order for there to exist the possibility of deciding between the competing christological positions of Nestorianism, docetism, etc., and the orthodox formulation of Chalcedon. If the very possibility of getting a minimal description of the christological reality is denied, how can one know what is 'orthodox' with regard to the nature of the reality under discussion? If the nature of the God-man is of the totally mysterious character claimed in certain quarters then it makes absolutely no sense to say who is talking appropriately about the God-man and who is not.

By enquiring what the minimal logical and linguistic conditions of adequacy are, and then asking that they be respected by mystery theologians, we are not trying to decide the truth or falsity of the mystery theologian's claim. That we might nevertheless elicit an answer to this is due to the indissoluble link which binds 'meaning' and 'truth'. The question being asked directly however is the more fundamental question: 'What do the claims of the mystagogues mean?' There is no real escape from this request. The reply: 'Believe!' will not do for three reasons: one does not just 'believe', one 'believes in' something; 'belief in' something entails 'belief that' something; and one has a *logical*

I

right to believe Z only if Z is warranted. Even to say with Tertullian *Credo quia absurdum est*, will not meet the challenge because even Tertullian must tell us what absurdity he is recommending.

The categories of adequacy, correctness, truth and falsity, orthodox and heretic, and many more, all disappear when the theologian adopts the mantle of mystery devotee. The tremendous price paid for the escape into mystery is not generally appreciated by those who seek to utilize this theological gambit. In order to carry on any sort of meaningful theological discussion we must be able to use the sorts of categories just listed. Yet in order to employ these categories we must have rules about language and logic which the mystery theologian, of necessity, must completely abrogate. It is important to point out that what our challenge forces upon the theologian is nothing but the responsibility of making sense.

Finally, the escapism of the mystery theologian is no virtue. In the *Leviathan*, Thomas Hobbes wrote: 'Insignificancy of language, though I cannot note it for false Philosophy; yet it hath a quality, not only to hide the Truth, but also to make men think they have it, and desist from further search.'[1]

IV

The second feature of non-theological mysteries which has already been mentioned is what we may call 'the Principle of Solubility'. This principle is the *a priori* assumption that such mysteries are soluble. There is a problem but the problem can be solved. What is the status of the 'Principle of Solubility' in theological mysteries? Simply put, the principle is rejected. Where the non-theologian asserts that the mysteries he investigates are, *in principle*, soluble, it is the assertion of the theologian that the mysteries he investigates (a curious word in light of the claim made by its proponents, but let it pass for the moment) are, *in principle*, insoluble. Take as paradigmatic the following statement from Gabriel Marcel's 'Metaphysical Diary': 'a genuine problem is

[1] Thomas Hobbes, *Leviathan*. Ch. 46.

subject to an appropriate technique by the exercise of which it is defined; whereas a mystery by definition transcends every conceivable technique'.[1]

What are we to make of this theological counter-move? What does it tell us about specifically theological mysteries, and does it clarify or confuse the issues? At first it appears that those who put forward this proposal are making an important and illuminating move in the clarification of religious language. By asserting that religious mysteries are inviolate to the probings of logicians, atheists, and heretics, to say nothing of the curious machinations of the believer, theologians seem to be making a genuinely important point. Not only is there merit in the proposal, but the proposers are in the very strong, indeed enviable, position of making a claim which is not apparently open to the ordinary critical reflections of philosophers and theologians. If one reproaches the mystery theologian about his use of language by pointing out to him that what he is saying does not correspond to ordinary linguistic convention, or any usually acceptable principle of significance, one realizes that he is already conscious of this point. The mystery theologian is not trying to conform to the standard models of linguistic propriety. The crux of his claim is that religious statements which use the notion of mystery conform to their own internal standards.

Upon reflection, we see that the strength of the mystagogue's position is much less than at first appeared. One begins to see that the enshrinement of mystery is not an important theological advance but an obfuscation which itself is in desperate need of clarification. The mystagogue's peculiar use of language involves far-reaching logical and epistemological implications of which he is unaware. First, the mystagogue's concept of 'mystery', and its corresponding concept of 'solubility', are framed in such a way that nothing could ever count as a solution to a theological mystery, and thus these concepts seem to have been emptied of any meaning whatsoever. In other words, the mystery theologian's understanding of 'solution' is deficient in that *every* sort of thing

1 Gabriel Marcel, 'Metaphysical Diary' in *Being and Having* (1949), p. 117.

which might conceivably be offered as a 'solution' is denied *a priori*. Thus the concept retains none of the significance we ordinarily attach to it. Secondly, let us consider the following argument: we ask the mystagogue to produce his concept of 'solution' in order that we may know from what standpoint he is criticizing our usage. For implicit in his criticism of whatever we may offer as a 'solution' is his maintenance of a different concept of 'solution'. Clearly he must have some such notion which he wields as a sword against us. At this point, however, the mystagogue is caught in paradox. If he is unable to reply to our question, or replies that he has no concept of 'solution', it becomes evident that his objections, which at first seemed so important, are of little account and can be disregarded. If, on the other hand, he offers us a meaningful concept of 'solution', he contradicts his most basic premise, namely, that we can never solve certain intractable theological problems because of their unique character, for example, the nature of the 'hypostatic union'.

Having made these objections, two other interesting and curious consequences of mystery theology remain still to be considered. The first is that it proves too much; the second, that it pays too high a price for its seeming inviolability. Let us now treat these curious consequences in turn.

What precisely is the critical import of asserting that mystery theology proves too much? Essentially the point being argued is that whereas the theory claims to make a contribution to the discussion and purports to illuminate the subject through its particular and extreme *via negativa*, in reality it does neither. There are at least three comparatively simple reasons for this unexpected turn.

First, by 'proving' that theological mysteries are insoluble in the sense of being totally unrelated to, or unaffected by, either existential or linguistic considerations, the theologian has proved only that his recommendations are vacuous. By destroying the dialectic between the mysterious and the known, the theologian also destroys the relevance and intelligibility of his own position. The proclamations of mystery theology do not illuminate either the nature of God's being, or any less grand aspect of our world. In the final accounting what difference at all do the propositions of mystery theology make either to clarification and progress in theology, or to an understanding of the furniture of the world?

Secondly, by denying *a priori* that any meaningful answers can be given to theological questions the mystery theologian subverts not only the realm of answers but also the realm of questions. By calling in question the legitimacy of 'answers' one also calls in question the legitimacy of 'questions'. This curious result occurs because the *a priori* exclusion of any possible answer being given to the question turns what seems to be a question on account of its grammatical form, into a 'pseudo-question'. The meaning of 'question' includes, *in principle*, answerability. Therefore, to deny the possible answerability of a question is to deny its true status as a question. This state of affairs undermines the possibility that mystery theology is a valid reply to theological questions. We recall Wittgenstein's saying: 'For an answer which cannot be expressed, the question too cannot be expressed. The *riddle* does not exist. If a question can be put at all, then it is also *possible* to answer it.'[1]

Thirdly, the previous two paragraphs raise, both as a logical consequence and as the most pointed crystallization of this line of criticism, the dilemma of whether the mystery theologian may even affirm that the referents which the term 'mystery' is intended to cover, can be said to be. What is proven by the mystery theologian is not his arguments, but the argument forwarded by the agnostic. In a sentence where the predicate place is taken by the words 'is a mystery', for example, 'the incarnation is a mystery', not only do we not know what the predicate of the sentence means but we do not know what the subject of the sentence means. The result of using 'is a mystery' in the predicate place cancels out both itself and the subject of the sentence (whatever the subject might be).

Just as Kant had no justification for claiming to know that the noumenal exists, the theologian who begins with the absolute

[1] Ludwig Wittgenstein, *Tractatus*, § 6.5 – the translation is my own.

otherness of God, or of the nature of the incarnation, is unjustified in claiming either that God exists or that the incarnation occurred. Either the various mysteries are unknown and incapable of linguistic formulation, or they are known to exist and are, of necessity, formulable, at least minimally, in propositional form. On their own general principles there is really no warrant for claiming either the existence of Kant's 'noumenon' or the theologian's 'mystery'. If we are injudicious enough to allow either into our ontology on the basis of the, *in principle*, unverifiable claims of either Kant or the theologian, we have opened the gates for an endless proliferation of entities, all now invested with ontic equality. The consequence of this would be to deny ourselves any chance of constructing a rule for deciding what does exist and what does not exist, and thereby also denying to ourselves the possibility of making the world intelligible.

The logically curious result of a rigorous defence of our model: 'For any ø, M is not ø', is that the defence cancels itself out. No category or predicate being applicable to M, M effectively drops out of the language. It must be quickly added that it is unusual to find a consistent employment of this model, as most theologians move, at the risk of self-contradiction, on two levels. It is usual to find that ø is ruled out by protectors of M on the basis of undeclared referential connotations ordinarily associated with the respective ø and M under review. One cannot, however, have it both ways: either the meaning of M is a mystery, in which case one cannot legitimately invoke the ordinary associations of M to dissociate it from ø; or the meaning and associations of M are at least partly known and it is on the basis of this knowledge that M is dissociated from ø, in which case the basic claim of the mystery theologian has been contradicted.

The other serious critical shortcoming of mystery theology is what I have called 'paying too high a price'. This shortcoming causes us to consider what is the precise import of the notion that one cannot ascribe predicates of any sort to the ultimate subjects of religious faith. It appears at first that this principle vouchsafes not only the mystery but also the teachings of the theologian himself. Not only can nothing count decisively, or otherwise, against the mystery, but nothing seems to be able to count against the teachings of the mystery theologian. However, this critical virginity which the mystery theologian assumes is too fragile a thing. The principles of significance which preserve and make possible the conditions under which the statements of the mystery theologians can be taken as meaningful statements, are intimately and necessarily connected to more general principles of linguistic usage. The proposition that no language or cognitive methodological procedure is capable of yielding a diminution of the mystery, calls in question not only the general principles of logic and language but also the concordant principles which underlie the propositions made by the mystery theologian. In other words, the possibility of articulating the specific propositions needed by the mystery theologian requires the possibility of coherent articulation in general. To drive a logical wedge between the former and the latter is to deny the structure which makes it possible for us to make the propositions of the former meaningful to ourselves.

The theologian forfeits too much when he claims that theology, or christology, is at heart a mystery. For in making his claim he commits himself to the paradoxical position of denying the justification for making even his own negative statements. What is the status of the statement 'God is beyond language', or 'the incarnation is the ultimate mystery'? If one denies the warrant for the entire class of statements which have, in our case, either 'God' or the 'incarnation' as their referent, then it follows that the statements in which our mystery theologian frames his account are also unwarranted as falling under that class of statement. If 'all X is not Z' is true, then 'some X is Z' is false.

We began this paper by stating the basis from which the claim of mystery theology is generated. That is, the qualitative disjunction believed to be necessarily inherent in all predicates applied to God from those applied to man. We predicate of the divine transcendental and experience-transcending attributes, while we predicate of man only those attributes commensurate with his limited nature and the space-time world he inhabits. Our analysis, however, reveals a serious dilemma. If it is the case that all ordinarily significant concepts are illegitimately employed in talking of the divine, then we have no significant or legitimate way of specifying any condition for the use of language in religious discourse. The conceptual product of the employment of such a principle of predication is, at best, some formal concept of an 'absolutely unconditioned X'. However, the necessary corollary of this formal notion of an 'absolutely unconditioned X' is the illegitimacy of drawing on orthodox theological disjunctions, such as finite versus infinite; temporal versus eternal; perfect versus imperfect, and so on. In fact, however, these disjunctions are called upon to justify the initial movement in the direction of mystery theology. The casual and unselfconscious employment of these traditional polarities by mystery theologians suggests that the principle of predication can be disregarded with impunity. This impunity is an illusion. The mystery theologian violates his own principles of significance and predication only at the price of making his claims nonsensical.

Without a doubt, we must find room in our conceptual scheme for limiting conditions, for circumscribing the boundaries of that world which we can make intelligible. Yet we must reject the senseless proposal of those theologians who argue that no linguistic proposition is, or ever can be, appropriate with respect to the divine reality. There are many things we do not know, and there are many things which we know but about which our ancestors had no conception. Nevertheless, this *learning* process must not be confused with the *ignoramibus* of the mystery theologian.

V

There is one more argument which has still to be considered. It belongs to the general family of arguments discussed in this paper yet at the same time is deserving of its own detailed criticism. I refer to what I call the 'asymptotic argument'. Consideration of the logic of this particular argument in relation to mystery theology has much to teach us.

It is sometimes suggested that religious language about God is asymptotic. That is, words used in theological propositions are not used descriptively or predicatively. When we say 'God is good', the word 'good' is not predicated of God in the same literally descriptive way as the word 'black' is predicated of coal in the proposition 'coal is black'. Moreover, when we say 'God is good', we use 'good' in a way analogous to, but different from, the way in which we use the same word in 'Rebecca is good'. Another way of putting this is to say that whereas we might affirm that it is *simply true* of coal that it is black, we never say of any theological proposition that it is *simply true*. Instead according to the asymptotic analysis of religious language, words, when used theologically, are not a 'perfect fit', but rather approach the objects of reference, or specific theological 'state of affairs', obliquely and in a manner which points towards, rather than describes them. Perhaps we can, through care and refinement, make theological language more and more appropriate but we can never – and this is a logical 'never' – construct a language which describes the objects of ultimate concern.

The propriety of this familiar theological gambit seems no more in question in mystery theology than elsewhere, and it appears at first sight that mystery theologians are no more and no less vulnerable than, say, Thomists who speak of analogical predication, or those theologians who hold that all religious language is symbolic in character. This, however, is not the case. Whatever the merits or defects of analogical predication, or of the argument that religious language is symbolic (two alternative asymptotic systems), the introduction of asymptoticity in defence of mystery theology is indefensible. The mystery theologian has committed himself in ways which make impossible the assimilation of his procedure with other theological procedures. The axioms with which the mystery theologian begins destroy the essential polarity which must exist for asymptotic systems to function.

By denying the possibility of being able to make any meaning-ful (and true) statements in theology the mystery theologian has cut himself off from any asymptotic defence, because, on the basis of his axioms the mystery theologian is, necessarily, unable to give any content, for example, to the term 'incarnation' in: 'The incarnation is a mystery', or again, to the term 'God' in: 'God is the ultimate mystery'. Any attempt to give content to either of these terms is self-contradictory and self-defeating. By the rules of the game, any statement that seems able to supply the needed explication of the terms 'incarnation' or 'God' is, *a priori*, inter-dicted, and this rules out the possibility of treating our two examplary statements as asymptotes. If we consider the form of an asymptote, the reasons why this is so will become obvious. A standard asymptotic model looks like this:

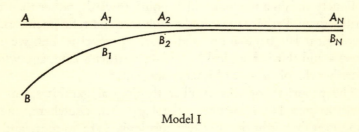

Model I

The line A and curve B continue *ad infinitum* to approach but never to meet each other. Consider now that in the legitimate employ-ment of this model in theology the theological reality, i.e. 'God' or 'the incarnation', takes the place of line A. Theological language, which can never apply to God literally, takes the place of curve B. Given the location and specification of A we can make meaningful statements about the asymptotic relation which ob-tains between A and B. This is the conditioned relation which is believed to obtain in systems of analogical predication and symbolic meaning.

If, however, we try to diagram the appropiate asymptotic model of mystery theology, we get the following:

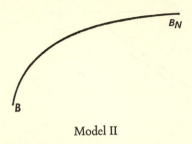

Model II

'But', comes the chorus, 'that is no model of asymptoticity. Where is the approaching line?' Now it is true that Model II is not an asymptotic model nor does it impart any information. Unfortunately, however, despite these crippling shortcomings, it is the appropriate model for the translation of the position of mystery in theology into the asymptotic mode. Following Model I, let the missing line *A* be the theological reality, i.e. 'the incarnation' or 'God'. Let curve *B* be the language of mystery theology. Then we come face to face with the central problem. In order to provide the asymptotic line *A*, we would have to be able to specify and locate it. Yet this procedure is not open. We cannot draw a line *A* which has a fixed reference and which will help us understand the relation between it and curve *B*. We do not have any warrant for even assuming the existence of line *A*. The mystery theologian has not argued for any principle which would allow for its construction. We have no justification for assuming that any asymptotic relation in fact obtains in mystery theology; on the contrary, we have *prima facie* justification that it does not.

Even if we leave this extreme conclusion aside for the moment for the sake of argument, and grant that the reality to which line *A* corresponds does in fact exist, we still cannot employ any asymptotic model meaningfully. For in any case where no more than the proposition 'God exists' is granted – the strongest

possible permissible form the mystery thesis can take – we have
the following unsatisfactory model:

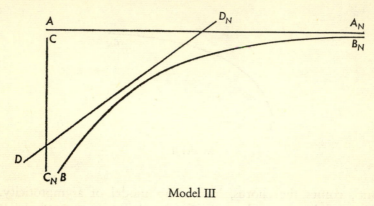

Model III

Breaking down this complex model into more simple sub-models
we have:

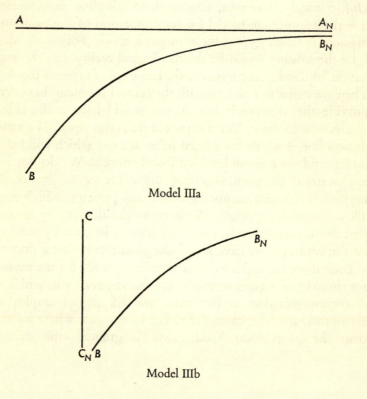

Model IIIa

Model IIIb

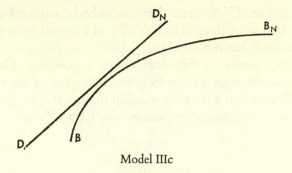

Model IIIc

This third model, however, provides no clarification or advance for the mystery theologian because there is no way to decide which of its three sub-models (a, b, or c) is correct or even *more nearly correct* than the other two. Translating this into an argument about religious language we see that mystery theology makes it impossible to decide which language is appropriate and which is not appropriate in talking about, for example, 'the incarnation' or 'God'. No statement or term can claim superior status in the theological vocabulary. Thus, when attempting to discuss 'God', for example, we can give no reasons for choosing the words 'good', 'loving', 'merciful', etc., over words like 'hateful', 'mean', or 'cruel', etc., as being indicative, however inadequately, of God's character or relational posture to man and the world. What we have in mystery theology is not a method of making at least one meaningful assertion about the divine, e.g. 'God is the ultimate mystery', but a method of meaningless mystification.

A final important point which this discussion of asymptoticity brings into focus is that of reifying mystery. It is an easy, but mistaken, step to treat 'mystery' in such a sentence as 'The hypostatic union is a mystery', as if it were 'a something when it is a nothing', to paraphrase an idiom of Wittgenstein's.

The confusion which results from supposing that all substantives are substances (again I echo Wittgenstein), is marvellously brought out in Lewis Carroll's *Alice Through the Looking Glass*: ' "I see nobody on the road", said Alice. "I only wish I had such eyes", the King remarked in a fretful tone. "To be able to see Nobody and at that distance too!"' To treat the term 'nobody' as if it referred to a very special sort of thing is to be guilty of a logical error that one can understand but not condone.

Scepticism regarding the relevance and importance of language and logic to theology brings to mind the saying of the wit who wrote: 'Where it is a duty to worship the sun it is pretty sure to be a crime to investigate or examine the laws of heat.'

VII

This essay began by raising the question of the alternative logic and usage of the word 'mystery' in non-theological and theological contexts. It was pointed out that the two uses were decidedly different. We have now had a much closer look at what the theological usage amounts to and where this usage of the word takes us. What recommendations can be made?

First, it seems obvious that it is a profound failure of theological nerve to adopt the epistemological position which asserts that neither ordinary language nor logic is relevant to theology. For the retreat into the mysterious is nothing but theological escapism. The feeling of certain men that they can say nothing about God is no warrant for the acceptance of this position as descriptive of the true situation. When theologians begin by assuming that they cannot make any true statement in theology, it is little wonder that they do not make any true theological statements in fact. When theologians begin with the axiom that religious language is a clumsy and inappropriate tool, it is no wonder that their language is clumsy and inappropriate. The retreat into the paradoxical and meaningless contortions of mystery theology is an uncalled for and unwarranted capitulation to the sophisticated attack of modern scepticism.

Secondly, and in the broadest possible terms, it is a fatal mistake to divorce theological and christological language from ordinary language. Whatever the peculiarities of theological discourse, it is not so peculiar that it bears no relation to anything else in God's world. To invoke some non-logical 'logic' as justification for talking nonsense is not to save but to sacrifice the integrity and relevance of the theologian's effort.

The point is well put by Mephistopheles:

> Have but contempt for reason and for science,
> Although they truly are man's best reliance,
> And let the Prince of Lies confound confusion
> By luring you toward magic and illusion –
> And you are on the road to hell.[1]

---

[1] Goethe's *Faust*, pt 1, lines 1851–5; a new translation by Walter Kaufman (Anchor Book, 1961).

15

THE APPEAL TO EXPERIENCE IN
CHRISTOLOGY

B. L. HEBBLETHWAITE

Much current criticism of traditional christology seems to rest either on an unexamined appeal to experience or on an over-valuation of the role of experience in determining the content of Christian doctrine. On the one hand it is suggested, by John Robinson, for example, that our contemporary experience of the world makes it impossible for us to retain, say, the two-natures doctrine of Chalcedon. That is to say, appeals to the this-worldly, secular, relativistic character of contemporary experience are supposed to clinch the *refutation* of the kind of christology enshrined in the creeds. On the other hand, historical studies are alleged, by Maurice Wiles, for example, to show that it was the early Christians' experience of redemption that largely determined the doctrine of Christ's divinity. In other words, doctrine in the ancient world was, at least in part, *established* by appeals to a particular kind of religious experience. It is far from clear that adequate consideration has been given to the question whether appeals to experience, secular or religious, can decide such issues one way or the other.

The question of *refutation* is ambiguous. Clearly there are discoveries that would refute Christian doctrine, the discovery, for instance, that Jesus never existed. Or again if Christian doctrine could be shown to bear no relation to experience whatsoever, that would be enough, if not to refute it, then at least to render it inconsequential. But these are not the senses in which it is claimed that our contemporary experience of the world makes it impossible for us to retain the traditional theology of incarnation. Behind the suspicion of such theology lies, rather, a general thesis about modern man's way of experiencing the world, which seems to be assumed or intuited rather than argued for. And it is the failure to analyse the concept of experience and the scope of appeals to experience that makes one dissatisfied with such appeals.

The inadequacy of experience-claims to *establish* Christian doctrine is more obvious still. Indeed it is widely agreed that the old appeals to Christian experience of redemption are insufficient by themselves to establish the divinity of Christ. What is less widely agreed is that in the nature of the case this must be so. An analysis of the concept of experience will show that appeals to Christian experience should never have been expected to decide the credibility of Christian doctrine. And an analysis of the nature and role of doctrinal syntheses will show that their relation to experience could never be that of conclusion to premiss.

It is not difficult to see why appeals to experience should be over-valued in the modern world. The collapse of the old author-ities – scripture and tradition – led theologians to look for a different basis for Christian doctrine, and there was a widespread tendency to take refuge in appeals to experience. But the reaction was too hasty. Appeal to experience is not the only resort when the old authorities are gone. The purpose of this essay is not only to show the inevitable inadequacy of appeals to experience, Christian or otherwise, but also to endorse a positive alternative, namely, appeal to the inner rationale of Christian doctrine. This must, of course, be accompanied by some indication of the real relation of doctrine to experience.

The bankruptcy of appeals to experience in christology is shown by the common tendency towards what has been called reductionism. Far from introducing a note of realism into a doctrinal system allegedly based on a mythological world-view, reductionism leads to a most unrealistic exposition of Christian belief. For the purely human Christ, however open to the will of God, cannot possibly carry the weight of significance which is still attributed to him.

I

What do we mean by 'experience'? The concept is a very complex one. The word itself comes from the Latin verb 'experior', meaning 'try', 'prove' or 'put to the test'. It comes to mean, as the dictionary tells us, 'the state of being consciously affected by an event', presumably because appeal to such a state is the most obvious way of testing some claim. To know something by experience is to know it by direct acquaintance, say, by one's own observation, rather than to have read about it, or been told about it by someone else. If I appeal to experience, I am appealing to first hand, personal acquaintance with the matter in question. The concept acquires a subjective side, when it is the felt or perceived qualities of the events experienced that are being stressed, and a more objective side, when interest centres on the actual events which have presented themselves to an individual or to a community. When Sir Maurice Bowra writes about *The Greek Experience* he is interested in the subjective side, in the way events in the world, indeed the world itself, and life itself, were felt and perceived by the Greeks. If, on the other hand, I ask a traveller about his experience in a foreign land, I am more interested in what he saw and in what actually took place – that is, in the objective side.

Mention of *The Greek Experience* indicates something of the concept's complexity. Clearly it is possible to talk about collective experience, if a group or generation or society is held to respond to particular events or to the world in general in a characteristic way. This shows that we are not passive recipients of identical impressions; but both bring to and extract from experience a variety of attitudes, presuppositions, and schemata of interpretation, which change from age to age. Not only do our subjective attitudes vary, but also what is to count as an objective event varies according to our interpretative presuppositions. The amount of interpretation depends on the scope of the experience-claim. There can be little dispute over a claim to have seen bright flashes and heard loud bangs. The claim that one has experienced a thunderstorm involves much more interpretation, whether it stems from general knowledge or from meteorological expertise. The claim that one has experienced the anger of Zeus applies a totally different framework of interpretation.

The problem then arises of the relation between these various claims, of whether they are mutually compatible or exclusive; and here one finds oneself arguing about theories and beliefs. But one thing is quite clear: this kind of issue cannot be settled by an appeal to subjective states; for it is the interpretation of subjective states that is in question.

Philosophers have attempted from time to time to fix the limits of experience, to delineate, that is, the area within which we may legitimately make experience-claims. It is very difficult to see how this can be done *a priori*. The most plausible attempt to do so was that of Kant, but he was only able to produce a watertight account of the conditions of experience by exaggerating the extent to which our conceptual framework, as it were, imposes itself on reality. Most modern assumptions concerning the limits of experience make the same mistake, only without Kant's self-consciousness. It is much better to make neither stipulations nor assumptions about the limits of experience, and investigate any experience-claim on its own merit.

The scope of experience-claims obviously varies in accordance with the nature of the object of experience – be it the external world, another mind, love, life in general, the world as a whole, or God. Let us take the example of religious experience. If I claim to know God by experience, I am certainly in the first place contrasting my knowledge with hearsay or the contents of a book. The question then arises, what is it to have experience of God? Clearly it is something different from experience of the external world, which can simply be checked by observation. It involves subjective states (more complex ones than those of perception) but cannot possibly be identified with them. To identify some experience as experience of God is to correlate my subjective states, my feelings and impressions, with a whole interpretative scheme given to me by my religion. This is not to deny the importance of my subjective states. I do not simply read about reconciliation and conclude that I am at peace with God. I am personally involved. The gospel speaks to my condition. My life is totally affected. Now I interpret this state of affairs as experience of God. The interpretative scheme makes sense of my subjective experience, and this enables me to construe it as experience of God. But the interpretation is not just read off the experience.

There are alternative ways of accounting for my subjective experience. There might be some psychological explanation, for example. If this were held to be a complete explanation, it would obviously conflict with my claim to have had experience of God. So the question of true or false accounts arises. The point to notice is that different interpretations involve different accounts of what my experience is of. The dispute is not over different ways of looking at the same thing. The subjective experience is not itself the 'thing' in question; nor is it agreed simply that 'the world' is the object of my experience. It is not a matter of there being an agreed set of uninterpreted facts which can be described now in secular, now in religious language. We are not talking simply about different ways of looking at the world, as though one could agree on what the world is and then disagree on how to evaluate it. Interpretation comes in long before we start talking about our experience of the world. (You cannot rule out the transcendent before you have started examining what might count as experience of the transcendent.) Religious language provides not just a possible attitude to the world and to life in the world, but includes a definitive account of what the world is in relation to the transcendent, and only because this account is believed to be true does the further question of appropriate attitudes arise. Moreover any particular experience, if it is claimed to be experience of God, can only be identified as such within the whole framework of interpretation which a given religion provides. It is no good bracketing the subjective experience, as it were, and scrutinising it in isolation, in the hope of perceiving its God-relating attributes quite apart from some framework of interpretation.

In what follows I use the term 'experience' largely in this subjective sense. I shall speak of 'the dialectic between experience and interpretation', meaning the way in which it is only some interpretative scheme which enables us to construe our subjective states as experience of something, and at the same time the way in which such schemes are both suggested and modified by experience.

II

I submit that Christian doctrine in general and christology in particular constitute such a total framework of interpretation. I emphasise the systematic nature of the interpretative scheme; for not only does experience demand interpretation, if it is to be identified as experience *of* something, but also it demands the whole framework, not just a particular part of it. Piecemeal attacks on individual doctrines based on the insufficiency of experience to establish them are therefore doubly mistaken. First, they ignore the inevitable gap between experience and interpretation, when viewed as premiss and conclusion. Secondly, they ignore the systematic nature of doctrinal syntheses – the interrelations of doctrine involved. This does not mean that experience is irrelevant, nor that all one needs is a tidy and coherent pattern of interrelated ideas. We cannot speak of the inner rationale of the interpretative scheme, without some indication of the way the system is applied in the interpretation of experience. The theologian is bound to be moving to and fro between experience-claims and doctrinal syntheses, but he must recognise the complexity of the relations between them, and especially this lack of one-to-one correlation between particular subjective experiences and particular doctrines. For the latter find their rationale within a whole, which is supported by experience only in the sense that it enables us to interpret our experience and construe it as Christian experience of God.

There is, of course, a fundamental historical problem here. The dialectic between systematic structures of interpretation and the particular experiences of individuals and groups extends across two thousand years of history. And so, in christology, we have not only to make sense of our own experience, and the experience of previous generations, but to relate both ours and theirs to the initial experience of the earliest Christians. We are not only concerned with the gap between experience and interpretation now, nor with this problem as one on which ideas have changed over the centuries, but also with the apparent inaccessibility of the historical facts behind the first Christian experience. Christianity seems to depend on particular facts about Jesus, but there is no direct access to the life of Jesus. However sure we may be of its broad outlines and salient characteristics, there can be no denying that they reach us already interpreted; and it is the already interpreted fact of Jesus Christ that provides the criterion for identifying specifically Christian experience of God as such.

It is also true that very great cultural changes have taken place between the early centuries, when the interpretative scheme of Christian doctrine was being worked out for the first time, and the present day. The enlightenment and the rise of modern science have greatly affected any attempt at total explanation, and particular discoveries have necessitated the revision of long established doctrines. The question of continuity across such cultural divides is the major question facing the church today. But two things should be remembered before we cut ourselves off completely from the experience and the interpretation of the early centuries or the medieval period for that matter. First, if Christianity is true, it is the same relation between God and the world that we with our cultural presuppositions are trying to articulate as they were with theirs. Secondly, we cannot make our own contemporary experience absolute. That would be to reject an old interpretative scheme simply by the wholesale adoption of a new one – namely empiricism. Few theologians actually argue a case for such a procedure. When Paul van Buren does so in *The Secular Meaning of the Gospel*, the resulting position is manifestly untenable.

If then there are continuities across the cultural divides of history, what is it that does make us develop and rewrite Christian doctrine? I shall argue that it is not so much some vague appropriation of modern man's view of the world, as critical reflection on the interpretative scheme itself, in the light of particular historical and scientific discoveries.

The systematic interrelation of Christian doctrines in a total interpretative framework is such that the rejection of a particular belief has very wide ramifications throughout the whole system and cannot be accommodated by piecemeal adjustments here and there. This does not mean that such large scale re-alignments never happen. One case where it has been necessary to rethink the whole system in the light of a particular change is that of the doctrine of the fall. The old model of original righteousness, fall and original sin has had to be rejected in favour of a new model of gradual creation, developing moral consciousness and a future goal. But this change has been forced upon us not by some I know not what modern way of experiencing the world, but by some highly specific scientific discoveries about the age and nature of the earth and the evolution of life on its surface. It should be noted in passing that no such difficulties attend the doctrine of creation; for its intelligibility and explanatory force are undisturbed by the recognition of the mythological nature of the stories in the book of Genesis.

If we were forced to reject the doctrine of the incarnation, there would certainly have to be a complete re-fashioning of the Christian framework of interpretation; for, as I hope to show later, the specifically Christian understanding of revelation and reconciliation – i.e. the Christian gospel – depends for its distinctive contribution wholly on the incarnation. But what conceivable scientific discovery, parallel to those which necessitated our abandonment of the doctrine of the fall, could demand abandonment of the doctrine of the incarnation? The case is entirely different. Would-be reductionists can only appeal to their own inability to conceive of what incarnation means, or to some general concept of contemporary experience which is supposed to rule it out. But the former is no argument at all, and the latter begs the question of the relation between experience and interpretation.

If appeal to experience alone can neither refute nor establish Christian doctrine, it is a fair question to ask how such a framework of interpretation arises, and by what criteria we are to justify or to develop it. The answer seems to be that the interpretative scheme is the result of inter-subjective reflection and argument within the community in the light of (a) previous interpretative schemes – i.e. those provided by the faith of Israel and by contemporary philosophies, (b) particular events – i.e. the words and deeds of Jesus viewed retrospectively in the light of the resurrection, and (c) the experiences, individual and collective, of belonging to the community. These latter, however significant and however exalted, could not possibly by themselves establish Christian doctrine. Rather it is the interaction of all three features – interpretation, event and experience – that creates and sustains a coherent system of doctrine which itself becomes the object of reflection and development in the context of cultural and philosophical change, and in response to particular historical and scientific discoveries.

Let us look at these three features in turn. In the first place, the whole process from the initial response of the disciples to Jesus, through the resurrection and the preaching and community life of the early Christians, up to the formulation of christological doctrine, takes place within the contexts provided in the first instance by the faith of Israel, and then by the various contemporary philosophical and religious ideas of the Hellenistic world. Now the faith of Israel includes already a highly developed framework for the interpretation of history and experience. This cannot be dismissed as a primitive and alien phenomenon with no point of contact with our contemporary experience. We have at least to explore the possibility that it represents a real response to genuine revelation, at however early a stage in the development of human self-consciousness this may have taken place. And if one presses back for the experiential grounds of Israel's faith, one eventually finds oneself postulating some combination of experience and reflection in a nomadic desert tribe of which one knows absolutely nothing, so loaded with interpretation is even the earliest record we possess of Israel's faith in its infancy. This attempt to look for uninterpreted experience behind the constructions of doctrine is now seen for what it is – a will o' the wisp – and an example of the genetic fallacy into the bargain. For doctrine is not rightly understood in terms of some original experience, but in terms of its ability as a rationally structured system to make sense of the actual relation between God and man.

Similarly Greek philosophy, however inadequate its comprehension of reality may now be thought to be, at least succeeded in fashioning a language in which real metaphysical problems

could be raised and discussed. And behind the language of christology, there are metaphysical issues – problems of the relation
between time and eternity, for instance, or that between immanence and transcendence; and there are inescapable ontological
problems involved if we are really talking about the relation
between God's reality and the world's reality, and not about a
particular way of looking at a world whose being and nature is
supposed to be thoroughly understood by contemporary man.

Certainly there are very great differences between the faith
of Israel and Greek metaphysical thought, but they both represent
developed ways of interpreting experience in the world, the one
in terms of divine revelation, the other in terms of rational
principle. Furthermore, if one believes in a real creator – creature
relation, it should hardly be surprising to discover points of
contact between revelation and metaphysical reflection. In fact
the Logos concept provided a very fertile means of bringing the
two interpretative complexes together.

Nevertheless, secondly, the peculiarly Christian contribution
proved to be a very distinctive concept of incarnation, which gave
a concrete and particular form to the more diffuse ideas of revelation which characterised the faith of Israel, and also to the general
rational concepts of the relation between the eternal and the
temporal which characterised Greek thought. Here it was the life,
death and resurrection of Jesus Christ that created, within the
context first of the faith of Israel, then of Hellenistic thought, the
doctrine of the incarnation. In particular, of course, it was the resurrection which enabled the life and death of Jesus to be construed
in more than human terms. It is not necessary to trace here the
development of christological concepts from Messiah-designate,
through the Logos and Heavenly Man christologies, right up to the
developed doctrine of the incarnation. What is important is to stress
the role of the particular events and especially the resurrection, as
handed down in the kerygma, and made the subject of theological
reflection, in evoking both the practical response of the Christian
community – its existence, life and worship – and the intellectual
response of christology.

The third factor behind the development of the characteristically Christian interpretation is, of course, the individual and group experience of the early church. Unless men's actual relation to God was transformed, and unless they actually experienced this new relation, whatever subjective form such experience took, any suggested remodelling of old interpretative schemes would have been inconsequential. In other words an interpretative framework must be found in experience to work and to make sense of that experience. It is not the case that the experience creates the interpretation. Neither does the interpretation create the experience. One would be tempted to say that it is the pressure of reality itself – the situation in which men find themselves, and the actual events that take place within that situation that creates both experience and interpretation, were it not for the fact that it is only through the dialectical interplay of experience and interpretation that men find themselves confronted by the real at all. So in the case in question it is the situation set up by the events of the life, death and resurrection of Jesus Christ, understood within the context of the faith of Israel, and yet transforming Israel's understanding of man's relation to God and that of the contemporary Hellenistic world, that makes possible, and is authenticated by, the early Christians' experience of salvation.

Now the developed structure of Christian interpretation is such that our Christian experience of God is understood to be both possible and intelligible, just because God both revealed himself to us and reconciled us to himself in a highly specific way – namely by coming amongst us and sharing our lot. There may be other concepts of revelation, which involve purely human mediators, or which consist in the direct impartation of certain truths or texts, but the Christian concept is that of a God who not only reveals himself to us by sharing our situation, but who in one and the same act achieves our reconciliation. In other words, for Christian interpretation, revelation and reconciliation come to much the same thing, just because the forgiveness and the love of God are shown so absolutely and concretely in his humiliation; nor can we distinguish showing and making real where reconciliation is concerned. For this is the way, according to Christian interpretation, in which God actually brings about our reconciliation, namely, by coming amongst us and loving us even at the cost of the cross.

The last paragraph has oversimplified the situation by leaving out the considerations, partly stemming from, partly constitutive of, trinitarian theology, which make us speak of the incarnation of the Son of God, rather than the incarnation of God *simpliciter*. Nevertheless, on the basis of the principle, *opera trinitatis ad extra sunt indivisa*, we need not hold back from making this simplification and speaking here of the incarnation in terms of God made man.

What is being stressed is the uniquely determining role of the incarnation in revelation and reconciliation, where the total framework of Christian interpretation is concerned. No doubt there is more to be said about how we are to conceive of the incarnation, and the reference to divine humiliation obviously points in the direction of a kenotic christology. But it should be clear now that we cannot abandon the concept of incarnation without destroying the whole fabric of the Christian interpretation, which involves the claim that God has related himself to the world in a particular way which we have to discover. It is not a matter of sitting back and thinking first about God and then about man, and speculating on how we might conceivably bring them together. The fact that God has come amongst us is integral to the Christian scheme of interpretation, not as a necessary deduction from some transcendental premiss, but as part of the dialectical process of letting brute fact change our understanding and bringing understanding to brute fact.

In the course of the continuing interaction between experience and interpretation, many false steps were taken and blind alleys tried out, as in the early heresies: either they led to incoherence, or they failed to make sense in terms of experience. But it was also the case, as it obviously still is, that many quite inadequate arguments were used, and false perspectives encouraged for a time, within more orthodox approaches. For example several of the Fathers found themselves arguing that unless the incarnate Son assumed a particular aspect of humanity, that aspect would remain unredeemed. The argument has no force whatever.

Presumably God could have redeemed man in quite some other way, or by divine fiat, and in any case redemption is not to be conceived of in such a mechanical way. We have seen that the Christian interpretation does not posit the incarnation as a divine necessity, but as the way which as a matter of fact – of grace, to use theological language – he has taken in revelation and reconciliation. Consequently one should be wary of attaching too much weight to the particular arguments which were used at particular stages of development. What matters is the inner rationale of the developed system and its ability to interpret experience. The detection of a weak or inadequate inference on the part of the Fathers does not necessarily discredit the system.

III

Talk of the inner rationale of the interpretative scheme does, of course, presuppose the intelligibility of the concept of incarnation, if the incarnation is held to be the lynch-pin of the specifically Christian framework of interpretation. Given its intelligibility it obviously has to be compatible with, or even, within the context of Jewish and Hellenistic thought, suggested by the known facts about Jesus of Nazareth; and it has to make sense of the experience of Christians, early and late. But, as was pointed out above, it is not a notion that could possibly be established by a series of experience-claims, any more than it could be refuted by some scientific discovery. There is of course, as was said at the beginning, a certain vulnerability – not to scientific discovery, as in the case of the doctrine of the fall – but to historical discovery, say, that Jesus never existed or was a murderer. But it is one thing to say that there are historical truth-conditions of the Christian doctrine of incarnation; quite another to say that it could ever be established by historical research. It is the intelligibility of the doctrine, then, to which we must finally turn.

It has already been suggested that some modern theologians find fault with the doctrine on quite inadequate grounds or on no grounds at all. Notably it is the appeal to the way modern man experiences the world that is held somehow to render the doctrine unintelligible. This woolly criterion does justice neither to what was said in the past, nor to what can be said today.

To take the latter point first. It is very difficult to see what objections to the doctrine of incarnation are not also objections to belief in God *tout court*. Given belief in God, it is far from clear how any experience, ancient or modern, can dictate how he is to relate to the world or make himself present in the world. Nor does this observation reflect a naive or mythological concept of God. For the argument that God must be thought of in such a way as to allow us to express his relation to the world in the language of incarnation is not much more than a formal argument. It prescribes very little in the way of a positive notion of God, except the basic open concepts of 'creator' or 'ground', which are necessary conditions of any meaningful talk of God. In other words the only concept of God ruled out by 'incarnation' language is that which interprets God-talk as simply a way of talking about the world – and that, I would claim, is not a concept of God at all. So long as it remains possible to talk about a relation between God and the world, it must be possible to consider the concept of incarnation. For incarnation means the *particular* presence of the eternal in the spatio-temporal world, the divine in the human, and there are no *a priori* grounds for ruling out that particularity.

It might be argued that, to talk meaningfully of incarnation we have to presuppose a personal rather than an impersonal concept of God and that this determines the concept of God more positively, and more mythologically, than I have allowed. There are two points here. The question whether personal language is presupposed seems to me to be a substantial issue between the religions of East and West, and not an issue concerned with the logic of theism as such. Secondly the suggestion that all personal language, in an attempt to articulate the structure of theism, is inevitably mythological, presupposes a 'closed' theory of language whereby all analogical predication results immediately in mythology.

Indeed it is the reductionists who seem to be operating with a mythological concept of God. For their rejection of the two-natures doctrine presupposes that it is possible to get a clear concept of divine nature, and then unite it somehow with our concept of human nature. Most of the difficulties in christology spring from just such a presupposition, as Bonhoeffer pointed out in his christology lectures. Not only is it the case that the logic of theism requires us to refrain from thinking that we can grasp the divine nature and therefore articulate precisely the relation of incarnation, but also the whole point of the doctrine of incarnation is that here the inexpressible is expressed, and what is beyond our understanding is given to us in a form which we can understand. There is no point in claiming that the humanity reveals the divinity, if the divinity is perfectly accessible apart from this revelation. The concepts of rational theism are in the nature of the case open and – in the technical sense – incomprehensible.

Consequently it is unjust to the scope of the old formulae to dismiss them on the grounds that they presuppose a mythological concept of God. Rather they are specifically designed to exclude the kind of arguments which follow from a supposed grasp of the divine nature. And if the orthodox indulged in such arguments at times just as much as the heretics, that is no reason for us today to throw out the whole interpretative scheme. For the basic insight holds – that it is of the essence of Christian theism that the eternal incomprehensible God is to be met and known in a particular man.

These reflections on the intelligibility of the concept of incarnation within the total structure of Christian theism are offered in the course of an essay on the appeal to experience in christology. I hope it will now be clearer why I hold that there is an alternative reaction to the challenge to the authority of scripture and tradition by the rational and critical thought of the last two hundred years. At first, as I say, theologians tended to take refuge in the appeal to experience. But experience turned out to be an inadequate support. Now the wheel has turned full circle and experience is being called upon to refute the classical doctrine of the incarnation and justify reductionism. But a closer examination of the concept of experience, and in particular a recognition of the continuing dialectic between experience and interpretation in any profound response to reality, will not only put a question mark against the suggestion that experience by itself can settle such questions one way or the other. It will also show something of the inner rationale of doctrinal syntheses and the way in which they in fact relate to experience. What we need in christology, as in all branches of theology, is an analysis of the internal structure of developed and developing doctrinal syntheses, together with an examination of the way they relate living traditions of religion and philosophy both to the life, death and resurrection of Jesus Christ and to individual and group experience in the past and in the present.

16

'SUBSTANCE' IN CHRISTOLOGY –
A CROSS-BENCH VIEW

D. M. MACKINNON

I

The use of the notion of substance in establishing the relation of
Christ to the Father, the doctrine of the trinity, and indeed the
relation of divine and human in the person of the incarnate Lord,
has come in for a great deal of criticism. Some of this criticism is
very well founded; thus one is perfectly justified in asking what
conceivable significance the proclamation of Jesus Christ as of one
substance with the Father can be thought to have for the members
of the average Christian congregation today. True, the phrase
occurs in the Nicene creed, traditionally said or sung at the
eucharist at least on Sundays and feasts; but in the context of that
confession the formal becomes suffused with the mysteriousness
of the creed's affirmations concerning the Son as its successive
clauses move towards the climactic assertion (in frankly mythological language) of his descent from heaven and his incarnation
by the Holy Ghost of the virgin Mary. When a modern preacher
or writer seeks to speak or write of the mystery of Christ's person,
and in particular his relation to his Father, he is not likely to avail
himself of the conceptual apparatus of substance, nature, etc.; he
will speak rather of, for example, a unique, even an absolute
openness of this man to the Father (ignoring the fact that absolute
is surely a metaphysical concept), or of the expression in this man
of God in human terms, almost suggesting to the uninitiated that
there has been poured out into Christ Jesus such amount (quan-
titatively) of the divine being as an individual human nature can
conceivably contain, *or* of the translation into terms of a human life
of the ways of God with men, presenting implicitly, if not explicitly, the life of Jesus as an acted parable of the creator's dealings
with his creatures, comparable to the parable of the prodigal son

(spoken to reproach the harshly legalistic) but infinitely more telling because it is acted out and is universal in scope. One may query the adequacy of one or all of the foregoing samples of currently fashionable christological discourse. But one will not fault speaker or writer with substituting one or other of them for the idiom of the *homoousion*.

Yet does the fact of their inappropriateness in certain communicational contexts constitute a case against the use of ontological categories in christology? It is sometimes said, for instance by Professor John Burnaby, that the formula 'being of one substance with the Father' does not occur in the scriptures of the New Testament, and that the intentions of those who introduced its use into theology can be adequately fulfilled by the adjacent acclamations of Jesus as 'God of God, Light of Light, Very God of Very God'. Certainly it might be thought a characteristic betrayal of the faithful on the part of theologians (a kind of idolatrous self-indulgence of their own expertise at the expense of its aim of *ministerium verbi divini*) that they lay upon successive generations the burden of mastering a particular metaphysical tradition or a crucial part of it.

I say metaphysical *tradition*: for it is important to see the doctrine of substance less as a precisely formulable dogma than as the name of a series of explorations whose very nature oscillates as they develop. Professor David Knowles in his *Evolution of Medieval Thought* (1962) has neatly characterised Aristotle as foremost among those 'who have sought to trace the veins and sinews of substance', and it is to Aristotle's investigations that I would briefly draw attention. It is not for nothing that R. P. J. M. Le Blond in his excellent *Logique et Méthode chez Aristote* (1939) entitles the section dealing with substance *L'Aporie de la Substance*. If at this point the reader is tempted to recall that Athanasius' philosophical background is Platonic rather than Aristotelian and that therefore it is a mistake to refer to Aristotle, he should also recall the extent to which Plato's theory of forms constitutes the background of Aristotle's discussions. The question 'What exists of itself?' (one of the questions Aristotle's analysis was certainly concerned to answer) was a question to which Plato in his middle dialogues had given an answer in terms of the forms. It was from Plato that Aristotle had learnt to ask this question and the student of Aristotle's *Metaphysics* and *Categories* is continually made aware of the pervasive significance for the later philosopher of his predecessor's enquiries. One is not employing an irrelevant teleology to the interpretation of Aristotle's relations to Plato if one says that in Aristotle's sustained engagement with Plato's ideas some of the ramifications of the latter became plain and that Aristotle is in fact a highly important commentator on the philosophical work of his predecessor. This though his commentary often takes the shape of a sustained and searching criticism.

This indebtedness to Plato undoubtedly has its bearing on the central crux of Aristotle's treatment of substance, *viz.* the extent to which he wavers between identifying substance with the individual natural thing in its concreteness (e.g. this oak tree, this domestic cat, Aspasia, Socrates) and with the form that makes it what it is (oakenness, domestic felinity, womanhood, manhood). It is as if he cannot make up his mind which of the two best merits being regarded as the nuclear or pivotal realisation of being: this because he finds the notions of individual thing, form, particular, universal, so obscure that their treatment daunts even his exceptionally pertinacious analytical intelligence. What certainly emerged from a study of the *Metaphysics* is that he believes that 'first philosophy', a very important part of philosophical enquiry, is concerned to give as comprehensive an account as possible of such notions as thing, quality, existence, causality, truth, which enter into discourse concerning any subject-matter whatsoever, which indeed seem uniquely pervasive in their exemplification. This account inevitably involves him in giving some account of their inter-relations; thus it is very well known that in his classical statement of the so-called 'correspondence theory of truth' Aristotle insists on the primacy of being over truth, and again, as we shall see, the primacy of substance (whether in the sense of concrete thing or of form) over quality and accident.

Because substance is for Aristotle the nuclear realisation of being, he alternates between characterising the subject-matter of metaphysics as substance or being *qua* being. What he sees the metaphysician as concerned with are aspects of the world that are at once totally familiar and everyday, and at the same time highly elusive and even mysterious in the paradoxical character that they immediately disclose to more minute inspection. For this same reason in his own metaphysical practice he seems to oscillate between the most strenuous abstraction, testing to the utmost the reader's power to follow his argument or see what he is getting at, and an attention to the ordinary and concrete that certainly disappoints the intellectual dilettante who picks up Aristotle's *Metaphysics* in the hope of enjoying the bold flights of a great speculative imagination. It is of course very hard indeed to characterise the fruits of Aristotle's analytical enquiries. To appreciate them at all (apart from the linguistic equipment necessary to master his extremely idiosyncratic, highly concentrated, Greek philosophical prose) one must, I suspect, have a feel for the sort of scrutiny of fundamental concepts I have mentioned; one has to be the sort of person whose curiosity is arrested by the highly pervasive roles fulfilled by the notions I have mentioned in discourse, and by the extent to which they are woven into the fabric of the simplest and the most complex factually referential assertions we make or beliefs we entertain about what is the case; one must be arrested by the various paradoxes of which we are made immediately aware when we ask questions concerning the relations of these notions to other concepts, often much less familiar, often much more sophisticated, and which demand a high level of advanced specialised education if we are to learn their correct employment (one has only to think of the key concepts of molecular biology or electronics). But these, if only because of the precision with which they may be defined, are somehow less elusive than the very familiar notions with which Aristotle in the *Metaphysics* is concerned; they find their niche both in the rarefied, technical discourse of the pioneering natural investigator or social scientist, and in the pitifully imprecise, yet still intentionally referential, descriptive statements of the man at the bar counter, or woman at the coffee morning.

It is a commonplace to point out that Aristotle's enquiries here trespass on the frontiers of the philosophy of logic. For instance his discussion of the difference between substance, quality and accident are often discussions of differences in predicating, of the differences between saying of Socrates that he is a man, that he is a philosopher, and that he is snub-nosed. All these propositions are of the subject-predicate form: yet there are crucially important differences in the way in which subject and predicate are linked in the three of them. To be a philosopher Socrates must be a man; but he need not be snub-nosed. Thus in the three propositions the ways in which subject and predicate are linked quickly emerge as fundamentally different. Socrates could not have been a philosopher without being a man. Yet Cimon was a man and not a philosopher. Neither Socrates nor Cimon could have been the one Socrates, and the other Cimon, without being a man. So we say that being a man is essential to the one's being Socrates and the other's being Cimon. Yet Socrates is a philosopher, Cimon is a general. We may say that it is hard for us to think of the two historical individuals without recalling the philosophical practice of the former and the military prowess and political commitment (*vis-à-vis* the relations of Athens, Sparta, Persia, etc.) of the latter. One might say that for the historian, whether of ideas or of the emergence of the Athenian *archē*, what is significant about Socrates and Cimon is the former's mission and the latter's leadership of conservative forces in Athens during a particular period of the Pentekontaetia. True, there is no part of Aristotle's ontology with which the modern reader finds himself less in sympathy than those parts in which he is exploring the principle of individuation. For the most part he seems to reduce it to a sheerly material factor, and to evacuate the uniqueness, for instance, of the individual person of the kind of significance we are tempted to attribute to it. This while of course at the same time insisting that manhood cannot beget manhood, only Agammenon Orestes, and if rejecting the claim of the historian to anything deserving to be called scientific knowledge, yet at the same time insisting on his concern with what Alcibiades did and suffered.

Again, when we come to the proposition that Socrates is

snub-nosed, can we forget, for instance, the consequences of facial deformity in the life of individuals? If we treat such predicates as *monon kata sumbebēkos*, do we not commit ourselves to the prejudice of exalting the formal and isolatable, that which is in an intelligible sense abstract, above the concrete detail which is deeply significant in the actual individuality of a human person. Yet a man *can* philosophise in spite of being snub-nosed, fulfil a highly significant role in his nation's affairs (as Wavell did in spite of shyness or as Aneurin Bevan did in spite of a speech impediment). We rightly dismiss impatiently the estimate of a university entrant's capacity that fastens on the Lancastrian or Glaswegian provenance of his accent. We are concerned with his potential as a student, and in such connexion we quite properly avert our attention from the place of his upbringing.

It will surely be noticed that this discussion has in fact taken the Aristotelian apparatus as its starting place, that while admitting serious weaknesses in the way in which Aristotle understood the relations of such notions as thing, individual, form, quality, etc., he was justified in fastening attention on these notions as notions we had to master if we were to understand what we were saying when we affirm or deny in certain ways. There are genuine discoveries to be made if we can overcome the paradoxes that quickly emerge when we drag into the light of consciousness the seemingly incompatible beliefs we hold concerning the most fundamental scaffolding of the world.

II

In further support of the case against the use in theology of the category of substance one inevitably hears quoted the chequered and complex history of the concept in post-Cartesian philosophy. In particular one finds in certain recent and indeed contemporary theological writing explicit reference to arguments contained in modern works both of speculative metaphysics and of analytical philosophy that the notion of event is more fundamental than that of substance, that in fact things in the sense in which living bodies, certain artefacts, human individuals (if one may treat the last as other than a particular species of living bodies) are to be regarded as 'logical constructions' out of events, the last being identified with momentary or short-lived occurrences, for instance flashes of lightning, sounds, mental images, what we would in ordinary speech regard as short-lived slices or phases of the history of persistent things. The late Professor C. D. Broad, in his well-known book *The Mind and its Place in Nature*, used the phrase 'instantaneous punctiform particulars' as a synonym for event in this sense. Of course certain events are thought of as forming groups, manifesting throughout a prolonged period of time a relatively unchanged *Gestalt-qualität* or pattern quality: for instance, King's College Chapel. Yet this fabric is constituted by the events that make up its history and when we are told that things of the sort I mentioned are 'logical constructions out of events', what is intended is that we should recognize things as definable in terms of events or sets of events, in a way analogous to that in which, according to the logistic programme in the foundations of mathematics, cardinal numbers were regarded as definable in terms of classes or sets (i.e. a cardinal number is, on this view, the set of all sets or class of all classes corresponding to a given set or class, the last being regarded as capable of ostensive definition). If such a programme could be carried out, arithmetic would be reduced to logic in the sense that the concepts of characteristically arithmetical entities, e.g. cardinal number, and of characteristically arithmetical operations, e.g. addition, subtraction, etc., would be defined in terms of characteristically logical notions and operations. So arithmetic would emerge as a compendious shorthand for a whole number of highly sophisticated logical patterns. If one generalises this highly sophisticated procedure of reduction or translation, one is able (I repeat, in the highly sophisticated sense of definition characteristic of such reductive analysis) to define things, etc., in terms of events, to treat events rather than things as an ultimate reference point of factual discourse. There are genuine arguments in favour of such a procedure; for instance, the nearly commonsensical recognition that individual things have histories, that if, for instance, one commits oneself to meeting one's friends tomorrow in King's

College ante-chapel at 4.45 p.m., one takes for granted that the chapel will still be there. This belief is well founded, but its grounds are *comparable* to those on which one bases one's belief that the 8.40 a.m. from Cambridge to Liverpool Street tomorrow will arrive on time. In the latter case one predicts that a process (*viz.* the train's journey) will be fulfilled in the period of time indicated; one's prediction concerns the process. Similarly, in the case of the arranged meeting one takes for granted the continuance throughout the interval of King's College Chapel as something going on. Things go on as much as journeys. What makes things things is the relatively self-containedness of the series of events distinguishing them. The form of King's College Chapel remains relatively unaffected throughout the centuries; whereas a sandcastle is obliterated by the incoming tide and one can quickly mention entities (say successive waves of sound disseminated as the organ in King's College Chapel plays a Bach Prelude and Fugue) which never coagulate to form a thing, while they yet possess a *Gestalt-qualität* in their relations one to another which makes them identifiable for what they are and not, for example, a series of variations on the national anthem, the Eton College boating song, or Parry's setting of Blake's 'Jerusalem'. One has only to think of the dramatic effect of a failure on the organist's part to play the right chord or of the background prevalence of a cipher on the organ to realise how much the identifiable character of the work played depends upon the occurrence of certain constituent sounds in their proper order and relation one to another.

No one who has studied the effort to reduce substance in the sense of thing to terms of event in the sense indicated will fail to acknowledge very important insights gained through the operation. But there are certain serious difficulties in supposing that the reduction has been complete.

When we say that 'things are logical constructions out of events', we are suggesting that to say there are in the world things and events in the sense in which there are electric fires and television sets is to be guilty of the same mistake as that of saying that there is in the world the House of Commons (when the phrase is not being used to refer to the Chamber as a determinate spatial volume) and the Speaker, the elected MP.'s, etc. In the case of the House of Commons we have that which is definable in terms of its members, etc.: definable in the special sense of being reducible to its members. It is in fact nothing over and above the members who compose it in their relations one to another, the Speaker *et al.* So with things we have allegedly to deal with what are reducible to events. The advantage of using the notation of things is one of extreme conceptual economy. The concept of the thing is the concept of the way in which various sorts of event are organisable or constructible: when of course it is recognised that this organisation or construction involves the discrimination of actual features of the world. The question then arises whether a world in which events were not so constructible would be in any sense a world for us, giving place to the deeper question whether the concept of event in the sense of 'instantaneous punctiform particular' is not a much more sophisticated notion than that of thing and of event itself in the senses in which we speak of events as happening to things. Is not the notion of event as something occurring in the history of a thing (e.g. the explosion of a gas installation) epistemically primitive? And if so, is not the notion of event parasitic on that of thing? Certainly it is very important to recognize that individual things have a history, that in fact their defining quality, that which makes a tom-cat a tom-cat, a chair a chair, a pin-cushion a pin-cushion, a man a man, a philosopher a philosopher, is a *Gestalt-qualität* which takes time to manifest itself, and that moreover the successful phases of the history of the individual thing in question are not conveyed by their antecedents in the way in which the conclusions of a syllogism in Barbara is conveyed by the conjunction of major and minor premise, or in the way in which the propositional function, some P is S, is conveyed by the propositional function, all S is P. There is an atomicity in the complexes we regard as substantial, a precariousness in their achievement that is reflected in the logical fact that we rely on induction in forecasting their future. But the existence of thing-wholes in the world provides the background for the elementary plotting of its processes: this though the more sophisticated our tracing of the invariant relations between these processes, the more exact and comprehensive our grasp of their form through effective use of the supposed microscopic structure of the familiar in the deployment of their relations, the more these wholes emerge as involved the one in the other.

III

To defend the use of the notion of substance is already to suggest that while initially Christian theological practice might be innocent of any self-conscious involvement with ontology, the simplest affirmation, for instance, concerning Christ's relation to the Father, must include the use of the sort of notions of which ontology seeks to give an account. If we think or speak of Christ as subordinate to the Father, or ask if he is subordinate, and co-equal, or argue whether as a person – understood in Boethius' terms as *individua substantia rationabilis naturae* – he is distinguished from his Father, we are immediately involved willy-nilly in the use of and reconstruction of ontological notions.

To write in these terms is not to write as an historian of the development of Christian doctrine would write; it is to comment on the history of doctrinal development, to imply that from the first, even though completely unself-conscious, commitment to the use of such notions as substance was inevitable. Too often those who write in general terms of the relation of Christian theology to philosophy imply that in their relation we have to reckon with a series of alliances, often ill-conceived, between individual theologians or more powerful groups thereof and this or that essay in speculative thought. Far too little attention is paid to the inevitable interplay between theology and the work of conceptual analysis which, as much as any essay in speculation, has belonged to the deepest concerns of philosophy. We cannot begin to understand and appreciate the *homoousion* unless we bear in mind that the doctrine of substance, properly understood, is a part of analytical philosophy rather than an essay in speculation. The person of Christ most certainly confronted the primitive church, as indeed it does the twentieth-century successors of that church, with questions that for their clear statement demand the use of just such notions as Aristotle explores in the *Metaphysics*. This because there is in these notions the peculiar ultimacy and the peculiar pervasiveness we have already tried to bring out and because (again to repeat what has already been mentioned) the person of Christ thrusts upon our attention the question how one identifiable historical individual shall be at once e.g. 'one thing' with the Father and yet subordinate to that Father in that that Father is greater than he. One can only dodge the use of these notions if one supposes that the doctrine of Christ's person is something that excuses rather than compels full intellectual effort in the attempt to grasp its implications. But if it is a mistake to suppose that the use of these notions can be avoided, it is also a mistake to forget that their employment must include the enlargement of their sense by reason of the totally novel use to which they are bent. Part of the failure to understand what is achieved by use of the concept of substance in christology both in respect of positive gain and in respect of limitation is due to a failure to recognise that the notion is now being used in ways to which the habitual routes of its employment offer no exact guidance. Something parallel to this indeed may be discernible where use of the notion of truth is concerned.

The use of the concept of substance in christology makes possible the over-coming of the seeming contradiction between two propositions, one asserting Christ's dependence upon the Father, the other his equality with that Father which sent him. There are those who immediately resent the suggestion that the theologian is concerned with propositions, let alone that he can find fundamental work in reconciling seeming contradictions between two propositions. Arguably indeed the question whether or not theology can dispense with the notion of substance is closely related to the question whether or not theology can dispense with propositions and with careful attention to the logical relations of involution and exclusion that obtain between them. To say this is not to suggest for one moment that fundamentally theology consists *simply and solely* in exercises in conceptual reconstruction aimed at making sets of propositions internally consistent; still less is it to say that faith consists in assent to propositions. It is only to insist that we have to make every effort to see where exactly the *skandalon* of the incarnation is, what is the actual paradox with which we are confronted once we have stripped away the cerements of ultimately unnecessary paradoxes in which we have wrapped it. To recognise the use of ontological categories as something indispensable in theological work is not for one moment to identify that work with the use of such categories in *rebus divinis*. *The part is not the whole.* But it may well be that it is a necessary part of the whole in question, so that the attempt to dispense with the use of such categories is to deprive theology of an element whose absence mortally affects its total structure.

It may be claimed for the *homoousion* that it makes it possible for us so to grasp the mystery of Christ's relation to the Father that we are measured by that mystery and not confused by the problems which we have set in its place. If we say that Christ's invitation to the heavy laden is not a *simulacrum* of the divine invitation but is *in fact* that invitation made concrete, are we not involved in something very close to the *homoousion*? Does not our recognition that we are so involved enable us to recognise the mystery of the invitation for what it is? Again, when in the fourth gospel Jesus addressing his Father said, 'Father, the hour is come', does not the *homoousion* enable us to recognise that that hour is indeed the ultimate hour because the agent of the action which belongs to it is the ultimate agent of that which the Father has appointed shall be done on earth by the one who was with him before the foundations of the world were laid, who is 'one thing' with him, yet always his obedient executant? Again, does not the *homoousion* enforce the radically paradoxical character of the great christological saying, 'I am in the midst of you as he that doth serve'? Christ's *diakonia* is presented not as a parable of God's regnant service of his creatures, but as that service itself become concrete. Does not the conceptual apparatus of substance provide the means by which the truly revolutionary paradox of what is affirmed in terms of action, event, etc., may be approached for what it is, and not dismissed as a kind of likeness, *homoiōma*, of the ultimate?

The above series of questions may help to bring out something of the role of the *homoousion*. The reader may begin to see its significance as an instrument for advancing our understanding to enable us see what it is that is at issue in the simpler, more direct, more immediately moving christological affirmations of the gospel. It is totally misunderstood if it is treated as a possible substitute or alternative to such affirmations. Its role is essentially complementary. One might go further and say that over against the simpler, yet more mysterious, evangelical affirmations, it is a second order proposition. That is, if we ask what it is about, we have to say that it is not about Christ, but about statements about Christ. It will be remembered that earlier in this essay emphasis was laid on the proximity of ontological investigation to work in the philosophy of logic. One could go a long way with the thesis that the *homoousion* gave men who had mastered it a surer purchase-hold on the relations of simpler, more immediately moving, certainly profounder theological affirmations. Yet if one says this, one has at the same time to remember that such insight is only won by a kind of enlargement in the sense of the concept of substance through its employment in christology. This enlargement moreover is certain reflection in the totally novel context of the doctrine of the person of Christ of the older tension between identifying primary substance with concrete thing, or with form. The distinguished historian of early Christian doctrine, Dr J. N. D. Kelly, argues powerfully that the substance of the *homoousion* is the form (or essence) which in the *Categories* Aristotle characterises as secondary substance. It would not be fitting for the present writer to challenge the judgment of one of the greatest contemporary English-speaking authorities on that history; but nonetheless he would dare to suggest that the historian who passes such a judgment should remember Aristotle's vacillation in respect of the locus of primary substantiality, and consider the extent to which in the effort to read the ultimate mystery of Christ's relation to the Father a comparable tension must necessarily be experienced.

IV

If, however, we turn from these general considerations to the contemporary theological scene, we have to reckon with signs of a flight from christology. Here I am not thinking of the criticism of christocentrism advanced e.g. by Professor C. F. Evans in his important paper 'Theology and Christology' in the S.P.C.K. symposium on the *Communication of the Gospel* (1961), but of a more pervasive tendency which suggests the preoccupation with the person of Christ in abstraction from the whole process of divine address and response in which that person has its setting or settings is to be guilty of a viciously disturbing abstraction. To some extent one can discern such an attitude in John Knox's study, *The Humanity and Divinity of Christ* (1967), and indeed in his earlier writings, not excluding his study of *The Death of Christ* (1959). This goes far beyond a repristinisation of the familiar tension between theocentric and christocentric spiritualities; such an emphasis might indeed be regarded as a central theme of Professor Evans' paper; but what we are now concerned with goes a very great deal further. It is not to even be regarded as a reaction against the radical christo-centrism of Karl Barth. It is much more the expression of an increasing belief that the person of Christ will not bear the sort of weight that in much classical theology, both ancient and modern, both catholic, evangelical and liberal, has been put upon it, but that this weight must be distributed more evenly throughout the Christian process as a whole. We ought not, it is argued, to be unduly disturbed by having to recognise how much the tradition of Christ's person is the product of the constructive religious imagination of the primitive and later Christian communities, relying admittedly in Knox's view on a mysterious 'memory' whose epistemological status remains very obscure, but which is regarded as unfettered by any law other than that of its own immanent and allegedly spirit-inspired development. It is suggested that it is in this spiritual tradition that Christian theology finds its most inclusive subject matter, that indeed Christ's person is an abstraction from the process which it has helped to create and to which in turn it owes its own elaboration and that we should eschew any suggestion of a definitive articulation of any aspect of Christ's person and work.

Now this approach, which is gathering a certain momentum (partly under the influence of *form and redaction criticism*) is one with which we must come to terms. It is arguable indeed that use of the categories of substance, etc., in the formulation of the classical christology, provided that we have become properly self-conscious concerning the function their employment fulfils, enables us to see precisely what is at issue here. When I was a student 35 years ago, it was often suggested that we needed in christology 'to use much more personal categories than substance, nature, etc.'. This because the older British liberal critics of the traditional christology, and indeed their continental counterparts (reacting against Hegel) who were not infrequently their inspiration,[1] were convinced of the centrality to Christianity of Christ's person, and rejected the use of substance in theology because it seemed to subordinate the concreteness of that person to Greek metaphysical abstractions. (It will not be forgotten that a very great orthodox theologian, Peter Taylor Forsyth, shared to the full the Ritschlian rejection of what he called 'Chalcedonism'.) But today may one not suggest that it is through obstinate adherence to the categories of substance, form, etc., that one is enabled to show what exactly it is that is being thrown overboard when we suggest that in fact the church's life, in which allegedly epistemological distinctions between subjective and objective are blurred, is the fundamental subject matter of the theologian's concern? (Even the ultra-montane for whom the church in Bossuet's phrase is 'the mystic Christ' has allowed that Christ stands over against his church, as judge of her stewardship of the sacraments in his abiding presence as one who is her Lord and servant.)

Now one must allow a certain validity to this protest in so far as it was a protest against the suggestion that through the use of the conceptual apparatus of which the notion of substance was

[1] This, though some of the greatest English modernists (e.g. Rashdall, Inge, Streeter, Major) were emphatically not Ritschlians. They were all convinced of the significance of metaphysics for theology, a tendency exemplified in Inge's avowed and Streeter's more circumspect Platonism, in Major's strong attachment to the Logos christology of the Alexandrian Fathers, and perhaps most strikingly in Rashdall's deep knowledge of, and respect for, medieval theology, shown not least in his sustained criticism of Gore's doctrine of the trinity as tritheistic.

the pivot we were enabled to reach something more ultimate in the economy of the divine self-disclosure and self-impartation than the person of Jesus Christ crucified and risen. It is not through the mediation of Christ's revelation of the Father that we are enabled to plumb the structure of being; but rather it is through the use of ontological categories that we are enabled to see precisely what it is that it may be confronts us in the person of Jesus. One must not forget the extent to which the older liberal theology to which I refer broke with orthodox tradition. But it remained continuous with that tradition in its insistence on the centrality of the person of Jesus and the kind of debates which it initiated turned on the way in which that person was most surely understood.

In the markedly different contemporary situation it is recognition of the significance of the debate concerning the *homoousion* that helps to remind us how greatly we diverge from the central theological tradition if we suggest that debate concerning Christ's person is somehow secondary in Christian theological argument. Whereas to an older generation the *homoousion* was something from which we should seek to free ourselves, today the very debates in which the use of the notion has its home is effective reminder that the understanding of Christ's person lies at the very heart of the Christian theological enterprise. Those who rejected the *homoousion* as a surrender of evangelical insight to the bondage of metaphysical abstraction were nonetheless deeply in its debt for the relentlessness with which it affirmed the centrality of Christ's mystery. We see today that if we abandon it we abandon not simply an outworn theology, but a whole tradition of argument, a whole sustained exercise in the work of faith in search of understanding that finds its reference point in that supremely significant theological affirmation.

Indeed this point began to emerge at a slightly earlier point in the history of recent christological debate. It is universally admitted that the nature of Christ's relation to his Father and to his brethren set the primitive Christians a variety of problems. It may be that initially their interpretation of this relation was in exclusively functional terms; it was the role or roles of Jesus which mattered, even as it was among the Son of Man's roles to disavow those who had turned in disregard from Jesus, in the hour of the former's glory, and to act as advocate for those others who had confessed him. Again, in the light of the Easter-event the disciples allegedly saw Jesus as designated himself to fulfil a certain unique role, or certain unique roles: even retrospectively as having in his life before the crucifixion such roles. But is this role or are these roles to be seen as matters of divine appointment, even as under the British constitution Lord Hailsham has recently been invested with the dignity or prerogatives of Lord Chancellor? Are they dignities bestowed on Jesus? Such is part of what is sometimes called adoptionism. Of course it may be the case that the first Christians were adoptionists or were sometimes adoptionists or were some of them adoptionists; it may indeed be that they saw things like that. Jesus was a supremely Spirit-endowed man. This was his essential dignity. But his followers presented this endowment to themselves in terms of a myth of divine adoption, of investment with a whole number of Messianic roles. Of course there are no such roles for anyone to fulfil: the description Son of Man has no more application than that of phoenix, chimera, medusa, etc. Jesus' function was to be bearer of the Spirit of God, its uniquely effective servant. If we like, we may speak of this function in mediatorial terms, provided of course we eschew the unnecessary mythology of suggested pre-existence. There is not that which is incarnate in Jesus except in so far as in moving from a Spirit to a Logos christology, we make bold to speak of the Word as incarnated in his life. We claim that the universally creative reason is manifested in him, concentrated to a point: so that we see in the small scale of an individual life that which is the ground of the world's ultimate and intimate order. If we call him the Word, we had better said manifestation of the Word. He is not concretely identifiable with the Word. To suggest this is to involve us at once in the theologico-metaphysical conundra relating to the situation of the Logos through whom the world is sustained in the period of its concentration to a point in the incarnate.

I have sketched a tendency that had already gone a long way

towards the attempt mentioned above to liberate Christianity from a kind of bondage to the doctrine of the incarnation. That tendency of course goes a good way beyond the sort of functionalism that I have more recently sketched. Indeed such a writer as Oscar Cullmann, who in his important study of *The Christology of the New Testament* insists on the use of functional as distinct from ontological categories, is mentioned explicitly by Professor Evans as a man committed to a christocentric viewpoint. In Cullmann the functionalist approach is defended as an obedience to the well-known theological maxim: *deum cognoscere dei beneficia cognoscere*. Yet if we eschew the kind of interrogation that the use of ontological categories imposes on us, do we not leave on one side the question whether or not we believe that a life has been lived of which we say that what we say of the deeds done in it, the words spoken, the sufferings endured, we say of that which belongs to one substantially identical with the Father except that he is Father and the liver of the life Son? These deeds, etc., are not fully characterized except as the deeds, etc., of the one who is the relation to the Father we call Son. Of course this faces us with the tremendous question how a particular act can be the act of one who is related to the Father, identical with the Father except in respect of this relatedness.

We are indeed being driven back towards a topic from which all except a very few theologians in the English-speaking world today fight shy, namely the doctrine of the trinity, and in particular the easily dismissed question of the relation of the essential to the economic trinity. To speak in more explicitly christological terms, we are raising the question of Christ's pre-existence. When we say that he pre-exists his incarnation, what is it that so pre-exists and what its pre-existence? If we follow some of the medievals and suggest that that which pre-exists is relatedness to the Father, relatedness that is quasisubstantival, we are in danger at once of making ourselves ridiculous in the eyes of those who would seek to bring theology into relation with the concrete by insisting on the sheer irrelevance to its essential business of futile ontological speculation. But what in the end is the service that ontology does to theology, ontology of the sort with which we have been concerned in this paper, except to tie it tightly to the concrete?

V

If I am asked what this paper suggests as the most fundamental task in christology to which it has pointed a way, I should wish to suggest that that task is the one of reconciling the use of the category of substance in the articulation of the christological problem with the recognition that it is the notion of *kenōsis* which more than any other single notion points to the deepest sense of the mystery of the incarnation. Those who have studied the history of ontology of the sort I have discussed in this paper are made aware that its enquiries move more consciously on the frontiers of the philosophy of logic, that some of its most certain fruits are discoveries concerning e.g. the manner of the linkage of subject and predicate in certain propositions. If we learn anything from the *homoousion*, it concerns less the manner of Christ's relation to the Father than the way in which that relation is to be understood; it is a second-order rather than a first-order christological proposition. That is to say, it is more something we say about what we say concerning Christ, than something we actually say concerning him that begins to lift the veil from the face of the God whom he discloses, with whom he is one.[1] For that we must use the language of *kenōsis*, but use it in closest relation to a reconstructed doctrine of the trinity. And for that reconstruction we shall certainly require to use ontological categories.

In gathering to a point the argument of this diffuse and complex paper, I should like briefly to raise some of the problems set by another notion which badly needs analysis in this context, namely that of dependence. Here again we have a notion which belongs at once to the philosophy of logic and to ontology; but it is also a notion which belongs to such concrete documents of the spiritual life as the concluding chapter of the late Dom Gregory Dix's, *The Shape of the Liturgy*. When speaking of the

[1] A reference to the treatment of the *magista genē* in Plato's *Sophist* would not be out of place here.

role of the Sunday eucharist in the religious life of Catholic Christendom, in language which Barth would not have hesitated to use,
he says, 'We depend upon Him for our very dependence.' What
is this dependence? How is it related to the dependence which in
an objective theology the believer affirms to obtain between
himself and Christ's atoning work?

It is indeed this latter dependence which for Dix gives shape and
form to our dependence upon God and is thought by him as
receiving concrete expression in the four-fold action of the eucharist. But many who would not share Dix's eucharistic theology
would agree that we receive from God through Christ's act the
manner in which our relation to him is given form, our dependence schematised for what it is.

These are very difficult problems; but they are problems on
which study of the notion of dependence developed in the fields
of the philosophy of logic and of ontology may have considerable
help to give. I mention *dependence* in this concluding section of my
essay for two reasons: first, it is just such another notion as
substance, *mutatis omnibus mutandis*, and therefore reference to it
may suggest other ways in which the essentially abstract apparatus
of ontology may further the more flesh and blood concerns of the
theology of Christ's person and work. Secondly, and this is much
more important, is it not the case that those who seek to subordinate christology to the church's achievement of self-consciousness in respect of her own spiritual life are in fact denying any
special dependence – relation or relations between the Christian
community and Christ's person and work? It may be that we have
to let such dependence (mysterious and obscure as it is) to vanish into
limbo; it may be that preoccupation with Christ's person is doomed
by the approaching failure of the 'new quest' for the historical Jesus,
if not before. Yet if *lex orandi* is in some sense *lex credendi*, it is still
Christ's person that raises the issue of the significance of the church's
existence more than that existence which raises and implicitly
answers the question of his significance. If we subordinate christology to the study of the church's life, aimed at a deep self-consciousness
concerning its inwardness, then the *homoousion*, the Chalcedonian
definition, etc., are reduced to the status of phases in that life, or

to that of abstraction from such phases. What matters is less what they affirm than the fact that men have subscribed to them. We can understand the subscription, not that to which subscription was demanded. The proper study of the theologian is ecclesiastical man! But may it not be that to insist that we attend not to the fact that these things are said, but to what by them was and is affirmed may have the effect of riveting our attention again upon the central figure, who in traditional faith gives rather than receives sense? At least the presence of these formulae help to keep this option alive and to raise, even in the late twentieth century, the crucial issue of the role of descriptive or analytical metaphysics in hermeneutics and theology.

APPENDIX

I. ON GOD AND SUBSTANCE IN ARISTOTLE

There is of course another part of 'first philosophy' that is concerned with supra-sensible substances (oak trees, cats, Aspasia, Socrates belong to the world the senses disclose to us), and especially with God. Indeed Book Λ of the *Metaphysics* is a short treatise on natural theology concerned both with God's cosmological role as unmoved first mover (a theme also dealt with in *Physics* Book 8 and in the *de Generations et Corruptione*) and in a most interesting way with God's characteristic activity which Aristotle characterises as *noēsis noēseos*. No account of Aristotle's doctrine of substance can be complete that does not reckon with his view of God as substance, and that he does so is made clear not only from *Metaphysics* Λ but also from his illustrative reference to the fact that good when predicated of God is predicated in the category of substance, made when deploying his very important doctrine of the analogical predication of good in *Nicomachean Ethics*, I, 6 – the passage in which he develops his sustained, if dense and complex, criticism of Plato's central metaphysical conception of the 'Idea of the Good'.

Indeed it is at this point that there emerges most sharply crucial exegetical issues concerning the relation between the analytical enquiries characteristic of Books Γ, Z and H of the *Metaphysics* and the theistic *Weltanschauung*, with the world pivoted on a God who is conceived as setting its processes in motion while remaining totally indifferent to, indeed oblivious of, its movement, the *prōton kinoun akinēton* who is in no sense properly regarded as a creator or even a *dēmiourgos* in the sense of Plato's *Timaeus* with the possibly redemptive role for which this divine being is cast, albeit at the cost of his metaphysical subordination. (The reference to the *Timaeus* owes a great deal to discussion with Mr Nicholas Reed.)

2. ON PROPER NAMES

At this point a proper treatment of the propositions in question would seem to demand some reference to Russell's distinction between grammatical proper names and logical proper names. When one says that Socrates is a man, is one not in fact asserting that the man called Socrates is a man, a proposition that we would dismiss as a tautology (in the vulgar sense as distinct from that in which e.g. Wittgenstein treated logically necessary propositions as tautologies of the two-valued propositional calculus) or a 'trifling proposition' (here to use the language with which Locke dismissed such propositions as 'oyster is oyster'). To argue in these terms is in fact to offer one account of what was intended when it was pointed out that neither Socrates nor Cimon could have been the one Socrates and the other Cimon without being men, that manhood is essential to their being what they are as Socrates and Cimon, *viz.* the men referred to by these names. What they are apart from their manhood seems to escape us immediately we ask what it is. Hence indeed Aristotle's unwillingness in very many places to follow the clear doctrine of the *Categories* in identifying *prōtē ousia* with the concrete thing; for what is that concrete thing apart from the form which makes it what it is?

INDEX OF NAMES